GW01451748

THE LIVELIHOOD OF MAN

THE
LIVELIHOOD
OF MAN

Economics in Theory and Practice

BY

HONOR CROOME
B.Sc. (Econ.)

AND

GORDON KING
B.Sc. (Econ.), B. Com.
Master for Economics at Dover Grammar School

New and Revised Edition

1969
CHATTO & WINDUS
LONDON

Published by
Chatto and Windus (Educational) Ltd.
42 William IV Street
London, W.C.2

*

Clarke, Irwin and Co. Ltd.
Toronto

First edition 1953
Reprinted 1954
Reprinted 1955
Second edition 1957
Reprinted 1959
Reprinted 1961
Third edition 1963
Reprinted 1965, 1967, and 1969

SBN 7010 0062 7

Printed in Great Britain by
William Lewis (Printers) Ltd.
Cardiff

PREFACE

IN writing this book we have had particularly in mind the needs of several classes of examinee: those taking Economics at the Ordinary level of the G.C.E., those who are in their first year of preparation for the Advanced level examination, and also those taking examinations set by various professional bodies. It is intended, however, that the book should be no less useful to young people (and their elders) who, while not preparing for any examination, require a simple but thorough introduction to the subject.

Our aim has been, first, to give a full and up-to-date picture of the economy of Britain and the modern world, such as is not elsewhere available in a convenient form, so far as we are aware, to the elementary student. And on the other hand, we have attempted to give a thorough grounding in elementary theory (with, in the last chapter, a glance into the further reaches of the subject), laying particular emphasis on two principles: the division of labour, and the necessity of choice between scarce alternatives.

We know from experience that senior pupils can be enabled both to grasp these principles, which are basic to all forms of economic organization, and to apply them to the analysis of current problems. Application, however, is often more difficult than a merely theoretical understanding. It is here, perhaps, that the teacher's personal role is most important, and we hope that this book, with its emphasis on practical institutions, may make his task easier.

We would urge that the teacher should make the fullest use of statistical material both to illustrate theory and to put descriptive matter in proportion. The teaching of economics should, we believe, be accompanied by some study of elementary statistical method and practice in the use of statistical sources.

H. M. C.
W. G. K.

PREFACE TO THE THIRD EDITION

IN revising this book for the third edition I have brought it up to date both factually and statistically in the light of the developments of the last ten years. In particular, a considerable part of Chapter V, the Economy of Britain, has been re-written and maps and tables have been brought into line with the most recent information. Some substantial changes have been made in the sections on Banking in view of the Report of the Radcliffe Committee. The achievement of convertibility of Sterling has also necessitated changes from the earlier edition.

In preparing this edition I have been particularly indebted to Mr. J. L. Croome and Mr. J. M. Croome for their many helpful suggestions. I should also like to acknowledge the help I have received from Dr. G. P. Wibberley.

W. G. KING

ACKNOWLEDGMENTS

THE authors would like to express their indebtedness to the following for much valuable criticism and advice: Mr. Thomas Birch, Rev. L. W. Langley, Mr. K. H. Ruffell and Mr. M. J. Harper.

Their thanks are also due to Dover Borough Council for allowing the reproduction of the Rate Demand Note (Fig. 28); and to Her Majesty's Stationery Office for the Population diagrams (Fig. 21), and for the questions reprinted from the Scottish Leaving Certificate specimen paper; and to the various examining bodies, both university and professional, which are listed on page 323, for permission to reproduce questions from their past examination papers.

Acknowledgment is also due to the Institute of Economic Affairs for permission to use figures from the Hobart Paper *Growthmanship* by Mr. Colin Clark.

CONTENTS

TABLES

DIAGRAMS AND MAPS

THE LIVELIHOOD OF MAN

CHAPTER I

WHAT ECONOMICS IS ABOUT

BEFORE beginning to study a new subject it is just as well to have some idea of the ground which one is going to cover; of the sort of things one will be concerned with and the sort of questions to which one will be looking for answers. If one asks 'What is the subject matter of economics?' one finds that a lot of different answers have been given, and in the advanced stages of the science these differences may be important. But for the kind of elementary study with which we are concerned, a very general, rough-and ready answer is good enough; economics has to do with *how people make their livings and arrange their spending.*

It has to do with shops and farms and offices and factories and mines; with banks and companies and Co-ops, trade unions and trade associations, and the organization of business generally; with money and prices and the cost of living; with lending and borrowing; with good and bad trade, employment and unemployment; with rates and taxes, Government spending and controls; with trade between different countries.

It throws light on questions like these: Why is America richer than Britain, and Britain richer than China? Why does almost everything cost more to-day than it did ten years ago? And why are some things so much more expensive than others?

B   1

Why do we pay taxes, and what do we get for them? Why does a bricklayer's mate earn less than a bricklayer, and a bricklayer less than an architect, and women, as a rule, less than men? What are stocks and shares and consols and bills of exchange and the sterling area and other such things mentioned in the 'City' columns of the newspapers? Why are some businesses very big and others very small? What causes slumps? And so on, and so on; this should be enough to give the general idea.

Making the Best of Scarcity. Can one pull these questions together a little and see what they have in common? Certainly they are all concerned with the business of getting a living, of supplying our wants in one way or another. But there is something more to be said about that. Something very obvious, in the first place; that we have to get a living because a living will not come to us of its own accord. If everything we wanted—food and clothing and shelter, comforts and amusements—was as free and plentiful as the air we breathe, there would be no need of farms and shops and factories, no need of wages and rents, no need of work, no prices and money—and no subject called Economics.

All these things, and the science which studies them, exist because, compared with what we want, with what we could easily use if we had the chance, there is *not enough* food and clothing and house room and transport and means of amusement, nor enough land and raw materials and human energy to produce them all. We have to make the most of the resources we have got; we have, in short, to get along as best we can with the fact of *scarcity*. We cannot eat our cake and have it too; we have to *choose*. We have to choose between working a bit harder and going without what the extra work would have produced; between this and that good thing which we would like; between more to-day and more to-morrow. Some of these choices we make entirely on our own—shall I spend this shilling on a magazine or a cinema ticket? Some we make jointly through our elected Government: how many new schools, how many new roads? In some countries almost all the choices are 'collective'—that is, government—choices; Russia runs her affairs like that. In others almost all the choices are private; the American Government settles far fewer choices than ours does, and a hundred years ago ours settled fewer still.

But whoever does the choosing, choice there must be; and a good deal of the subject matter of economics is the way in which, when someone chooses *this* rather than *that*, the effect of that choice is passed back through shops and warehouses and factories, City offices and banks and shipping lines, and joins up with other choices to settle the way in which the world's scarce resources, land and material and human beings, shall be used.

The Division of Labour. What has just been said leads to another point. When we choose *this* rather than *that* we generally do not, like Robinson Crusoe, immediately turn to and produce it ourselves. Having chosen our own jobs, we stick to them, and let others get on with doing other things. We *specialize*; that is, we break up the great over-all job of getting a living into very small bits: which is why we live so much more comfortably than Robinson Crusoe.

To put a Christmas pudding on an English table the mother of the family has probably spent some hours working in the kitchen. But before she begins her work flour has been ground in Liverpool from wheat grown in Canada, spices have been brought from the West Indies and currants from Greece and raisins from Australia, sugar from Mauritius and suet from cattle reared perhaps in Ireland or the Argentine; ships have been built to bring them, engineers have worked on blue prints, and steel workers in furnaces and rolling mills; and miners have hewn the coal with which the iron is smelted to make the steel. Prospectors have sought out the oilfields which yielded the fuel which powered the ships, and merchants have organized the trade, and wholesalers have split up the cargoes into handy consignments for the grocers, and grocers have stored them and arranged them on their shelves, keeping a supply always ready (unless something, somewhere along the line, has gone wrong) for the housewife to walk in and ask for whatever her pet recipe tells her she needs. (And that recipe book started life as a tree in Newfoundland, an idea in a writer's mind, a printing press in a building—but one could go on like this for ever).

The short name for all this complex process is the *Division of Labour*; and, once again, it forms a major part of the subject matter of economics. When we study the organization of the Bank of England, or the way a Joint-Stock Company is set up, or the process by which the money of one country is exchanged for the money of another, we are not just learning a string of facts but finding out how all the world's different jobs are keyed together, what makes all the independent parts of the system fit—and also what may check or interrupt its working.

The Limits of Economics. Studying these things, we are bound to find some questions coming up which are not strictly economic; questions of right and wrong, questions of human feelings, of beauty and ugliness, of better and worse ways of life. 'Social justice', for instance; is it tolerable that some should be much richer than others? or is inequality only wrong when it means actual suffering for the poorest? These are moral and political questions; economics has a lot to say about inequality, but it cannot give the whole answer. And attitudes to life: is it better to be thoroughly concentrated on 'bettering oneself', on getting more and more and having more and more to spend, or to be easy-going and leisurely and keep on doing things in the old way? One can learn from economics a good deal about how higher standards of living are won and of what has to be given up for them, but not whether this or that increase in standards is worth having at the price of this or that amount of upset. (One example of this kind of question comes up over married women with young families going out to work to raise the family income; and it is easy to think of others.)

In the early days of economic thought (economics is a very young science; it hardly existed a couple of centuries ago) there was a good deal of confusion over what was and what was not its proper business; and some of that confusion still lingers, particularly among people who are not themselves economists. One piece of confusion needs clearing up before one can really get started on the subject: and that is the meaning of the word

production. Dimly, in the backs of our minds, we are apt to
think of production as making things, actual things, and in
particular the things which we personally think are useful. We
think of farmers as producers, and of miners, and of factory
workers; perhaps we are not so sure about the people who
move things from place to place, and still less sure about those
who store them, and sort them out, as merchants and wholesalers and shopkeepers do; we may be even more doubtful
about such people as doctors and teachers, whose work, however useful, is concerned not with things but with services, and
we may be inclined to brush aside altogether those—actors,
artists and singers, for example—whose job is not to cure or to
teach, but to make life brighter. As for those whose work
results in something of which we actually disapprove, we find
it quite difficult to call them 'productive'—think of a tee-
totaller's view on brewery workers and barmaids, a high-
brow's views on pop singers or a lowbrow's on modern
sculptors.

Now, all this kind of distinction has to be dropped in
economics. *Any work which results in something for which someone is willing to pay* is production, never mind if it is growing
things, or making them, or moving them, or storing and sorting them, or organizing any of these processes from a desk; or
rendering services, whether 'essential' or of the kind one could
do without at a pinch. And that holds good whether these
things and these services are recognized as valuable by everybody, or by only a few, and even if a number of people regard
them as downright bad.

Having said so much about what economics is concerned
with, about the questions which it can and cannot answer, and
about the confusions one has to avoid when studying it, we are
ready to begin that study itself.

CHAPTER II

HOW PRODUCTION IS ORGANIZED

THE business of production, the business of supplying consumers (that is, all of us) with what they want, is very
differently carried on in different parts of the world and has
changed a great deal over the course of history. There are countries even to-day where one can see the productive process going
on in the simplest possible way as it has gone on from pre-
historic times. In the South Seas there are islands where the
people living in coastal villages live almost entirely on fish
which they catch with home-made spears and nets from home-
made canoes; inland the people are farmers, and every so often
the farmers and the fishermen meet, with songs and ceremonies,
to exchange fish for maize and vegetables, and go home again,
while the women make baskets and clay pots and weave fabrics
for the few clothes and mats they use, and the children mind
the pigs. That is all the productive process amounts to, year
after year and generation after generation.

But we are mostly concerned with our own sort of society,
with the modern Western world where people have specialized
and learned to use machines and to trade (as one must when
once one has specialized) and to use money (as one must if one
wants to trade). A good way of beginning the study of that
society is to look at the different kinds of business unit, the different kinds of *firm*, which handle production; the organizations into which people are grouped in order to get a living and
whose heads decide what shall be made, and how, and when,
and where. In a modern community like Great Britain they
come in all shapes and sizes, from the one-man corner shop to
the enormous nationalized industry with about three-quarters
of a million workers and hundreds of million pounds' worth of

equipment; some suit one kind of business, some another. We shall see later why some must be big and some little, why some are owned and controlled by private persons and others by officials acting for the public, how they grow and change and split up and vary their activities. To begin with, here is a list of the different kinds.

Types of Enterprise: the One-Man Firm. The oldest kind of enterprise, and that of which there are most to be found, is the one-man firm, where a single person owns and controls the business. He may be actually and literally single-handed, a cobbler or window cleaner or jobbing carpenter or free-lance journalist; or he may be an employer of others, a farmer or small factory owner or shopkeeper. The important and distinguishing thing about him is that he carries the whole responsibility on his own shoulders. Within the framework of the law of the land, it is his affair and no one else's to decide what goods (or services) the 'concern' shall produce, what price it is worth his while to pay for premises and tools and materials and hired labour, if any, and what it is most profitable to charge for what he sells; whether to move or stay where he is, whether to change his methods or not, how much to advertise, and so on. He owns the whole affair; how much money can be sunk in it depends entirely on what he can put down out of his own pocket or personally persuade his family, friends and banker to lend him. All the profits are his, and so are all the losses; and if at any time he goes bankrupt, that is, makes such heavy losses that he cannot pay his debts, everything that he owns— not only his business but his private belongings—can be sold up for his creditors' benefit.

Retail Shops: Large- and Small-Scale. The commonest kind of one-man firm is the small retail shop, which can be started without a great deal of capital or specialized knowledge. It is estimated that in 1961 there were 580,151 shops in Britain, of which 84 per cent were one-man concerns. But if one looks not at the number of shops but at the volume of trade, one gets a very different picture. In the same year, out of a total retail turnover of £8,949,000,000, 25 per cent of this was handled by 10 per cent of the big shops. Before the 1939–45 war, the big shops' share was growing; concerns like the Co-ops and the great chain stores, Boots, Woolworths, Timothy White's, and so on, had a good many advantages over the small man and could make a profit even when selling at prices which to him would mean a loss. These advantages still exist; war-time and early post-war rationing, price control and allocations reduced them, but since these ended the big firms have resumed their expansion. The development of the 'self-service' type of store has put the small man at a further disadvantage.

It is worth looking at the advantages which the big shop enjoys over the small, because the same question, or others very like it, keeps on cropping up in other forms of production. The big shop, with its big turnover, can afford to employ highly qualified workers to do special jobs—knowledgeable buyers, skilled sales assistants, clerks, accountants, display artists, stockroom managers, and so on, whereas the owner of a small shop can only draw on his own abilities and is unlikely to be first rate at every aspect of his job. The big shop can buy in large quantities—and that suits makers and wholesalers who are likely on that account to give bigger discounts than they do to the customer who buys in dozens rather than thousands. It can raise extra capital, when wanted, more easily; its credit is more substantial than that of the little man. All these things cut down the big shop's costs per unit of goods sold and so make it possible for it to offer better value to the customer.

But there is another side to the matter. If all the retail trade of a neighbourhood is concentrated in one big shop, then, obviously, all the neighbourhood has to come to that shop—which may be a long way. Convenience counts, and the little man supplies it. Moreover, the little man can know all his customers personally, advise them in their purchases, help a small child sent in on an errand, be a neighbour as the big impersonal chain store can hardly be. Here we are slipping into one of those social questions where economics fails to give the answer —which is more important, neighbourliness and personal relations, or a bit more buying power for every shilling spent? But one can say that people value the personal touch, and are often willing to pay for it by going to the small independent trader even when he offers less choice and fewer bargains.

Farming: the One-Man Concern. In farming, where (judged either by turnover or by the sheer weight of numbers) the small concern is predominant, another set of influences is at work. Here the owner, or the responsible manager, must be right on the spot; one cannot farm by routine or according to standing orders. The vagaries of the weather, and the unpredictability of nature generally, mean that important decisions have to be made from one hour to the next, without delay for consulting higher authority. There is a French proverb which says that 'the master's foot is the best of fertilizers'—and there is a limit, varying of course with the kind of cultivation, to the amount of ground the master's feet can get over. That limit keeps the size of farms down and makes the one-man concern the typical farming business unit. The 315,000 individual family farm businesses in England and Wales in 1959 compared with only 32,000 partnerships and 7,000 joint stock companies engaged in farming.

Of course the one-man concern—in the sense of one-man ownership and control—may itself vary a great deal in size. But as the able and ambitious independent business man tries to expand his business he soon finds that single ownership and control is a handicap. To keep all the strings of control in his own hands means uncomfortably stretching and dividing his energies; to borrow money for expansion, once he has tapped all the possible lenders who know him personally, is difficult; and the more the business grows, the more forbidding is the risk of failure. So expansion sooner or later means a change from this simplest form of business organization to something more complex—a partnership or a private or public joint-stock company.

The Partnership is not such a common and important form of business as it used to be. It is mainly found, outside commercial circles, among professional men; e.g. doctors, solicitors, or chartered accountants, whose practices are too big for one man to handle. The usual arrangement is for two or more persons each to contribute a sum of money for the promotion of a business or practice. The partners (of whom there may by law be not more than twenty, or ten if their business is banking) arrange among themselves the proportions in which profits shall be divided between them; that division will usually be in proportion to the capital which each has subscribed. The act of any one partner is binding on the firm, so that all are collectively responsible for one another's obligations and liabilities incurred in the firm's business. Each, therefore, is individually liable for the firm's debts; which means that if the firm gets into financial difficulties and is unable to meet its debts out of its existing resources any one or more partners may be legally called on to pay the debts out of their private means.

Partnerships have the advantage of providing a means of the expansion of the one-man firm. They draw on the capital and credit of several persons instead of one; they can combine the benefits of different kinds of experience and personal ability. But the heavy risk entailed on the partners by unlimited liability for the firm's debts, and the restriction on their entry into, or withdrawal from, the firm, and the difficulty of maintaining the partnership where death duties on a partner's estate are heavy, are disadvantages only to be escaped by passing from the partnership to something more complex and working under different rules.

The Joint Stock Company. That something is the Joint Stock Company. When a firm has '& Co. Ltd.', or just 'Ltd.', after its name, that means that it is a joint-stock company and that *the liability of its members is limited.* Under limited liability, which has been legalized and defined by a number of Acts of Parliament between 1869 and 1948, no shareholder can lose more than the amount which he has invested in his shares. If the company fails, its creditors cannot force him to make good its debts out of his other property, as they could if he were sole owner of a one-man concern or a member of a partnership. He knows where he is; he knows the worst that can happen. That makes investment a much more attractive proposition; and the joint-stock company finds it correspondingly easier to raise money by drawing in new members.

Company Promotion. When a one-man firm or partnership is turned into a joint-stock company, the procedure is as follows. The existing assets of the firm, held by the owner or by partners, are valued at a certain figure. To this figure there is added the amount of additional capital which the founders of the new company think they need. This total amount, representing the capital of the new company, is divided into *shares*, usually of £1 each. (We shall see later that there are several different kinds of shares, giving different rights to their holders.) Of these shares, a part is allocated to the original owner or owners in proportion to the assets of the parent firm. The rest are then sold to new shareholders—people who, having money to spare, see a prospect of profit in the new company's activities. (If the company is a *public* one, the minimum number of shareholders is seven and there is no maximum. If it is a *private* one, there need be no more than two shareholders and there must not be more than fifty; also, a private company's shares must not be offered for sale to the public generally, but must be sold privately.)

Possible subscribers are attracted by issuing a Prospectus—these are frequently published in the daily papers and contain a full statement of the nature and objects of the new company. Every company must have a Memorandum of Association, which states the official title of the company (followed by the word *Limited*), the situation of the registered office, the amount of 'authorized capital', the number of shares and the objects of the company. This last is usually a very comprehensive list covering every possible form of activity in which the company might wish to engage; it is important, because a company may not legally do anything which is not included in the 'objects' clause.

Every company must have its Articles of Association. These are the rules for the conduct of the company, governing such matters as the issue, transfer and forfeiture of shares, the holding of meetings, the powers and qualifications of directors, and the keeping of accounts.

When a copy of the Memorandum of Association has been filed with the Registrar of Joint-Stock Companies, and the Registrar has satisfied himself of the company's *bona fides* (good faith or genuineness) he issues a Certificate of Incorporation, which gives the company its legal existence as a corporate body, with a legal 'personality' of its own. When this is done, the company can allot shares, collect their purchase price, and if all other necessary legal formalities have been complied with, set about its business.

The law concerning company promotion is strict and complicated; it has to be, because experience has shown that without legal safeguards company promotion provides a very happy hunting ground for crooks. Fraudulent promoters have induced people to buy shares in bogus companies which were never intended to function; assets and prospects have been misrepresented; money subscribed for solid-sounding enterprises has been diverted to wild-cat schemes. It has been said that it will probably never be possible to give 100 per cent protection to the born gull against the born shark; but the shark has a more difficult time nowadays than he used to.

Types of Securities. One becomes a member of a company by buying the shares (certificates of part ownership) which it issues. Shares may be of different kinds to suit the requirements of different people. *Preference shares* are those having first claim on the company's profits. They are thus safer than other kinds; but this advantage is balanced by the fact that the dividend on them is usually limited to about 6 per cent on their nominal value. Sometimes preference shares may be *cumulative*—that is, if the company does not earn enough in one year to pay the preference dividend, then those arrears must be paid off in later years before anything is paid on other types of shares. *Ordinary* shares, often referred to as 'equities', receive any profits left after the claims of the preference shareholders have been met. If the company does badly this may be nothing—the ordinary dividend is 'passed'. If it does moderately well the ordinary shareholders may get about the same return as the preference shareholders. But if it is really successful the ordinary shareholder is the one who gets the full benefit of success. He takes the biggest chance and gets the biggest reward; he is the chief risk-bearer of the productive process. Some firms also issue *non-voting ordinary shares*.

As an alternative to increasing its capital by selling additional shares, a firm may sometimes *borrow* money. The shareholder and the lender are in quite different positions. The money paid in for shares is never paid back by the company to the shareholder—if he wants to turn his share back into cash, he must find someone else (through the Stock Exchange or otherwise) to buy it from him. Moreover, if there are no profits there will be no dividends. Loans, on the other hand, must be repaid by the agreed date and the interest on them must be met, profits or no profits—if necessary by selling the firm's assets. The shareholder is a part-owner; the holder of a debt certificate is a creditor.

Because of this priority enjoyed by loan charges, and consequently the lesser risk involved, the rate of interest on a loan is generally less than the return which people reckon to get on the capital they invest in shares. The former may be around 6 per cent (we shall see in Chapter XII what pushes interest rates up and down), while dividends may be anything from zero to 100 per cent or more on the nominal value. Loans to companies are usually known as *debentures* and are almost always issued in stock units, often of £100. Sometimes firms issue a hybrid type of security known as *convertible debentures* which carry an option to convert into shares at a future date. Public bodies, local authorities and governments, also raise loans by issuing stock in £100 units; though these are never called debentures, they are much the same thing. (These loans, too, are discussed in Chapter XXI.)

Advantages of Joint Stock Organization. The modern joint stock company has a great many advantages over other forms of business unit. First, the principle of limited liability, because it enormously reduces the risks of ownership, makes it

sensible instead of appallingly rash for the man with a little
capital to invest it in industry instead of merely putting it in a
bank. Before limited liability, the only people normally willing
to invest were those who could keep a personal eye on their investment; so firms could in general only draw on the capital of
those who personally knew and trusted their owners. (In general, but not always. There were tremendous waves of speculation from time to time, such as the South Sea Bubble of 1720,
and very ruinous they were for the unlucky.) Then, too, unlike
the member of a partnership, the shareholder in a joint-stock
company can get his money back by selling his shares to someone else. He may not get it all back, because if profits are low,
and dividends small or nil, no one will pay much for the privilege of sharing them; but he may on the contrary get much
more, because if the company is thriving the prospect of a
share in its profits will look extremely attractive to the buyer.
Moreover, the continual rise in prices in recent years has led
people to buy shares, in preference to fixed interest-bearing
securities such as government stocks, to provide a 'hedge' for
protection against the decrease in the value of money.

Altogether, then, the joint-stock, limited-liability organization makes it possible for the man with energy and ideas and
technical and commercial skill, but not enough capital, to join
forces with the people who have capital—perhaps, individually,
only a little capital—but whose energy and ideas or skills are
occupied in other fields altogether. It makes it possible for investors to spread their risks instead of having all their economic
eggs in one basket. It makes for flexibility and easy growth. It is
useful even for the medium-sized concern; for the really big
one, the kind which must start on a large scale or not at all, like
a steel works or oil refinery, it is just about indispensable. The
only alternative, for the very large-scale concern, is one which
needs separate discussion; and that is public ownership and
control by a local authority, a public corporation, or a government department.

The Co-operative Movement. One form of business organization stands rather apart from those discussed so far; and

that is the Co-operative Society. In this country it is very important indeed in retail trade, but hardly appears elsewhere; other countries have farmers' co-operatives, which buy fertilizers and equipment and sell produce, builders' and printers' co-operatives, and others pursuing different occupations, but even taking the world as a whole the consumers' retail co-operative is much the most frequently found.

It has an interesting history, beginning back in the 'hungry forties' of the nineteenth century. At that time the workpeople in the new factories and mines were often grossly cheated by those who sold them their necessities. Very often it was the factory owner or mineowner who owned the shops—known as 'tommy shops'—and they would pay their workers not in cash but in vouchers which only the 'tommy shops' would take. This was called the 'truck system'. Then the owners could make an extra profit out of their compulsory customers by selling them shoddy goods at fancy prices, including adulterated foods and short-weight deliveries. If the worker was in debt to the shops, as often happened, he was tied hand and foot to his job. A pathetic description of the sufferings of the workpeople under this system is given in Disraeli's novel *Sybil*.

It was to remedy this state of affairs that the co-operative movement was started. A little group of weavers in Rochdale —the 'Rochdale Pioneers'—decided to set up a co-operative store, buying their own stock-in-trade, wholesale, selling honest goods at a fair market price, and returning any profit to members in proportion to their purchases—that is, as a 'divi'. They grimly saved, for several years, the twopence a week a head to which each had pledged himself; and when they had twenty pounds between them they laid it out on oatmeal and flour, sugar and soap and on a few other staples and opened their tiny store in Toad Lane.

Others had tried before, but they had made the mistake of trying to sell at cost price, leaving no margin for wastes and losses, and had failed accordingly. The Rochdale Pioneers succeeded. Year by year the devoted members ploughed back the best part of their 'divi', increased their stock, enlarged their premises, and attracted new recruits. To-day there are over a thousand separate retail co-operative societies in Great Britain, some big ones with many branches, like the London Co-operative Society, whose membership runs into the hundred thousands, others with a single shop and only a few hundred members. In 1962 there were thirteen million members, and the total value of co-operative retail trade was over £1,050 millions. That means that nearly a third of the families of Great Britain belong to the movement.

The retail societies have their own wholesale organizations, the Co-operative Wholesale Society, set up in 1863 to beat an attempted private-business boycott, and the Scottish Wholesale Society, dating from a few years later. These have branched out into flour mills, tea plantations, the manufacture of clothing and furniture and many other things, banking, insurance, and building society business. All these, and the retail societies themselves, are legally limited liability companies; but they pay no 'dividends' in the usual sense. Their members, as shareholders, get a fixed return on their shares—there are no big shareholders, £1,000 being the maximum allowed; the profits go back, as in the days of the Rochdale Pioneers, to the members *as purchasers*. This dividend on purchases comes each year to about £59 millions.

For a good many reasons, co-operation has not thriven as a way of organizing actual manufacture. A co-operative factory, when the workers are the owners, is apt to run into problems of discipline, to have difficulty either in finding first-class managing ability within its own ranks or in attracting it from outside, and to need more capital to begin with than it can conveniently raise. Also, producing for the general market in competition with private enterprise involves taking risks which co-operative enterprise is generally not willing or able to face. The C.W.S. factories thrive on their assured "co-op" market, but they are not themselves "co-operative" in the sense of being owned and managed by their workers. Ownership and management are in the hands of officials representing the consumers.

Co-partnership and Profit Sharing. There is, however, a half-way organization which attempts to combine the co-operative spirit with the more successful private-enterprise structure, that is the *profit-sharing* firm in which the employees are given shares in the concern as well as wages, get dividends in the same way as ordinary shareholders do, and sometimes have representatives on the Board of Directors. There are an increasing number of these, and where the profit-sharing system has taken root it has done a great deal to abolish the cleavage between workers and owners and give the former the feeling that the firm is *their* firm instead of merely their boss. Here, however, in this matter of feelings and loyalties and responsibilities, we are once again getting outside the economic field. And indeed it must never be forgotten that all these organizations, from the cobbler's shop on the corner to Imperial Chemical Industries or the C.W.S., are groups of people whose work is part of their life and whose relations with one another are those of human beings and not of cogs in a machine.

CHAPTER III

PUBLIC ENTERPRISE AND CONTROL

ALL the forms of enterprise discussed in the last chapter, apart from the co-operative movement, have one important feature in common: they are run by private persons acting according to their own lights, on their own responsibility, for their own profit. (In a big joint-stock company the managers who actually control things are employees, not owners; but they are still working for private profit—that of the shareholders, who own the company and can in the last resort decide its policy by coming together at a meeting and voting for a new Board of Directors.) This kind of organization of economic life is what is called the *free enterprise system*, or, in its developed modern form where a great deal of privately owned equipment is used, *capitalism*. But it does not extend over the whole of economic life; it never has. A certain role has always been played by the State and by lesser public authorities; and in modern times that role has greatly increased in importance in all parts of the world.

Profit Motive and Public Benefit. This question of the frontier between public and private enterprise, of how much trust one can put in the profit motive and of just when it fails to provide what the public needs, is one which is apt to raise people's political temperatures. Mercifully, however, it is perfectly possible to set out the arguments and facts without getting involved in the question whether business men are greedy bloodsuckers or whether the people who run nationalized industries are incompetent tyrants. One can begin by taking a look at this all-important profit motive. Really it is just one variety of the general economic motive with which we are all concerned whether we are business men or professionals or manual workers; the motive of self-betterment. The business man looks for the best profit he can get, the wage earner, singly or through his union, looks for the best wage, the actor or author or journalist looks for the manager or publisher or editor who will give him the best contract. They all try to act in the way which will *pay* best—allowing, of course, for the fact that some jobs are so distasteful that people avoid them even when pay is high, and others are so pleasant, or so exciting and hopeful, that a very small return still makes them seem worth while.

One way or another, directly or indirectly, everyone engaged in the economic process is supplying something to the con- sumers. Now, under free enterprise, the consumer decides how to lay out his income and what it is worth his while to pay for each of the different kinds of goods and services he buys. If he sees several sorts of the same kind of thing on the market, he will buy the one which seems to him the best value for money, If he is very short of one kind of goods, and has plenty (or is less short) of another, he will buy the kind whose want he feels more intensely. So the business man who offers better value for money than his competitor will generally get more custom, and make a bigger profit, than that competitor, and the business man who supplies what people most acutely lack, and most want, will get more customers and make a bigger profit than the business man who offers them something they want less urgently. Very broadly speaking indeed, the profit motive works towards a state of affairs in which the consumer gets what he wants as cheaply as it is possible to produce it. And the fact that the business man (whether independent owner or director of a joint-stock company) who gives the consumer what he wants as cheaply as possible can expect a bigger profit, means something else too; it makes it worth his while to offer higher prices for the materials he uses and higher wages to the workers he employs, and so to attract resources and energy away from where they are less useful to where they will count for most in the process of satisfying the consumer.

The business man who supplies the wrong things at high

prices, on the other hand, makes losses until he learns better, and so his suppliers and his workers tend to turn elsewhere for better prices and better pay. The consumer, as it has been said, is king; and it is through the profit motive that he rules, because satisfying him is the only way to make profits. However thoroughly self-seeking the business man may be, his best move from his own point of view is to provide what the public wants —to work, that is, for the public benefit.

Where the Profit Motive Fails. There was a time when this very simple picture of the working of the profit motive was accepted as a good enough reason for leaving the profit motive alone to guide business men and workers and consumers. But as sensible people of all parties have come to realize, it is a very incomplete picture. Later, we shall have to look at the details, and see how price changes come about and affect the way consumers and business men behave; and that is not nearly as simple as the last paragraph might make one think. Just now, the question we have to consider is—where, if anywhere, does the profit motive break down as a means of getting the consumer's needs met? Because there, at the point where it breaks down or falls short, is where public enterprise and control has to step in.

Community Needs. Everyone agrees that there are some needs, and very basic and important needs too, which private enterprise cannot meet at all; some things which can only be bought by everyone clubbing together to buy them, as we do, in effect, when we pay taxes to the Government or rates to the local council to finance their activities. A single consumer can buy five shillings' worth of handkerchiefs or potatoes; he cannot, obviously, individually buy five shillings' worth of police protection, or guided weapons, or high roads, or lighthouses. So these things cannot be supplied in the way of business. They have to be managed by the Government. Then there are other needs which, left to ourselves, a great many of us would not fill adequately either from our own point of view or other people's. A single consumer can buy education, or the services of doctors and hospitals; but if he does not, or cannot, buy enough of these things to safeguard a certain basic standard of education and health for his family, they not only suffer themselves but become a nuisance and a danger to other people. So again the State has to step in—how far, is a political question to which different countries give different answers—and supply education and health services free or below cost price, up to a point where everybody can be sure of getting that minimum. A single consumer can buy (or rent) house room; but if he and the landlord and the builders are left to settle things entirely between themselves their activities can result (as the industrial towns of Great Britain show too well) in acres and acres of insanitary eyesores, which blight the lives not only of their first inhabitants but also of later generations. Anything which the consumer needs but which cannot be individually bought; anything which, because of poverty or ignorance or reckless-ness, the consumer cannot be trusted to buy in sufficient quanti-ties, or at a sufficiently high standard, for the general good; anything falling into either of these two classes must be either supplied by the State or made cheaper by State subsidies.

Monopoly. But that is by no means the whole story. Some of the rest of the story—the story, that is, of the unsatisfactoriness of unmixed and unqualified free enterprise—will have to wait; notably the 'social justice' side of it, the question of the way free enterprise distributes wealth and poverty. Another part of the story which must wait is that which has to do with currency and banking and is all tied up with the problem of booms and slumps (we shall see about this in Chapter XXII). But one im-portant reason for preferring public to private ownership and control in certain kinds of industry, other than those men-tioned above, arises when private enterprise is for one reason or another not *competitive*. When the working of the profit motive was discussed a little earlier, it was pointed out that when business men failed to give as good value for money as their competitors they lost custom, so that every business man's desire for profits led him to give as good value for money as he could. This sounds splendid. But if he has *no* competitors, if he is alone in the field, he can if he chooses keep his prices high, supply poor quality goods and services, brush aside new ideas when they look as though they might be troublesome, and make what is called a *monopoly profit* out of his customers. He can in fact, behave just like the tommy-shop owners mentioned in the last chapter. He need not necessarily; but he may.

Public Utilities. Now there are many kinds of enterprise in which there cannot be effective competition, and in which accordingly the profit motive cannot be trusted to lead business men to give the best value for money. The supply of gas, water and electricity, for instance—there may be hundreds of firms supplying these services, but the consumer can only deal with the one covering his neighbourhood. (Why can there not be several gas companies supplying one street and so giving the consumer a choice? Partly because the roads would be 'up' continually for construction or repairs of mains; partly because duplicate mains would be so ridiculously expensive; partly because, as it happens, large-scale gas production is much cheaper than small-scale. And the same goes for electricity.) Then railways present much the same picture, even in the open country duplicate railway tracks are ridiculously wasteful. So the single railway company serving a particular route would, if the profit motive acted alone and uncontrolled, have travellers and shippers on that route at its mercy.

Wherever this situation arises in an essential industry, wherever economic or other forces make competition impossible, public authority has to step in and exert some sort of control. And—though here we are getting on to controversial ground—in some cases the simplest, least expensive and most efficient way of exercising that control may be to buy out the private owners and run the industry by public enterprise; that is, to *nationalize* it.

The Development of Public Enterprise: before 1919. Public enterprise is of many different types; the chart facing this page shows the main kinds.

Historically, its development over the last hundred years

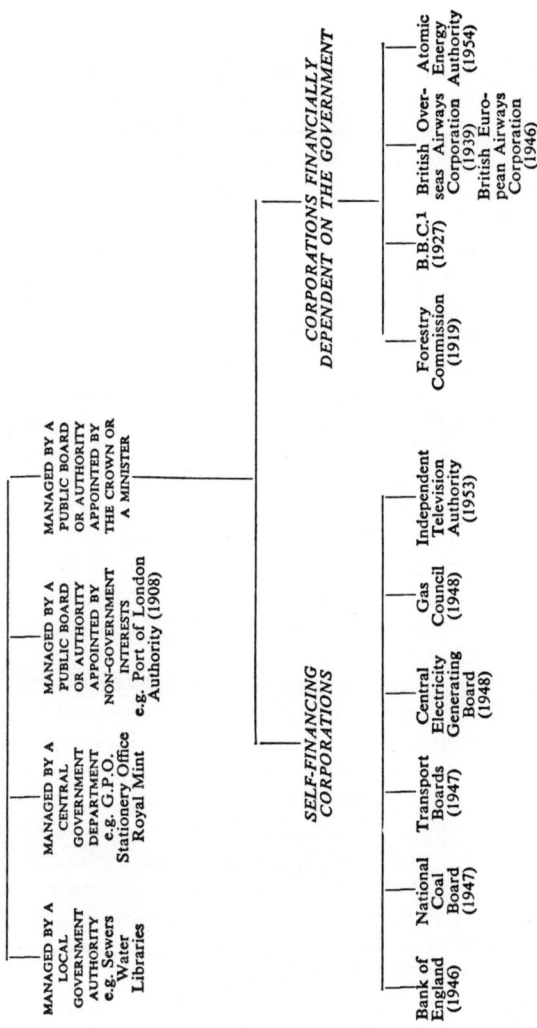

| MANAGED BY A LOCAL GOVERNMENT AUTHORITY e.g. Sewers Water Libraries | MANAGED BY A CENTRAL GOVERNMENT DEPARTMENT e.g. G.P.O. Stationery Office Royal Mint | MANAGED BY A PUBLIC BOARD OR AUTHORITY APPOINTED BY NON-GOVERNMENT INTERESTS e.g. Port of London Authority (1908) | MANAGED BY A PUBLIC BOARD OR AUTHORITY APPOINTED BY THE CROWN OR A MINISTER |

SELF-FINANCING CORPORATIONS

Bank of England (1946)

National Coal Board (1947)

Transport Boards (1947)

Central Electricity Generating Board (1948)

Gas Council (1948)

Independent Television Authority (1953)

CORPORATIONS FINANCIALLY DEPENDENT ON THE GOVERNMENT

Forestry Commission (1919)

B.B.C.1 (1927)

British Overseas Airways Corporation (1939) British European Airways Corporation (1946)

Atomic Energy Authority (1954)

1 The B.B.C. is only partially dependent on Parliament financially, for it receives no subsidy, but the proportion of licence fees it obtains is decided by Parliament.

FIG. 1—TYPES OF PUBLIC ENTERPRISE

falls into three fairly clearly marked periods: from the mid-nineteenth century to 1919, from 1919 to 1945, and from 1945 to the present day. During the first of these periods it was, initially, kept down to a minimum. People had almost boundless faith in the profit motive and a deep distrust of officialdom. Roads, sewers, fire services, and of course national defence and coinage, were recognized to be the business of public authority; so were the mails. But the problem of inducing gas and water and railway companies to give good value was tackled either by an uphill endeavour to encourage competition, even when it was quite unsuitable, or by laws which made such companies answerable to special bodies of public officials who acted as guardians of the public interest and who were known as *Statutory Commissioners*.

Growth of Public Enterprise. Later in the nineteenth century the local authorities (particularly the County Councils or County Boroughs created under the Local Government Act of 1888) widened the sphere of their activities and began to supply such services as elementary education (and, after 1902, secondary education as well), public libraries, parks, baths and washhouses, and in general to meet a number of those wants which private enterprise was unable or unwilling to meet on an adequate scale.

By that time the shortcomings of unmixed private enterprise, of the 'capitalist system', had become so obvious that some people were beginning to feel that it ought to be swept away altogether and replaced by State ownership and control of 'the means of production, distribution and exchange', i.e. all property involved in the productive process. This was the Socialist point of view, dating well back and owing much to the writings of Karl Marx. In the 1890s a non-revolutionary Socialism found a particularly clear and influential voice in the *Fabian Society*. It was, however, still very much a minority point of view; public opinion thought Socialism hopelessly impractical.

Public opinion had, however, moved a long way since the days when private enterprise was supposed to be the answer to practically all questions of economic organization. In 1908 an interesting new form of public enterprise made its appearance in the shape of the Port of London Authority, which was a *Representative Trust*. Up to 1908 a conglomeration of different bodies, private and public, had been concerned with the administration of the warehouses, the wharves, and the river. These were private individuals and firms—warehouse owners, dock owners, shippers, merchants and public bodies including the Board of Trade, the London County Council, the Admiralty and Trinity House. All had an interest in the smooth running and efficient co-ordination of the Port's business; all agreed, in the end, that they could only get smooth running and efficient co-ordination by having one competent authority for the whole Port. The solution was a Board of twenty-eight to thirty members *representing* the different interests concerned, whether suppliers, or users of the Port's services; a Board whose business it was to direct the administration of the Port with the help of an executive staff.

Here there was no actual transference of ownership, nor was there any political theory involved. The 'P.L.A.' represented a commonsense, compromise solution of a particular problem; not, it is generally agreed, a solution which could be applied to every sort of undertaking, but unmistakably successful in this particular case.

Public Enterprise, 1919–39. Between the two World Wars there were important developments in the field of public control. It was more and more generally recognized that that field existed and was a great deal wider than nineteenth-century opinion had believed. Nevertheless, very little property was actually transferred from private to public ownership during these years; none of the measures concerned really involved nationalization.

The first public body to be created during these years was the Forestry Commission. World War I had shown up our timber policy; Britain was seriously short of timber, and although about a million acres of potential forest land were available, no serious planting had been done for many years. The returns on the heavy capital outlay needed in forestry are, in general, too slow to attract private enterprise; here, evidently, was a gap to be filled. So the Forestry Commission of eight members was set up in 1919, with the duty of developing forestry and a Treasury grant to finance its work.

The war had also shown up our system of electricity distribution. Very largely because of the nineteenth century's fear of big concerns wielding monopoly powers, this was a patchwork of small enterprises, working to different standards, and far below the best practicable efficiency. To pull it into shape the *Central Electricity Board* was appointed in 1926. The CEB was a first-class example of compromise between public and private enterprise. The Board *controlled* the generating stations, but did not *own* them. The final distribution of electricity to the consumer, what one might call the 'retailing' of electricity, remained in local hands. But the 'wholesale' distribution—the country-wide 'Grid' with its four thousand miles of high-voltage transmission lines—was owned and controlled by the Board.

In 1927 the advance of wireless telephony from the experimental stage reached the point when a decision had to be taken about its future control. Broadcasting can, technically, be left to private individuals and firms, as it is in the United States, with the programmes financed by advertisement; and the argument about whether the American system or ours gives the best results is still going on. In Britain, however, it was decided that the public would be better served by a public corporation, holding a monopoly of the right to broadcast and financed by wireless licences; and so the *British Broadcasting Corporation* was set up, a Government creation, but with directors appointed by the Crown in Council, and free to pursue an independent policy with only the slightest and most general control by the Cabinet or Parliament. (In 1954 the B.B.C. monopoly was modified by the establishment of the Independent Television Authority. This leases television transmitting stations to private firms, which finance their programmes by advertisements under closely defined rules.)

In 1933 it was the turn of the London passenger transport services to be reorganized under public control. Up till then the

London area had been served by a number of different companies and authorities running the various bus, tram, Underground and suburban railway services. But as London spread and sprawled and the streets grew more congested and the traffic problem more acute, it became clear that an overall co-ordinating authority was needed, to plan and direct the system as a whole. For this purpose the *London Passenger Transport Board* was formed. Actual ownership remained private, though the old shareholders got a different type of security instead of their original shares. But the control of the huge new concern was vested in a public Board, its directors appointed by the Minister of Transport and chosen so as to give fair representation to the various interests involved. Once appointed they, like the directors of the BBC, were free from direct day-to-day control either by the Minister or by Parliament.

Public Enterprise, 1945. All these extensions of the field of public enterprise had been carried out by Conservative Governments. The Labour view, which was bound up with a deep distrust of the profit motive, was that they should be carried much further; that the greater part, if not all, of the key services and industries of the country should be nationalized. The form of nationalization which the Labour Party favoured was not (as in some countries) direct ownership by the State and control by a Civil Service department—the method used, for instance, in the Post Office. It was a development of the pre-war Public Corporation, a step onward from the London Passenger Transport Board. Not only the control but also the ownership of these industries was to be transferred from the private shareholders and directors to a Board or Corporation appointed by the appropriate Minister. (The Bank of England, like the BBC, had a governing board appointed by the Crown.)

This development was basically different from anything that had happened before 1945. It arose from a real change in public opinion and Government policy. The inter-war Boards had been set up to do a job which private enterprise could not do; these were set up to take over a job which private enterprise

was already doing. Moreover, the inter-war Boards had not
actually deprived anyone of their property; these did, compen-
sating the losers but giving them no choice. (Whether compen-
sation was, in this or that industry, too small, about right, or
too much, remains a matter of heated argument.) The following are the main industries and services affected.

Industry or Service	Title of Corporation	Date of Formation
BANK OF ENGLAND	No change in title	1946
COAL	NATIONAL COAL BOARD	1946
CIVIL AVIATION	BRITISH OVERSEAS AIRWAYS BRITISH EUROPEAN AIRWAYS	1946
TRANSPORT, i.e. railways, road haulage, docks, inland waterways, hotels, L.P.T.B.	TRANSPORT COMMISSION RECONSTITUTED AS SEPARATE BOARDS	1947 1963
ELECTRICITY	BRITISH ELECTRICITY AUTHORITY reorganized as CENTRAL ELECTRICITY GENERATING BOARD and AREA ELECTRICITY BOARDS	1947 1958
GAS	GAS COUNCIL	1948
TELEVISION	INDEPENDENT TELEVISION AUTHORITY	1954

Under the Road Transport Act of 1954 road haulage mainly
reverted to private enterprise through the progressive
re-sale of the Road Haulage Executive's assets.

FIG. 2—NATIONALIZATION, AFTER 1945

The Political Background. This difference is partly a difference in the motives and general ideas of the people who put
through the changes, partly a difference in the circumstances.
The Labour Government of 1945 distrusted the profit motive
as thoroughly as the Governments of a hundred years earlier
had trusted it; they believed that quite apart from the special
case of monopolies, and of services which could not be supplied on a business basis, it was a good thing for the productive
process to be carried on with a direct eye to the public good
rather than by individuals looking to their own advantage.
Also, for reasons which will be more possible to understand

when we have studied money and banking and taxation and employment, they believed that it would only be possible to avoid booms and slumps when the productive process was shaped by far-seeing experts at the centre of things, and that this shaping and guiding job could only be properly done when at least the more important basic industries were directly under public control. (On this point most economists, though not all, disagree with them.) There were other reasons peculiar to Socialists, too—political reasons, the feeling that private ownership of basic industry gave too much personal power to the big business man, the belief that so long as private owners held that power it would be impossible to get far towards that levelling-out of differences of wealth which was so important a part of Socialism. But here we are getting off the economist's proper ground.

Britain's Post-War Difficulties. Apart from the special attitude of Socialists to these matters, however, there were also the special circumstances of post-war Britain. For one thing there had been heavy wartime economic losses; particularly, much of the property built up overseas in the previous hundred years had had to be sold to pay for wartime imports. That made it important for the right things to be produced—not just the things individuals felt they would like here and now, but the things which would help put Britain back on her feet again in the long run, like new equipment and docks and factories and railway rolling-stock. Then, too, it was just precisely the basic industries like mining and rail transport which most needed an overhaul (because for various reasons they had had very lean years before the war and had got run down) and which, because they were in such a bad way, were least likely to be able to get the capital they needed from private investors. Finally, all through the basic British industries the size of the firms concerned and of the plant they owned was, by world standards, too small for the most efficient working; they needed to be regrouped and co-ordinated to get the *advantage of scale*, an expression about which there will be more to say later. Under private ownership this did not seem likely to happen.

The Case for Nationalization. Taking together both Social-ist reasons and others, nationalization was supported on these grounds:

1. Because of the untrustworthiness of the profit motive.

2. In order to curb the power of the individual rich men and so make possible an advance towards equality.

3. In order to help the central planners iron out booms and slumps and keep employment high.

4. In order to carry out long-term planning to raise the national output of wealth each year.

5. In order to ensure that industries which needed a great deal of new capital should have the whole credit of the State to back them.

6. In order to reorganize and re-group undertakings so as to reap the advantages of large size without incurring the disadvantages of private monopoly.

The Case Against Nationalization. Some dangers pointed out by people who disagree with nationalization are:

1. Without the profit motive—and without the fear of per-sonal loss—those in charge of an industry are likely by degrees to get slack and fall short of the highest efficiency.

2. The fact of being responsible, however indirectly, to a Minister and to Parliament may make directors and man-agers over-cautious, too anxious to justify themselves, too much bound by routine and precedent, and altogether too unwilling to take the kind of risks which economic progress involves. Moreover, on matters of day-to-day administra-tion they are put quite outside public control.

3. Where the losses due to mistakes fall on the taxpayer, it is likely that the wrong policies will be pursued far beyond the point at which private enterprise would have seen the error of its ways.

4. Though large scale has its advantages, these are out-weighed after a certain point by unwieldiness and internal red tape, thus difficulties of administration arise.

5. A serious mistake by the executives of a nationalized industry has much worse effects than the mistakes of inde-

pendent business men because all the industry's eggs are in one basket.

Time will show how—in each industry—pros and cons finally balance out.

There are also semi-political questions: What about the worker's freedom when there is only one business which he can work for? What sort of training in responsibility and leadership is possible where nobody can be his own master? What about the power of the big public Corporation, bigger than any private business, to override the individual whose interests stand in its way? But these, again, are not really suitable for discussion here. They are only mentioned because the way people feel about them is apt to give a slant or twist to the way they look at the economic side of the matter, and to make decisions about nationalization a matter of party feeling rather than of judging (as one surely should) each particular industry's case on its merits.

State Control of Private Enterprise. Of course the State intervenes in the productive process in plenty of other ways besides directly owning or controlling particular industries. All through the last century, but particularly during and since World War II, there has been a steady increase in government control over the working of the economic system.

Some of these interventions, particularly the earlier ones, were aimed at making free enterprise work better, at helping to ensure that the economic choices mentioned in the first chapter were really free and made with open eyes. Laws regulating weights and measures, setting a standard of purity for food and drugs, making untrue descriptions of goods a punishable offence, were of this kind. Others aimed at protecting the weaker party to a bargain—like the Factory Acts, which forbade first very young children, and in the end all children, to work in factories, and laid down rules about safety, cleanliness, ventilation and so on, and limited the hours which women and young people were allowed to work, and provided for the employment of Factory Inspectors to see that these rules were obeyed. Later on, this sort of intervention on behalf of the weaker party went further, laying down minimum wages in certain trades where the workers were too helpless to bargain for themselves (the first measure of this kind was the Trade Boards Act of 1909); and controlling the prices of some necessities which might otherwise have risen to famine heights—the Rent Restriction Acts passed during World War I were among the most important laws of this kind; or laying down special rules to govern the behaviour of monopolistic concerns —the Railway Rates Tribunal dated right back to the mid-nineteenth century.

These interventions have not always been on behalf of the *buyers* of goods; sometimes the seller has been the weaker party (like the workers protected by minimum wage legislation, who are sellers of labour). During the 1930s several laws were passed preventing people from selling things *cheaper* than a minimum figure, because in times of bad trade a few desperate price-cutters can make it almost impossible for their fellow traders to get a living. (Later on, when we have seen how prices get settled in a free market, we shall be able to discuss the pros and cons of this kind of control.) The many new price controls imposed during World War II and maintained for several years after were, however, almost all aimed at protecting the consumers. So, of course, was rationing, which is another matter more easily discussed after the general question of prices in the free market.

Post-War Controls. Another kind of control, almost unknown before World War II, is that which gives power to Ministers, or officials representing them, to decide whether or not such and such a piece of business should go through, such and such a building be erected, such and such a loan be granted, such and such a purchase of raw materials or fuel be permitted. During and immediately after the war there were some 52,000 of these controls, which aimed at fitting the activities of privately owned and managed business into the national plan and at spreading out the effects of particular shortages. Most of these were regarded as temporary and were abolished as conditions eased; but a few, mainly on certain types of foreign exchange transactions, still remain, and as we shall see later the principle of Government intervention of this type is not likely to be dropped.

Another new departure since World War II was the formation of the Monopolies Commission in 1948 with the purpose of enquiring into the effects of restrictive trade agreements. The Restrictive Practices Court was set up in 1956, and all restrictive trade agreements must be registered with it. If it is considered that an agreement may be against the public interest, the Court may call on those concerned to justify it. If it is not justified, the Court can order it to be ended.

We have now looked at the bones, as it were, of the business world; at the different types of private business from small to large and the rules under which they work; at the public enterprises which supplement, or replace, private business where the public interest appears to demand it; at the various types of control by which, outside the field of public enterprise, the State changes the course of events which the unmixed profit motive would bring about. The next chapter discusses the principles on which the productive process is divided up between these different units, between different sorts of workers, and between different parts of the world.

D

CHAPTER IV

THE DIVISION OF LABOUR

IN Chapter I it was noted that our economic civilization rests on a complicated and world-wide division of labour; on specialization of workers, local groups, nations, climatic areas. It is now time to look more closely at this characteristic.

Isolated Man. It is possible, just possible, to live entirely without division of labour. Robinson Crusoe (even though he was, under another name, a real person) is hardly a proper example, for he began his solitary life with a store of tools and weapons and ammunition which were the products of a civilized community and which he could not possibly have produced for himself, But some years ago there was an adventurous American who, by way of experiment, went to the edge of one of the great forests of Maine, took off every stitch of clothes except his trousers, and walked empty-handed into the woods to live, if he could, for a year by his own wholly unaided efforts. He succeeded. He found water, and drank it in his cupped hands; he built a shelter of fallen boughs, and thickened it with moss; he lay in wait with a cudgel for porcupines, and cooked them on a fire made Indian-fashion with a fire-stick; before winter he had made himself, from lichen and from the skins of animals caught in deadfall traps, enough clothes (of a sort) to save himself from freezing to death. And he emerged, battered, bearded and triumphant, to prove that the thing could be done.

Now the difference between his standard of life in the woods —the hunger and cold and endless discomfort, the unremitting labour, the knowledge that an unseasonable change of weather,

34

a shift of game, an illness, even so slight an accident as a sprained ankle, could mean destruction—and the standard which he enjoyed in his normal life, is the measure of what the division of labour means in the modern world. The same abilities, the same natural gifts, the same strength, the same qualities of application and ingenuity, which would just, but only just, keep him alive when he was alone, enabled him as part of a modern community to live in a warm and comfortable house, eat varied, ample and tasty food, dress in clothes whose softness, sturdiness and fit suited whatever occupation and climate he found himself in, be whisked from place to place at high speed without exertion, and enjoy recreations, amusements and comforts of hundreds of different kinds. He was just the same man in both sets of circumstances; it was the division of labour, his ability to fit his work in with other people's, which had made the difference.

Primitive Communities. Turn from this eccentric adventurer to the kind of primitive community mentioned in Chapter II, and the difference is already enormous. Simple as is their division of labour, some division does exist. The men fish, the women cook and weave; those whose skill lies in the making of tools or weapons or the building of canoes concentrate on using that skill; it is someone's business to tend the communal fire, it is the business of some special group to keep the communal meeting-house in repair. So instead of just managing by good fortune and unremitting labour to struggle through a single year they live and thrive happily and healthily enough generation after generation.

Theirs is, however, a desperately poor and insecure life by our standards. Their diet is monotonous, their houses flimsy, their clothing only adequate so long as the weather favours them; when disease strikes them they have no defence, and a crop failure or a storm smashing their boats means literal starvation. Only in those parts of the world most richly favoured by Nature do such primitive communities have any leisure in which to enjoy themselves, amuse themselves, and develop many arts and skills other than those strictly concerned with keeping alive. Yet there is no evidence that man by man and woman by woman these primitive peoples are any less naturally gifted than the comfortable citizens of a modern community. Again, it is the degree of the division of labour which makes the difference.

The Advantage of Equipment: Machinery and Tools. This may seem a little sweeping. After all, the biggest and most obvious difference between the primitive and modern community is the difference between the kinds and amounts of equipment they work with. Two men may both be specialists in the making of roads. But if one has a crude pickaxe and the other is driving a bulldozer there will be, to put it mildly, a difference in the amount of road-making they can do. Two others may be weavers; one sits at a hand-loom, throwing the shuttle to and fro, the other tends sixteen or even thirty-two power-looms, each of whose shuttles moves many times as fast as the single hand-thrown shuttle. And so on. *But the development and use of equipment, from simple tools to such giant industrial plants as are found in, for instance, the iron and steel industry, is itself the result of the division of labour.* Scientists and technicians have specialized in working out their principles and designing them, groups of specialized workers have made them, and meanwhile (for otherwise the work could not have been done) others have been producing the food and clothes, and consumer goods generally, which these workers for the future need to keep themselves going.

Of course the more equipment is available, and the more each specialized user of that equipment can produce as a result, the more human energy is available to work for to-morrow and the day after instead of for to-day, and thus to produce still more equipment and liberate still more energy; and the more possible it is to take out some part of the gain in leisure and enjoyment; and—an important point—the shorter the period of each worker's life which has to be devoted to actual production, so that instead of children having to start working and earning as soon as is physically possible they can spend their growing years in learning and developing and acquiring skills and finding out where their abilities lie. So the effect of specialization is that of a snowball, gathering impetus and growing faster and faster.

Simple Division of Labour: by Trades. The first and simplest kind of division of labour is that of trades—carpenter, farmer, smith, fisherman and so forth. It is in itself enough to raise the standard of productivity, and hence the standard of living, a long way above that of a community of unspecialized families. Jack-of-all-trades is master of none, and the 'master', knowing thoroughly the complex of jobs on which he has concentrated, and having (with any luck) chosen the kind of trade to which his particular abilities are suited, will produce more than the 'Jack'. Moreover, the 'master' can afford a full outfit of tools for his single trade; the 'Jack' cannot possibly afford all the tools of all the trades, and must make do with something much sketchier.

Division of Labour by Jobs and Processes. But division of labour by trades is only the beginning. Trades can be split up into single jobs, and these in turn can be split up finer and finer into different processes to which different workers can devote their whole attention. Adam Smith, in a well-known passage of his famous book *The Wealth of Nations*, shows very vividly the enormous increase in output which results from this kind of division of labour. He found that in so small and specialized a trade as the making of pins there were no less than 'eighteen distinct operations, which in some manufactories are all performed by different hands. One man draws out the wire, another straights it, a third cuts, a fourth points it . . .' and so forth. Even a small 'manufactory' which, employing only ten men, had to assign more than one process to some of them, could turn out by these methods some forty-eight thousand pins daily, or four thousand eight hundred a head. 'But if', says Adam Smith, 'they had all wrought separately and independently, and without any of them having been educated to this particular business, they certainly could not each of them have made twenty, perhaps not one pin in a day.' Division of labour carried on from the *job* to the *process* had in fact multiplied output several thousandfold.

As one might guess from his style, Smith wrote a long time ago. In 1776, when his book was published, manufacturing firms were still small units, and many processes of production now carried on in factories were carried on in homes and home workshops. In the following years the factory system began to appear in the cotton industry, as the growth of the market for cotton goods stimulated the invention of new machinery and this new machinery proved too large to be housed in workers' homes. From the cotton industry it spread to others; as first water and then steam power was applied to work the new machines, larger factories proved more economical than smaller. And once a number of workers were gathered under a single roof, the way was open for further division of labour, from job to process, in trade after trade. This movement has continued to the present day, and, as machinery has grown more and more elaborate, processes have been more and more subdivided. As the task of each worker has become more specialized it has also often become more simple, mechanical, and consequently boring: a poor sort of occupation for a complete man with a complete set of faculties, all of which must lie fallow except for the single skill of tightening, say, a single bolt on an object moving past him on a production belt. (Boredom may, in fact, actually reduce efficiency, thus offsetting some of the gain from specialization.) But the output of goods per head, and the standard of living which that output implies, have risen enormously. So has the amount of leisure in which the over-specialized worker can, if he chooses, live as a complete person. Humanly considered, this increase is not all pure gain—but here, once again, we come to the borderland when economics alone cannot answer our question.

Gains of Specialization. To sum up, then: division of labour makes it possible for each worker to concentrate his particular natural ability on the job he can do best and to avoid those he can do least well. (This is particularly important in the skilled occupations, most important of all in the professions.)

By experience and repetition, at any level of skill, it increases the worker's proficiency. Practice makes perfect.

It saves the time which any worker doing a number of different jobs must lose in turning from one to the other; in readjusting his mind, fetching and putting away different tools and materials, and so on.

It allows special tools and machinery to be used full time instead of standing idle while the worker using them is otherwise occupied. This in turn makes it worth while to make and instal elaborate equipment which increases output. All this means a much greater output of wealth per head and so a higher standard of living.

It makes it possible to provide for the future. Unspecialized workers can only work for the future (make tools, build houses or boats, drain land) while they can draw on stores of consumable goods which they themselves have built up; and stores are apt to be perishable and certain to be limited. With the division of labour, some can concentrate on long-run projects, others can meanwhile support them. (Here we run into the question of money and savings; but that must wait.) Moreover, it is much more possible to save, that is, to divert energy and resources to the future rather than the present, out of the greatly increased output per head which follows from the division of labour.

Primary, Secondary and Tertiary Production. Looking at the pattern, as it were, of the division of labour, one finds that it is possible to divide the great variety of different ends to which it is directed into three main kinds. There is what is called *primary production*—raising crops and herds, fishing, lumbering, mining coal and metals, quarrying; the kind of production which results in raw materials and foodstuffs. There is *secondary production*, which is broadly the same as manufacture—the working up of primary products into their finished form. And there is *tertiary production* or *service*, which includes transport and storage and all kinds of office work and professional services. In Great Britain there are about 24 million workers (the rest of the 52 millions making up the whole population either have not left school, or have retired, or are housewives working in their own homes, outside the labour market, or are disabled from work for one reason or another). Of those 24 millions, under 2 million are engaged in primary production, about 12 million in secondary, and about 10 million in tertiary services. Of course the dividing line between actual workers is not perfectly clear cut. Mining is obviously primary production —but the National Coal Board has to employ typists and accountants and managers and 'service' workers of all kinds as well as face workers. Retailing is obviously tertiary production —but a big shop will employ a whole staff of carpenters, for instance, in its packing department. Still, it is perfectly possible to look at two different countries, or at the same country at two different times, and say that the proportions between the three chief kinds of production are different.

Historic Changes in the Economic Pattern. They do vary, very widely, over different parts of the world and different periods of history. By and large—there are exceptions—the less economically developed a country is, the greater the proportion of its total activity which goes into primary production. When one comes to think of it that is natural enough. People must eat. If they can only just manage to produce enough food to keep going, they cannot spare much time and energy to produce other things. (The aborigines of the Australian desert and the pygmies of Central Africa cannot spare any; they go naked and have no houses.) But as a community's knowledge and equipment improves so that they can produce more food, their stomachs do not expand to match. They eat better, they enjoy more variety—but they take out more and more of their increasing gain not in extra food but in more and better clothes and houses and general amenities.

Look at a cornfield in England at harvest time. Round and round the field there moves a tractor pulling a combine-harvester which cuts the wheat, swallows it up, ejects the straw, pours the grain into bags and throws them out ready for transport and storage; a single man is driving the tractor, another tends the combine, and in a single day they will have reaped and threshed perhaps 14 acres. Then look at a picture of the same

field being reaped in medieval times. A whole line of workers
—men, women and children—are toiling across it with sickles,
working from dawn to dusk, and returning on their tracks to
bind the fallen swathes. Later they will have to thresh it by
hand—more long hours of work. Where are their descendants
to-day? Just two are riding in that tractor; of the rest, some are
perhaps making the machines which the modern farmer uses;
they are serving primary production at one remove. But others
are making things which have nothing to do with primary production; things of which their ancestors had never heard, like
wireless sets, or which only kings and nobles enjoyed, like soft
fabrics, or which the medieval worker might just aspire to as a
luxury, like leather shoes. And others are not making things at
all, but moving them about so that they are available everywhere; or following professions; or helping in one capacity or
another with the organizing job—business and administration
—which the division of labour makes necessary. And the
children will not be working at all; with every adult worker
producing so much more, their labour can be dispensed with.
   In some parts of the world—notably in China, India, Indo-
nesia—the harvest scene remains much more like the second
picture than the first. These countries are short of equipment
and knowledge, so most of their energies have to be devoted to
sheer necessary primary production. Others, like those of Central Europe, occupy a half-way position. But one must not jump
to the conclusion, because backward countries have to stick
pretty closely to primary production, that the argument works
the other way—that all primary-producing countries are backward. Far from it. Though a country, or a region, may stick to
primary production because it cannot help it, it may also do so
because its primary production is so tremendously efficient that
it has a great deal of primary produce to export in return for
the manufactures of other countries. If one takes China as an
example of the first kind of primary producing country, one
can take New Zealand, with its mutton and wool and dairy
produce, as an example of the second kind. China has about
the lowest standard of living in the world, and New Zealand
about the highest, higher even than that of the United States.

Changing Patterns of Consumption. Over the world as a whole, however, one can see the rule works itself out: as production in general rises, primary production forms a smaller and smaller part of the total. One can see the same effect from another angle by looking at individual family budgets; the bigger the income, the less the proportion of that income spent on food and fuel, that is on directly consumed primary products. Tastes differ, of course; some people are more interested in their stomachs than others; but the general rule holds. (Anyone who chooses to imagine how his family would spend twice the income they have now will soon come to the conclusion that they would not double their food bills. They might eat more and better, but almost certainly not all that much more and better.)

The Growth of Tertiary Activity. And—this is not so obvious nor so simple—much the same argument applies to the different proportions of secondary and tertiary production. As production in general rises, tertiary production—service and transport—takes up a larger and larger proportion of total resources. This is partly because the same increased specialization which makes the rise in production possible calls for a great deal more transport and organization than the simpler kind which it replaces.

Someone has to be responsible for dovetailing the different jobs and processes in a factory—enter the manager or a complete managerial staff, unheard of in a small workshop where the owner does any necessary managing of his two or three assistants without moving from his own bench. Someone has to keep track of what each process or component costs and what each item sold brings in—enter the accountant and his office staff, again unheard of in the small unspecialized enterprise. Someone has to link the different specialized enterprises together so that each can get supplies of what it needs and find a market for its products; enter the transport services and merchants, which indeed have always existed, but which are far more important in the modern world than in the old world where people and regions specialized less and were more self-sufficient. Someone has to make the goods available to the consumer, who cannot possibly collect them from where they are made and would find it difficult and expensive to order them direct from the maker; enter the shopkeeper, in larger and larger numbers, and behind the shopkeeper the wholesaler who does for him exactly the same job as he does for the general public. Someone has to tell the public what is available and at what prices—enter the advertising agent.

As the social and economic fabric grows more complex, and everyone comes to depend more on everyone else, and people live more closely packed together, Government has to play a more and more active part—enter more and more Civil Servants, more and more local government officials, and, on the side of business, more and more people whose job is simply to deal with these. One may say that the work done by all these people is the price of specialization. In particular cases the price may be so high that the gains of specialization are wiped out—so high that more would be produced, net, by a simpler division of labour which involved less organizing and rushing about and telephoning and writing of letters and drawing up of schemes and regulations. When people talk about 'masses of unproductive workers' and 'red tape', they may be talking nonsense—because it should be clear by now that organizing and lubricating the division of labour is just as necessary a job as any other—but they may be putting their finger on a weak spot and pointing to a piece of organization so complex that it makes more work than it saves.

But this *necessary* increase in 'tertiary' production is not the whole story. There is also the tertiary production which comes about because energies have been released as production increases, the tertiary production which forms part of a higher standard of living. Medical services and holiday travel, the theatre and cinema, entertainment generally, education of every kind, the provision of news and literature and art—one can think of many more kinds of production which are desired for themselves and not just as a means of getting more actual things made and into the consumer's hands. And these kinds, too, tend to increase more than proportionately as the standard of living rises. And of course—awkwardly enough as we found in Britain after World War II—a country which has grown poorer has to reverse the process; more resources are needed in primary production, fewer can be afforded in service industries, and this reversal may be very hard to bring about.

How Natural Resources Shape the Pattern. Concentration on primary, secondary or tertiary production or on particular kinds of any of these does not, as has been pointed out already, depend entirely on the stage of economic development which a country has reached. It depends also very much on that country's resources and situation.

One cannot, for instance, have industrial development without power. A country or locality which has easily accessible coal, or oil wells, or water power easily convertible into electricity, is obviously better placed for industrial development than one which has little or none of either. Coal can be imported, so can oil, and so within limits can hydro-electic power, but their transport costs money. The same is true of raw materials, particularly the iron ore which is the foundation material of all mechanized production; but it matters most with coal, the oldest source of large-scale power, and so, in general, major industrial development has taken place close to the coalfields of the major industrial countries. One can see this correspondence clearly in appropriate maps of the United States, Britain and Europe.

Even more obviously, the nature of production depends on climate. One cannot grow bananas in Britain, nor run fur-farms in the tropics, nor carry on any economic activities at all at the North Pole or in the middle of the Sahara or Gobi deserts. Short of such flat impossibilities, it takes much less effort and equipment per bushel to grow wheat on the Canadian prairie than on a hill farm in Wales, and many more costly devices to make a factory or mine tolerable in tropical Africa than in Lancashire. (One of the richest coalfields in the world, the Wankie field in Rhodesia, can be exploited at present at only a fraction of its capacity, partly because it is too hot for even the African workers.)

Communications. Then there are communications to be considered. Where there are natural harbours and waterways, convenient routes through hills and forests, few impenetrable natural barriers, trade can expand and industry can enjoy cheap access to materials and markets; and the more important cheap transport is to any given industry, the likelier it is that that industry will grow up where communications are good, and not elsewhere. Whether communications with the source of raw materials, or communications with the final market, matter most, depends on the product. Steel works use many tons of coal, of ore, and of limestone to produce every ton of finished steel, and finished steel travels easily; so nearness to markets matters little beside nearness to sources of material. The canning of fruit, vegetables and fish uses perishable, hard-to-move raw materials and transforms them into something which will keep indefinitely and travel easily: so the same argument applies. But when the finished article is costlier and more awkward to move than the raw materials (as with furniture or radio sets) nearness to the final market counts for more. The heavy engineering industry in which Britain led the world for a hundred years benefited not only by Britain's native coal and iron resources but by Britain's coastline with its deep-water ports— to which, as it happens, our coal seams lie very handy. Before World War II it cost less to carry coal 500 miles by sea from Newcastle to Hamburg than 200 miles from the Ruhr by land.

Localization of Industry. Of course climate, natural resources, communications, and historical influences all work together. Given a start, industries grow; once industrialized, the whole economy develops faster and faster. Beside *natural advantages*, in fact, one must set *acquired advantages*. In a steel town, people talk steel, think steel, almost breathe steel; a tradition of craftsmanship, a familiarity with everything that has to do with steelmaking, come naturally to them. Technical training facilities grow up; special transport, special banking and insurance practices, subsidiary industries supplying machinery and tools, others offering a market for by-products, marketing experts, auxiliary enterprises of all kinds, develop and cluster round. A firm working in such surroundings has a great advantage over one set up elsewhere, even when the natural resources elsewhere (perhaps discovered later) are just as good.

Moreover, an established industry generally specializes within itself in a way which increases the advantages of the division of labour. The West Riding of Yorkshire, broadly speaking, means wool; but within the West Riding the west and north with Bradford, Halifax and Keighley produces mainly worsteds. The east and south concentrate mostly on woollens. There is further specialization within these areas. Bradford is not only the commercial centre but has most of the combing machinery and about a third of the worsted spindles. Huddersfield produces both high-grade worsteds and fine woollens, Dewsbury and Batley mainly cheap woollens. Another form of specialization has developed in the motor industry in the Birmingham-Coventry area. The motor manufacturing firms—those whose names appear on the completed car—tend to confine themselves to the job of making engines and of assembly, while the manufacture of chassis frames, carburettors, electric equipment, windscreens, and so forth, is carried out by separate firms producing for many different makes of cars.

Industrial Inertia. As one might guess from this account of the 'localization' process, industries often hang on in the area where they began long after the original reason that brought them there has disappeared. The pottery industry of North Staffordshire is a well-known example of this. It was set up originally to exploit the local clay for rough earthenware. It has long ago turned its main activity to the making of fine chinaware from 'imported' Cornish china clay; but it stays where it began. It is too deeply rooted, its 'acquired' advantages have grown too important, for a shift to be worth while.

Changes in Industrial Location. Nevertheless, industries do move, and old centres find new rivals. Britain's long start and all the advantages which that start gave her have not prevented even bigger and more efficient engineering and textile industries, for instance, springing up in Germany, the United States and Japan. (Early starts cut both ways; later starters learn from the first-comer's mistakes, and begin right away with the latest techniques.) Within Britain itself, there has been a tendency since the end of World War I for the older industrial areas to decline in relative importance and for the Midlands and the London area to expand industrially. Population in the Midlands and around London has grown faster than in the country as a whole; that in South Wales has actually decreased. (See Fig. 4). This is partly because certain industries which had begun in the Midlands happened to be the ones, which, during that period, have expanded most (notably the Midland motor and electrical engineering industries); and partly it is because the basic industries of the north and of Wales were, on the contrary, precisely those which suffered the most from depression and unemployment between the wars and from which, therefore, workers tended to drift away. Partly it is because, as it has become increasingly possible to substitute electricity for steam power, industry has become less dependent on coal and hence on nearness to the coalfields, and has been able to think more about nearness to markets (remember what was said on page 45). Numerous new industries, based on recent inventions and unknown before World War I, have been located near to their markets to produce goods now in general use because of rising standards of living: particular examples are new food-stuffs and electrical apparatus.

Over-Specialization. Up to World War II the question of where a new industrial enterprise should settle was decided entirely by the business men concerned. Now—this is all part of that increased measure of public control discussed in Chapter III—government policy takes a hand. Business men are not actually ordered to build in this region nor (as a rule) forbidden to build in that, but every encouragement is given them to set up works in those areas whose existing industries cannot be counted on to offer sufficient employment. These areas, the Development Areas, were the worst black spots of unemployment during the depression years; their story shows the seamy side of specialization. An area which is thoroughly and entirely specialized has all its eggs in one basket; if anything serious happens to its markets (like the decline in foreign demand for British cotton goods and coal and ships) there is no handy alternative industry to take up the slack as workers are dismissed and plant closed down for want of orders. So in the long run it may be wise to let some of the possible gains of specialization and localization go; to encourage diverse industries as a kind of insurance against uncomfortable changes.

The Limits of Specialization. Apart from this question of risk, how far can the division of labour between people and areas be carried? What are the limits? We may leave aside for the moment the difficulties which may arise as a particular firm expands—difficulties of technique and of management about which there will be more to say later. Apart from these, the most important limit is the *size of the market*, that is the number of possible buyers of the thing or service being produced. One may take Adam Smith's pin-makers, for example; it would have been no use ingeniously organizing eighteen different processes in order to produce forty-eight thousand pins a day if there were only, say, half a dozen tailors to buy them. A modern business man, too, may be perfectly well aware that he could produce a thing more cheaply by switching over from comparatively simple, small-scale methods to the highly mechanical mass production which pushes division of labour to the furthest point; but unless he can expect a correspondingly big market the switch would be a costly mistake. He would be left with his cheaply produced goods on his hands. Of course, the cheapening itself will enlarge the market for that particular product—as it gets cheaper more people can afford it—but there are at any given moment obvious limits. Whatever the manufacturer may do to attract customers by advertising, and to make things easy for them by hire-purchase, there must come a time when the market becomes 'saturated'—when people simply do not want to increase their spending on his product, however attractive the terms, because they are so well supplied with it that they would rather spend on other things of which they are shorter. So, though the division of labour can to a certain extent create its own market, the size of the market which it serves at the beginning sets a limit to its growth.

The larger the market, the more division of labour is possible, the more cheaply the article can generally be produced. *Big markets and cheapness go together.* That is one reason why the United States, with a potential internal market of 160 million purchasers, can produce some things so much more cheaply than Great Britain, with a potential internal market of only 50 million purchasers. It is also a very strong argument in favour of doing away with obstacles to international trade such as tariffs. This was one of the reasons for setting up the European Economic Community (Common Market). When every industry has the whole world for its possible market, every industry can take the fullest advantage technically possible of the division of labour, and there is more produced for everyone to consume. Certain countries with a tiny internal market nevertheless produce certain things more cheaply than anyone else by using mass-production methods or particular highly-specialized skills for the world market; Swiss watches and Swedish ball-bearings are examples of this. With cheap transport and without trade barriers, national frontiers and the size of national population need matter very little.

Even with a world market wide open, however, certain trades are never likely to carry the division of labour to mass-production lengths; the whole world could not offer enough demand to justify the mass production of glass eyes, or stuffed snakes, or, for that matter, the very highly-specialized scientific instruments which only a few highly-specialized scientists could use. And—this is an important point—it is not nearly so easy to mass-produce services as to mass-produce goods. Division of labour may multiply the output of a metal worker by hundreds; it does comparatively little to multiply the 'output' of a teacher or doctor or administrator. And as we have already seen that increasing division of labour actually calls for an increasing amount of services, it is obvious that there is quite unmistakable limit to the gains, in leisure and standard of living, which

E

it can bring about even in a perfectly peaceful and united world market.

Disadvantages of Specialization. So much for the limitations to the division of labour. But there are also actual disadvantages in pushing it to extremes. We have had hints of these already. There is the monotony of repetition work, so much less satisfying in itself than a skilled craft. (One should remember, however, that even before the days of mechanization there was plenty of work just as monotonous, far more strenuous, and carried on for much longer hours. Imagine being bottom man in an old-fashioned saw-pit, pushing and pulling twelve hours a day at a cross-cut saw in a shower of sawdust!) Then there is the necessary standardization of the product. Adam Smith's pins must be uniform in size, shape and quality: if these are varied, time will be lost and the advantage of specialization will disappear. Differences in design, for any machine-made product, call for readjustments in machinery or actual changes of equipment. In shoemaking, for instance, new lasts must be set up, in engineering processes new dies must be made. This adds to cost and limits the benefits of mass production, so producers stick to the single standardized product as closely as they can.

Standardization may not matter in the least for pins and may be a positive advantage to the consumer of many other products (think of electric fitments), but more personal belongings are another matter. Clothes, furniture, shoes, pottery, toys—we generally like to be individual about these things and choose them to suit ourselves. We could all dress much more cheaply if the only clothes made were uniforms—but even the much lesser degree of standardization imposed by the war-time and post-war 'Utility' system led many people to complain of drabness.

Specialization and Unemployment. But perhaps the most serious disadvantage of the division of labour is the resulting danger of *unemployment*. A man producing for his own needs will never be unemployed—though, as we have seen, he will

probably live considerably more poorly than even an unemployed worker drawing benefit in a developed community. A
man producing for the needs of a small local group, working to
order or for customers whose requirements he knows at first
hand, is very unlikely to be unemployed unless he chooses to
be. But production for a wide market involves a risk; it is
necessarily production 'on spec'. The producer must estimate
what demand will be months or even years ahead, perhaps on
the other side of the world. (The greater the degree of mechanization, the greater the scope for error, because the further
ahead plans must be made. The machines themselves must be
ordered, made, delivered and installed before manufacture
can begin). Business men's estimates may be out, or demand
may change or cease unexpectedly, or other producers, of whose
intentions the business man was unaware, may capture the
market—or, of course, a government may slap on a prohibitive
tariff or tighten its licensing arrangements, or suddenly change
a tax rate or its production policy for aircraft or weapons. Any
of these circumstances are likely to cause unemployment.

This might not matter very much if the workers who lost
their jobs could quickly turn to something else. But the same
developments which have made them workers for distant markets have made them specialists at that work—we have seen
how the two things hang together—so that they cannot easily
take up another occupation; particularly, as we have seen,
when the whole neighbourhood or region is specialized in the
same trade and consequently finds itself in the same boat.

Apart from the unemployment arising from unforeseen
changes in the market, there is that which arises from the very
progress of the division of labour: *the technological unemployment*, as it is called, which comes about when improved
machines save labour by displacing workers. This, while uncomfortable for the workers concerned, is only a temporary
price paid for the whole process of industrial advance. From
the long run point of view, the displaced workers are being
liberated to produce something else—like the dozens of reapers
who once harvested the field now worked by a single tractor.
They are pulled back into employment by a number of forces

set in motion by the very change which pushed them out. Some extra labour will be needed to make and to service the machines themselves; some will be brought back to work more machines as cheaper output brings bigger sales and consequent expansion in the industry; some will be employed by other industries, whose products are meeting with a new demand because people buying the cheaper goods of their original industry now have more money to spend on other things.

This process—automation is its latest form—has gone on throughout modern industrial history; and more and more workers have found work with more and more labour-saving machinery to produce more and more goods and services—for their own consumption. But of course it is uncomfortable, sometimes tragic, for the particular worker who is unlucky enough to be slow in finding a new place in industry; and it is generally agreed that society as a whole, which benefits from technical change, owes a living to those individuals on whom the price of that change happens to fall.

Specialization and Social Isolation. Here we are obviously drawing away from economics towards questions of social justice and social responsibilities generally. Another borderline matter of the same kind is the problem of the specialized community which is so wrapped up in its own speciality and its own affairs that it gets cut off from the rest of the world. Through no fault of their own, but because of the nature of their work and their geographical isolation, the coal miners of this country have rather drawn away from the rest of the community; so they tend to misunderstand and suspect other people and to feel (perhaps rightly) that other people misunderstand and suspect them. Better education can help here, of course, but this is another reason for wanting to diversify economic life, to encourage different industries to settle in regions which would otherwise be too closely specialized.

Specialization and Strategy. Finally, specialization by *nations* carries with it some political and strategic dangers. A country which devotes most of its resources to producing a

comparatively small range of goods, exporting these in exchange for all the rest of its essential needs, may as a result
enjoy a much higher standard of living than it would do if it
refused the advantages of the large market. But if war breaks
out and some of its suppliers are on the wrong side, or overrun
by the enemy, or cut off by blockade, the results may be catas-
trophic. Many of the countries of Western Europe, and particularly Great Britain, are specialized in industrial production
to a point which makes them dependent on other lands for
their essential supplies of food and raw materials. Even short
of war, a change in world market conditions (such as a falling
off in the demand for their exports, or an increase in their suppliers' own consumption of food and materials) may be a
severe blow to them. The two world wars and the crises following them have shown how vulnerable Britain's position is.

On the other hand, the industrial power which Britain had
built up by specializing, and could hardly have built up otherwise, did prove adequate to produce the ships that beat the
blockade, the planes that beat off the invaders, and the sinews
of war in general; it is a very wide-open question at which
point the strategic disadvantages of being specialized really do
outweigh the strategic advantage of the wealth and strength
which specialization brings.

CHAPTER V

THE ECONOMY OF BRITAIN

T HE last chapter showed the general principles which govern
the division of labour between individuals, groups, and
different parts of the world. How have they worked out in our
own country—Great Britain? It is the business of this chapter
to give—broadly of course—a kind of bird's-eye view of the
way in which people in the British Isles get their livings.

Great Britain a Country of Town Dwellers. It is fairly
certain that more than three-quarters of the readers of this
book will be town dwellers and only a minority will live in the
country. If one classifies the inhabitants of England and Wales
according to the sort of local government area in which they
live, one finds four out of five living in 'Boroughs' or 'Urban
Districts', while even among those living in rural districts a
good number travel into towns every day to earn their living.
(Hence rush-hour traffic on suburban lines and bus routes.)

This is a higher proportion of town dwellers, and consequently a greater density of population, than is found in almost
any other country in the world. Average densities (people per
square mile) of a number of countries are shown in the following table:

TABLE I—DENSITY OF POPULATION IN VARIOUS COUNTRIES

Belgium	775
Japan	650
Great Britain	567
Italy	389
France	202
United States	50
Norway	27
Australia	3

The reason why so many British people are townsfolk can be easily guessed from the figures of primary, secondary and tertiary production given in the last chapter and from what was said there about the localization of industry. Most British workers earn their living not by growing things but by making and selling them—which means working in factories, mills, workshops or offices. Since industrial and commercial establishments are extremely difficult and expensive to run in isolation, that means towns. And since people working in industry and commerce need others to perform for them all the services necessary to a modern community—retail distribution, transport services, electricity, gas and water supplies, building, education and entertainment—every concentration of population concerned with a basic industry attracts a further concentration to serve its needs.

A series of maps (Figs. 7, 8, 9, 11, 12, 13) in this chapter shows the main regions where most of the population are engaged in mining and manufacturing. If one compares these with the accompanying population map (Fig. 3) one sees that these are also the regions of densest population.

Gains and Losses of Concentration. Football enthusiasts will discover that the big League clubs are almost exclusively confined to these same heavily populated areas—because a dense population is needed to ensure a sufficiently large 'gate'. And what goes for first-class football goes for many other things too. Only by coming together in towns can people enjoy the best facilities for education, for cultural activities like music, art and drama; or, for that matter, a wide choice of friends and acquaintances. The village bus and the growth of broadcasting and television have helped the countryman in these respects, but the town dweller still has an advantage.

On the other hand, dense concentration has its disadvantages. Towns are smoky (much smokier than they need be technically—but smoke-abatement devices, even if they save money in the long run, are expensive to install) and smoke is bad both for health and for the standard of living. 'Besides contributing through fog to traffic disorganization, accidents

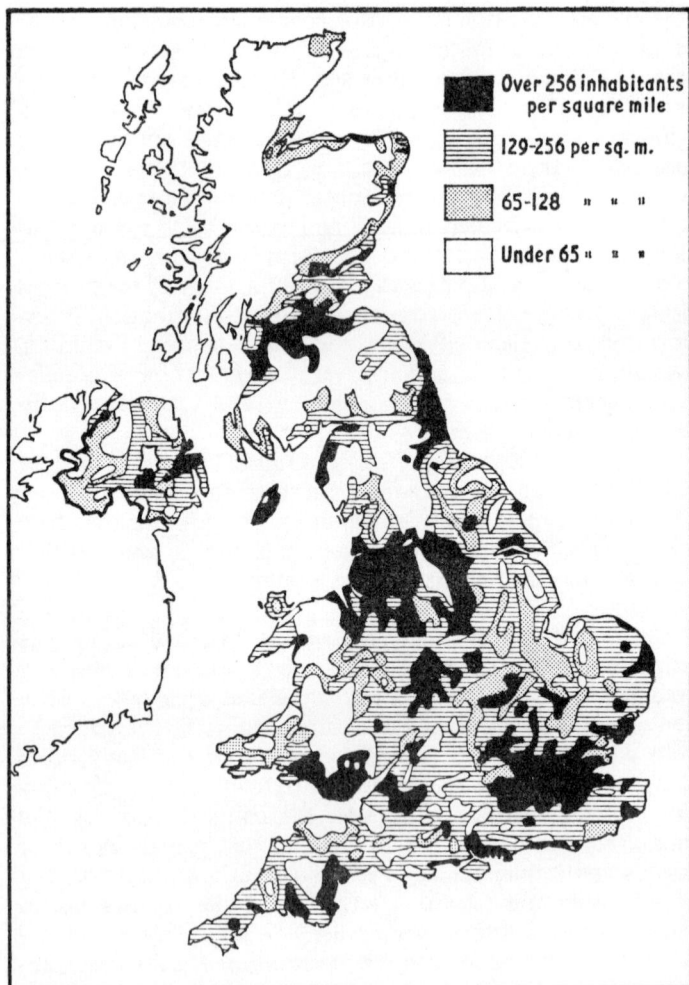

Over 256 inhabitants per square mile

129-256 per sq. m.

65-128 " " "

Under 65 " " "

FIG. 3—DISTRIBUTION OF POPULATION IN THE U.K., 1951

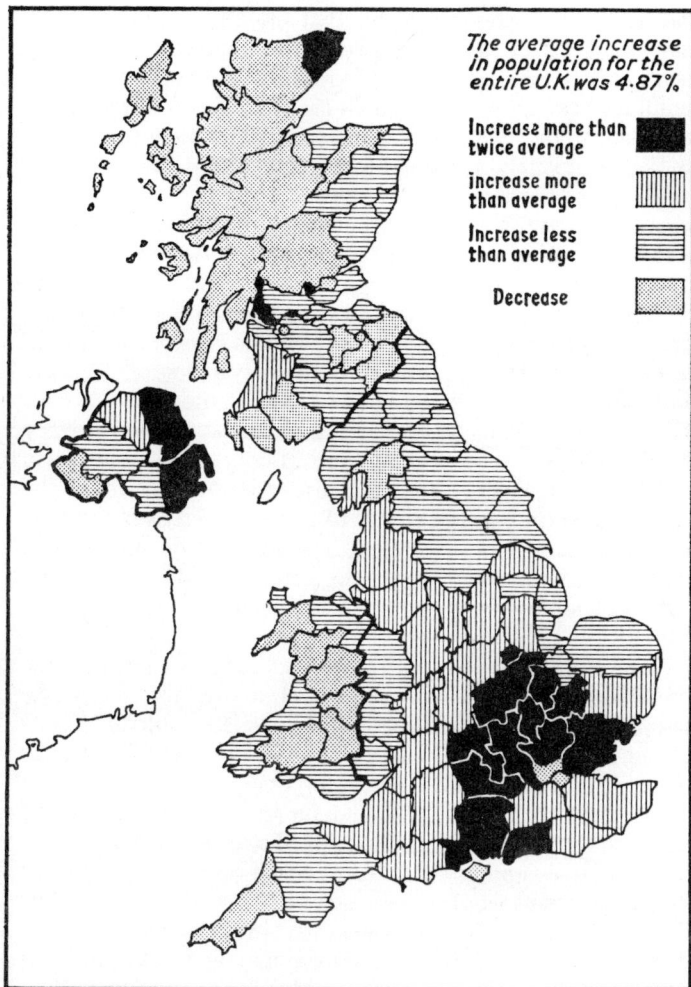

FIG. 4—DISTRIBUTION OF POPULATION IN U.K.:
Changes, 1951–61

and delays, it is unquestionable that smoke costs the country many millions of pounds a year, quite apart from its detrimental effects on vegetation and the fabric of historic and other buildings.' (*Royal Commission on the Distribution of the Industrial Population*, 1940.) The Clean Air Act of 1956 bans 'dark smoke' completely and empowers local authorities to ban all smoke from the chimney of any building in 'Smoke Control Areas', but unfortunately, progress in dispelling smoke has been slower than the Beaver Committee on Air Pollution envisaged.

Noise is another drawback to town life; so is crowding. A good many people, of course, like noise and crowds rather than otherwise, but statistics of nervous and psychological ailments show that town dwellers do suffer, even if they are not consciously aware of it, from the lack of that quiet and privacy which country dwellers enjoy. And of course crowding has a perfectly recognizable economic cost of its own; compare the expense of getting so many tons of traffic moved over a mile of road in Birmingham or Manchester, with that of moving it in open country; or the time spent in getting to and from work by a village shop assistant and her counterpart in London.

Town Planning. It is with questions such as these that the art of town planning is concerned: How big must a town be before it can support a theatre or a first-class football club or a technical college? How can its industrial and residential areas be sited so as to cut down travelling time for the workers and at the same time keep noise and fumes out of their houses? How are through traffic and local traffic to be prevented from getting in one another's way? How much open space is needed to rest the townspeople's eyes, ears and nerves? There are few if any towns in which it is not possible to see evidence of fearful mistakes made in the past before town planning was thought of —particularly in the industrial north of England. In putting those mistakes right and in preventing fresh mistakes in the future, there is room for the work of economists, architects, traffic experts, medical experts, administrators, and ordinary sensible citizens—for town planning raises an enormous number of social and technical as well as of economic problems. Various Town and Country Planning Acts have in recent years given both the central government and local councils very considerable powers to determine which areas shall be 'developed', i.e. built upon, and where industries shall be located.

The Balance of Town and Country. There is a wider social problem which should be mentioned here even though it is not strictly an economist's business. Is an urban society—that is a nation consisting overwhelmingly of town dwellers—an unbalanced society? Some people think that urban and rural life each have their own particular contribution to make to a nation's civilization. Each type of community has its own strength and weakness; therefore, they say, it is undesirable that a nation's population should be weighted heavily in one direction or the other. This is an argument quite separate from those which we considered in the last chapter—those concerning the economic risks of specialization and its possible strategic disadvantages in wartime. It would still hold good, if it holds good at all, in a perfectly stable and peaceful world. In this respect, as in the strategic and economic respect, Britain took a chance on specialization. Other countries which might have become equally industrialized decided differently. Which decision was right? Economics cannot answer.

Occupations in Great Britain. Now to look more closely at the pattern of specialization in Great Britain—the pattern of occupations and the geographical layout of industry. In December 1961 there were 23,923,000 men and women in civil employment, distributed among the various occupations as shown on page 60.
The 8,938,000 engaged in manufacturing industries were distributed as shown on page 61.

Coal. Almost the only important source of natural wealth which we possess, apart from the soil, is coal. Most of our industries depend in some degree upon it. It is still, directly or indirectly, our most important source of *power*. In industry and

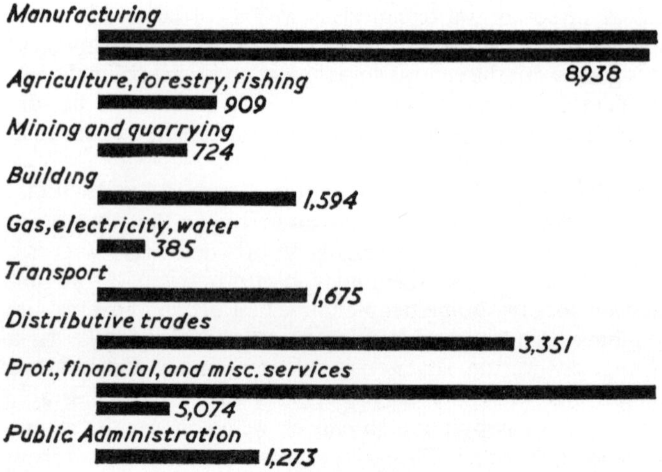

Manufacturing

Agriculture, forestry, fishing   8,938
909
Mining and quarrying
724
Building
1,594
Gas, electricity, water
385
Transport
1,675
Distributive trades
3,351
Prof., financial, and misc. services
5,074
Public Administration
1,273

FIG. 5—DISTRIBUTION OF WORKERS IN CIVIL EMPLOYMENT
(*in thousands*)

for the generation of electricity much more coal (measured in tons) is used than oil, although consumption of the latter is steadily increasing. As we lack mountains, we have little hydro-electric power. Atomic power generation, however promising, is still comparatively in its infancy. Coal provides the necessary *heat* for most of the basic metallurgical industries—iron-founding and steel-smelting—and keeps our houses warm and lit and cooks our food. Its *by-products*, which range from fertilizers through dye-stuffs to nylons and aspirins, are widely used in the chemical industry. Serious coal shortage could still mean complete dislocation of industrial life.

For reasons to be discussed shortly, British coal output is now little more than two-thirds of the peak annual figure of 287 million tons reached in 1913. The fuel-using industries have expanded and so, with an increasing population, has the domestic demand; but these users have learned to burn coal more efficiently and also some have switched to oil, consumption of which has risen.

The decline in our overseas coal trade is particularly regret-

Engineering, shipbuilding, and electrical goods

2,392

Chemicals and allied industries
531

Metal manufacture
620

Bricks, pottery, glass, cement etc.
345

Vehicles
887

Metal goods, not elsewhere specified
556

Textiles
821

Leather goods and fur
62

Clothing and footwear
564

Food, drink, and tobacco
815

Timber, furniture etc.
289

Paper, printing, and publishing
619

Other manufacturing industries
303

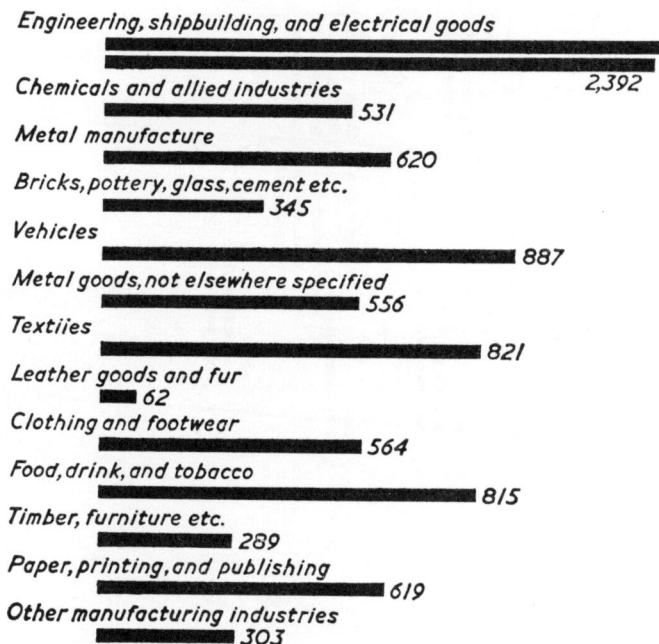

FIG. 6—DISTRIBUTION OF WORKERS IN MANUFACTURING
INDUSTRIES (*in thousands*), DEC. 1961

able because it has meant our losing what used to be a very
important advantage to our shipping; coal made an outward
bulk cargo for British shipping, to match the inward bulk
cargoes of foodstuffs and raw materials, so that shipping costs
were covered both ways and shipowners were in a position to
quote very cheap freight rates for general cargo and so to
attract most of the world's custom. Now, many ships sail from
Britain not only in ballast but with nearly empty bunkers and
refuel elsewhere.

The Coalfields. Three large coalfields—Northumberland
and Durham, South Wales and Monmouthshire, and York-

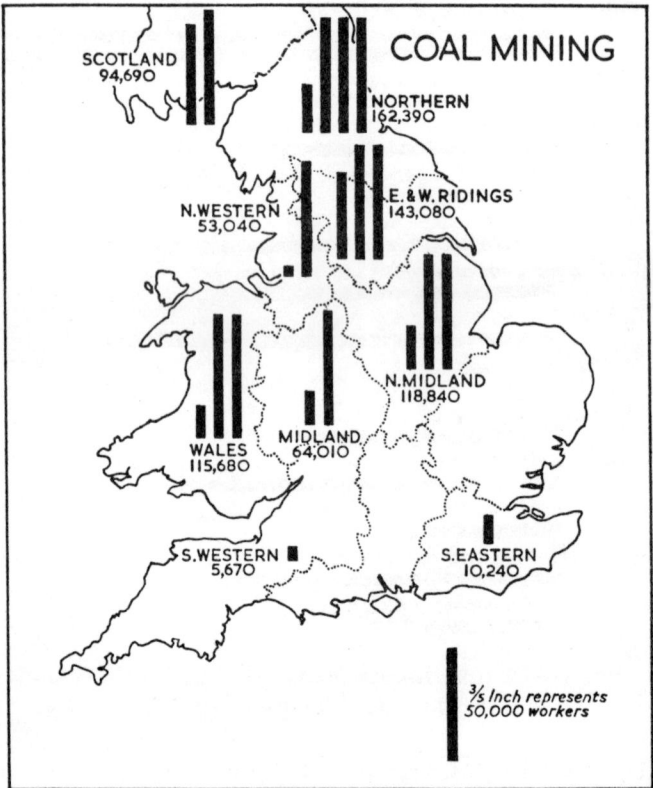

SCOTLAND
94,690

COAL MINING

NORTHERN
162,390

N.WESTERN
53,040

E. & W. RIDINGS
143,080

WALES
115,680

MIDLAND
64,010

N.MIDLAND
118,840

S.WESTERN
5,670

S.EASTERN
10,240

3/8 Inch represents
50,000 workers

FIG. 7—THE COAL INDUSTRY: REGIONAL DISTRIBUTION
OF WORKERS, 1959

shire, Nottinghamshire and Derbyshire—produce over two-
thirds of the total output. Other coalfields exist in Lancashire,
Warwickshire, Staffordshire, Lanarkshire and Cheshire, while
small quantities are obtained in North Wales, West Cumberland, Somerset, Gloucestershire and Kent. The type of coal
produced and the purposes for which it is used vary from area
to area. Much of the Welsh coal is anthracite, especially

valuable for steam-raising, and in the past it was the coal from this area and from the north-east coast which was chiefly exported. Derby coal, on the other hand, is better for household use.

Different areas also differ widely in their conditions of production. Some coalfields have wide, easily accessible seams of coal, so that men can work them comfortably and use machines at the coal face. Others, for geological reasons, have narrow twisting seams where miners must work lying squeezed up in cramped positions. Some are nearly worked out, so that only the least accessible seams are left; others are newly opened, with plenty of coal near the surface or the main shaft. Some are a patchwork of small pits planned in the old days of mining before steam power and modern ventilation; others have had from the start the full advantage, in planning their layout, of modern mining techniques. Consequently costs of production are much higher in some areas than in others. At the ruling price of coal, some pits, and some fields, make handsome profits; others sell every ton of coal at a loss. Should all the least efficient pits be closed and both workers and expensive equipment be concentrated on making the best use of the more efficient? That sounds like a sensible answer, but it does not look so sensible to the miner who is asked to leave his village and who knows that there is still perfectly good coal at the bottom of the pit.

The Inter-War Slump. Much of the coal industry's trouble is the result of the bad times which it passed through between the wars. Between 1920 and 1939 demand both at home and abroad slumped badly, and unemployment rose to shocking heights; during the great depression of the early 1930s many Welsh pit villages had four out of five breadwinners out of work. This was partly because Continental coalowners had improved their methods and cheapened their prices to a figure at which British coal could not compete, partly because oil was being increasingly used instead of coal, especially to power marine engines, partly because many of our foreign customers had developed hydro-electric power, and partly because British industry in general—the main home customer—was also depressed for various reasons which will appear later. The situation was complicated by the fact that so much of the cost of coal consists of wages. The 1920s and 1930s were on the whole a period of falling prices, and in order to attract custom it would have been necessary to reduce coal prices to match; but that could hardly be done without reducing wages, and that was a step which the miners not unnaturally fought tooth and nail. It was a reduction in miners' wages, aimed at winning back foreign markets, which touched off the General Strike of 1926. The miners lost their fight—and the bitterness of that fight has not died away even a generation later.

Coal Shortage. During and immediately after World War II the position was transformed. Instead of coal begging for customers, customers were begging for coal, supplies fell far below the amount demanded at the prevailing price. The main reason for this shortage was the fall in the number of miners. Hundreds of thousands, particularly among the younger men, left the industry for good during the depression years; and memories of unemployment, the discomforts and dangers of the miners' work, and the opening up of opportunities elsewhere in a time of full employment, led those who remained to discourage their sons from following them in the pits.

Nationalization of Coal. In 1947 the control and ownership of the coal industry was taken over by the National Coal Board (see page 28) under the Coal Industry Nationalization Act of 1946. The Board undertook a vast programme of re-organization, re-equipment and research. Reorganization, by concentrating production in the best pits and authority in larger management units; re-equipment with new coal-cutting, conveying, cleaning and other machinery; research into more economic methods of obtaining coal. The shift of men and equipment from low to high yielding pits has been slowed by the social difficulties mentioned earlier, and the new structure of authority has not fulfilled all hopes. But the output of coal per man working has steadily increased, mainly due to greater mechanization, particularly power loading, so that though the number of miners employed has continued to fall, the total output has declined less. On the other hand the demand for most types of coal has slackened considerably, partly because users have turned over to oil, and in some years since 1959 the National Coal Board has held embarrassingly large stocks, especially of small coal.

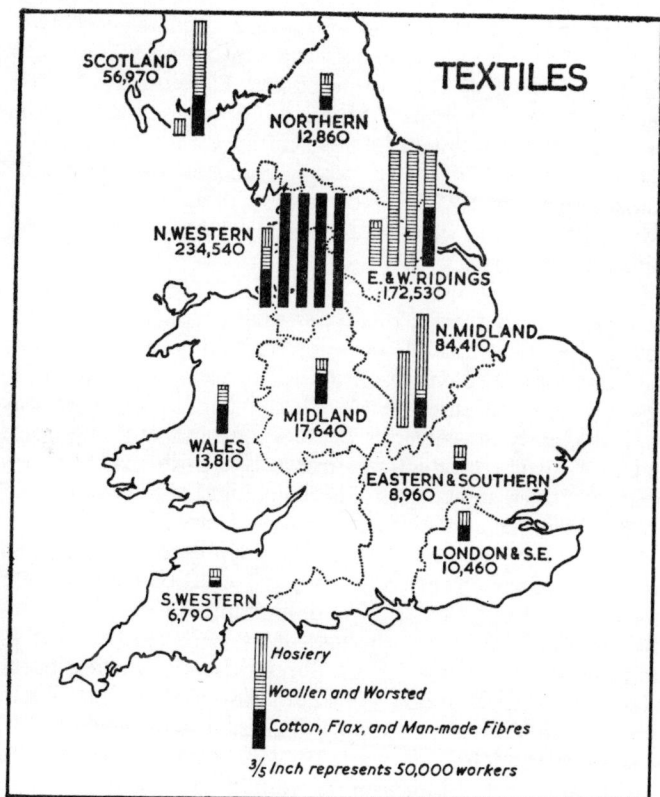

FIG. 8—THE TEXTILE INDUSTRY: REGIONAL DISTRIBUTION
OF WORKERS, 1959

F

Textiles. From the fourteenth century until the early part of this century textiles of some kind played a major part in our industry and export trade. Until the end of the eighteenth century, wool goods, both woollens and worsteds, were of major importance. In the nineteenth century the growth in production of cotton yarn and cloth, chiefly in Lancashire, contributed much to make Britain the greatest industrial and trading nation in the world. Over a third of our exports just before World War I were textiles and Lancashire supplied nearly two-thirds of the entire world export trade in cotton goods. Now all this has changed. The cotton industry has shrunk till it is a shadow of its former size. Man-made fibres—rayon, nylon, Terylene, etc.—developed in this century by the chemical industry have revolutionized some branches of the textile industry, notably hosiery. Now although the quality of our textiles, particularly worsteds, is high, they are among our less important exports.

Cotton. Apart from a relatively small output in west Scotland, almost the whole of cotton production is concentrated in east Lancashire and on the borders of surrounding counties. It grew up there because the Manchester and Bolton area was from the early seventeenth century onwards an important centre of fustian production (fustian is a cloth made from a mixture of linen and cotton). The availability of pure water and a humid climate were also contributory factors.

The industry has declined steadily since World War I when the output of woven cotton goods was over 8,000 million linear yards. In 1961 output was 1,237 million linear yards. This contraction has been due to the loss of overseas markets and to the development of man-made fibres. Many countries, particularly the United States, the South American countries and India, set up industries to supply their own needs, while Japan, by using cheap labour to work Western machines, captured a considerable part of Lancashire's tropical and oriental market. In recent years the British industry has met stiff competition in its home market from cotton goods imported particularly from Commonwealth countries in Asia.

As a result of this contraction significant changes have taken place in the organization of the industry. There is no longer the high degree of specialization by firms in the different stages or grades of manufacture. Originally firms specialized not only in the spinning or weaving or finishing processes but confined themselves to spinning just a certain range of counts or weaving only flannelettes or shirtings of a certain quality. Now there is much more integration in the industry.

The future of the cotton industry lies probably in concentrating on high quality products and in combination of cotton with synthetic fibres. The contraction of the industry, since 1945, has been accompanied by an expansion in the north-west of other industries notably chemicals (including man-made fibres) and engineering.

Woollens and Worsteds. About three-quarters of the workers employed in the woollen and worsted industries are concentrated in one area of the West Riding of Yorkshire, although there has been some tendency in recent years for the industry to spread to new centres, notably Darlington, Rotherham and Belfast. 'Woollens' are made from short-fibred wools; 'worsted' from long-fibred wools. There are considerably differences, however, in the structure of the two industries. The manufacture of worsteds, like that of cotton, is divided up among firms specializing in different processes; worsted spinning takes place in large mills specializing in particular types of yarn, while worsted weaving uses a variety of yarns. Moreover, a large proportion of worsted yarn is worked up outside the worsted industry proper, going to the hosiery market or to overseas buyers.

In the woollen industry, on the other hand, it is usual for all processes to be concentrated in one mill. This is partly because the products of the woollen industry are more varied in type; great variety of type, as we have seen, gives less scope for large-scale specialization. Further, most of the woollen yarn is used immediately by the weavers and does not go out to other branches of manufacturing industry.

British woollens and worsteds are generally recognized as the best in the world, and these industries suffered less from foreign competition between the wars than did cotton. They did suffer from the general depression, both at home and abroad, but they kept their labour force reasonably intact. In recent years the output and export of woollens have not contracted or expanded in any spectacular way.

Outside the West Riding, there is the tweed manufacture of Scotland (including the famous home-spun and hand-woven tweeds of the Scottish islands) and there are small centres of production scattered over England and Wales, such as Witney (specializing in blankets), Buckfastleigh and Chipping Norton. Before the mid-nineteenth century, indeed, woollen cloth manufacture was found anywhere where the water was naturally soft and where sheep were abundant—British wool was already famous when Britain was semi-barbarous—but the industry now works mostly on imported wool from the Southern Dominions.

Man-Made Fibres. This branch of the textile industry has grown up since World War I: it started with rayon and then, since 1945, expanded rapidly with the development of nylon and Terylene, these being the three best known synthetic fibres. Whether, as was said, 'the rayon stocking did more to bring about democracy than any political reform' may be arguable, but shopgirl and duchess undoubtedly appear far less different in their dress since both have been able to buy cheaply clothes made with synthetic fibres. The structure of the industry is radically different from that of the older textile trades. Synthetic fibre production requires elaborate machinery and the vitality of the industry depends on continuous technical progress and research whose cost can be borne only by very large firms. So (as one would expect) manufacture of filament and yarns is done on a large scale in factories controlled by a few firms, such as Courtaulds and I.C.I., though their product is also made up by a number of small firms. The industry is widely dispersed where an adequate labour force and an ample supply of good water are available, the principle centres being the North and West Midlands, Lancashire, Yorkshire, Cumberland and certain parts of Wales.

Other Textiles. These include the carpet, linen, jute and hosiery industries. The ordinary consumer sees very little jute, but as the raw material for sacking it is essential to a number of industries. Hosiery includes not only stockings and socks but knitted garments as well. It is concentrated mainly in the Nottingham area, and has enjoyed a steadily expanding output in recent years.

Iron and Steel. Before World War I, three quarters of Britain's iron and steel was produced in three areas: the northeast coast, South Wales and Lanarkshire. These regions are still important by reasons of their nearness to the ports (to which iron ore comes) and to good supplies of high-quality coking coal. Other regions, however, have grown in importance as technical progress has made it economically possible to work the low-grade ores of the Lincolnshire-Northamptonshire field. This field has become the chief centre for the production of steel tubes. Other important areas are Sheffield, with its traditional specialization in special steels, Lancashire, which had concentrated on sheet steel and wire, the West Midlands and West Cumberland.

During the nineteenth century British inventors and business men (generally the same people) were pioneers in developing new methods of iron and steel production. (The most important advance of all, the discovery of a way of using coal in iron-founding, was the work of two eighteenth-century founders, the Darbys of Coalbrookdale.) Britain was the world's iron foundry as she was the world's workshop; and on the foundation of British supremacy in iron and steel was built a corresponding supremacy in engineering, from shipbuilding to bridge and railway construction and from textile machinery to locomotives. Indeed, it was with equipment brought from British workshops, and with railways built by British engineering firms that most of the other countries in the world began their modern industrial careers.

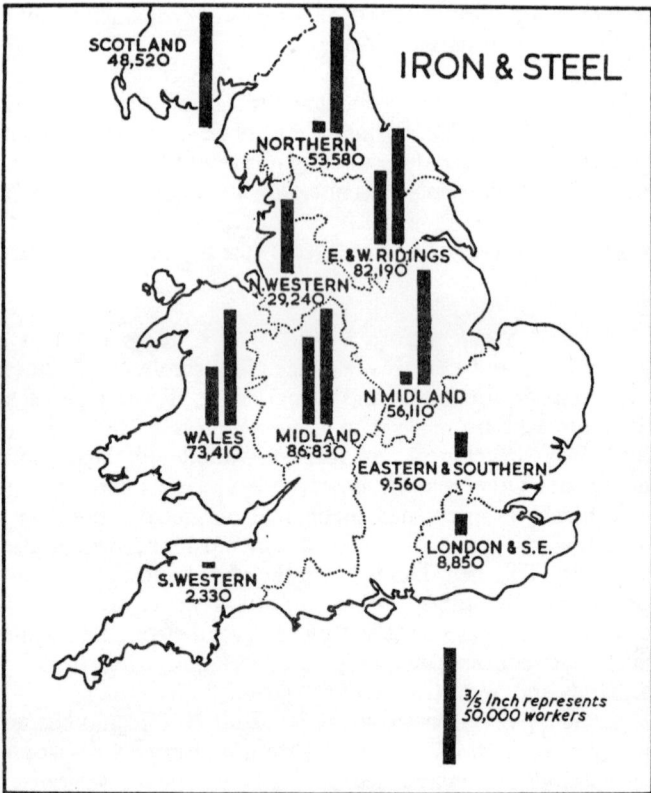

FIG. 9—THE IRON AND STEEL INDUSTRY: REGIONAL
DISTRIBUTION OF WORKERS, 1959

Depression and Foreign Competition. Some of those
countries were apt enough learners to better instruction. Towards the end of the century the United States and Germany
were not only fully exploiting the techniques developed in
Britain, but developing new and better techniques of their
own; and their industries soon exceeded ours in size and out-

put. Between the wars the British steel industry suffered a severe depression, with unemployment as bad as that in coal. There was foreign competition by larger, more up-to-date and better-organized concerns; there was the world-wide slackening of demand during depression (depression always hits the steel-using engineering trades hardest, because in bad times no one wants to invest in expensive new equipment, or even replace the old); and there was the particular depression of the British shipping industry, previously a wonderful customer, because of the decline in international trade. During the 1930s a good deal was done to restore the efficiency of the steel industry by scrapping out-of-date and run-down plant and reorganizing the industry in larger units. In particular, two very large steel works were constructed, one in Lincolnshire and the other in South Wales. Much more recently very large plants have been constructed at Margam and Llanwern in South Wales and another in Lanarkshire. Great Britain still remains among the leading iron and steel producing countries of the world, although the U.S. and U.S.S.R. are considerably ahead of us in the quantity of steel they each produce. After 1945 steel shortage was a handicap to British industry and for a number of years demand for all kinds of steel tended to exceed supply. From 1959 increase in capacity brought a better balance, indeed stocks, of heavy steel particularly, accumulated as demand began to fall below output.

Large-Scale Production. Steel production, for reasons which we shall see more fully in Chapter VI, can be most economically carried out in large-scale plants performing all the processes from the raw material to the semi-finished, or even finished, product. This means control by a single firm of coal and ore mines, coke ovens, blast furnaces and rolling mills, and possibly engineering works as well. Concentration of control has increased throughout the industry's history; with comparatively few separate firms left, monopolistic under-standings have grown easier. (World War II, enforcing close co-operation, strengthened this trend.) Distrust of monopoly power was the chief reason for the Labour Government's

nationalization of the industry in 1950; and the de-nationaliz-
ing Act of 1953 provided for some public safeguards.

Motor and Cycle Engineering. This is a new industry
which has grown up almost entirely in the last fifty years.
Measured by its labour force, over half of the industry is con-
centrated in the west Midlands, especially in the Coventry and
Birmingham areas. Other important centres of production are
Oxford and the Greater London area.

Both cycle and motor manufacture started in a small way
and in the hands of a large number of small firms. In both,
however, mass-production methods yield enormous economies, so those firms which by technical superiority, imagination
and organizing ability developed a lead were rapidly able to
lengthen it. A major proportion of the total output of cars is
concentrated in two firms. Specialization between firms, however, has gone further than this would seem to imply, since
different parts are manufactured by different specialist concerns and assembled by the firm which gives its name to the
finished vehicle.

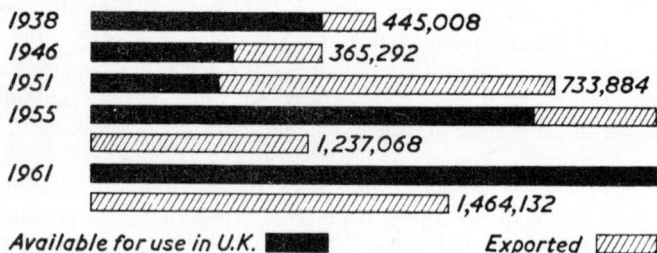

1938	445,008
1946	365,292
1951	733,884
1955	
	1,237,068
1961	
	1,464,132

Available for use in U.K. ▬▬   Exported ▨▨▨

FIG. 10—PRODUCTION OF MOTOR VEHICLES FOR HOME
AND EXPORT, 1938–61

The recent expansion of the motor-car industry and its contribution to our export trade since 1946 is illustrated in Fig. 10.
The low proportion of home sales in the early post-war years
was imposed by official controls making supplies of steel con-
ditional on a high export ratio. Although exports were hit in
1951 by restrictions imposed by some overseas countries in

financial straits, and again in 1955 by a stiffening of foreign competition, they have subsequently continued to expand.

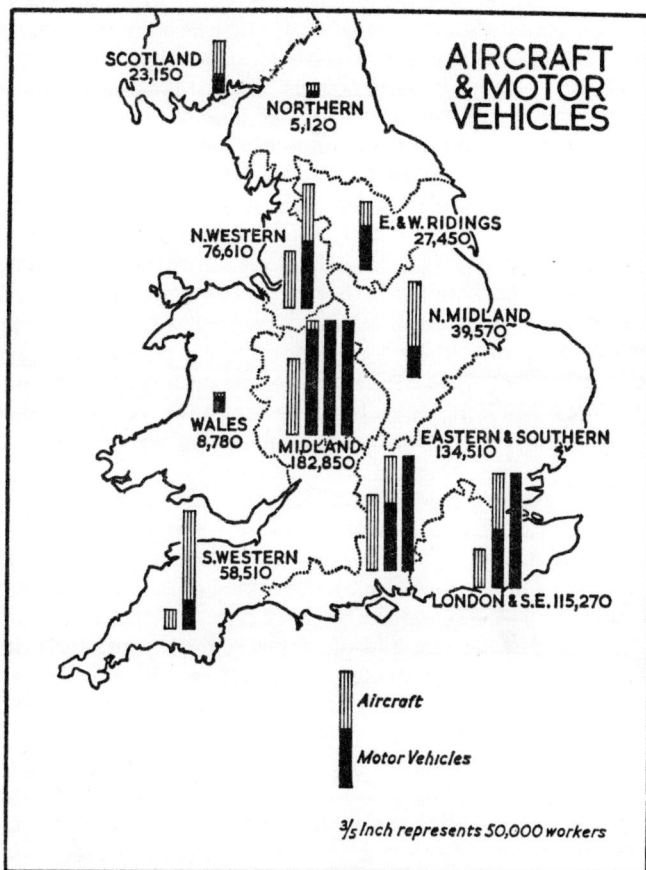

FIG. 11—THE AIRCRAFT AND MOTOR VEHICLE INDUSTRIES: DISTRIBUTION OF WORKERS, 1959

The Aircraft Industry. This industry grew up during and after World War I. Some of the major producers of aircraft developed out of established engineering firms, e.g. Vickers, Bristol Aeroplane Co. (originally started to build electric tramcars) and the English Electric Co. Other firms such as de Havilland and Handley Page were started solely for aircraft construction. As is the case with most industries developed during this century there is no very marked localization.

Since the production of efficient aircraft is of supreme military importance and depends on a vast amount of continuous research, this industry attracts a large amount of government financial assistance, particularly for scientific research. In recent years hundreds of millions of pounds have been spent in this way. This has of course helped the industry commercially as well, and a considerable export trade in both commercial and military planes has been built up. The industry is, however, particularly vulnerable to changes in government policy. For example, in 1959 the industry suffered a decline through the reduction in orders for military aircraft. As a result it was reorganized by consolidating the various firms into five main groups.

The Engineering Industry. If shipbuilding and the manufacture of electrical goods are included, this is Britain's most important industry from the point of view of numbers employed ($2\frac{1}{4}$ millions out of a total working population of about 24 millions in 1962) and the value of its exports.

Because of their size and importance, the motor, cycle and aircraft industries are treated separately in this chapter; but even with these excluded, engineering really consists of a whole range of allied industries, producing a very wide variety of products. These include engines of all kinds, boilers, ships, machine tools, and every kind of mechanical equipment used in industry and agriculture. Another branch is electrical and electronic engineering, which comprises electrical machinery, wires and cables, telegraph, telephone, radio and electronic apparatus, batteries and accumulators. Constructional engineering, e.g. the building of bridges, dams and docks, occupies another section of the industry. Engineering is thus not only an industry in itself, but an essential substructure or handmaid to all economic activity in a modern economy.

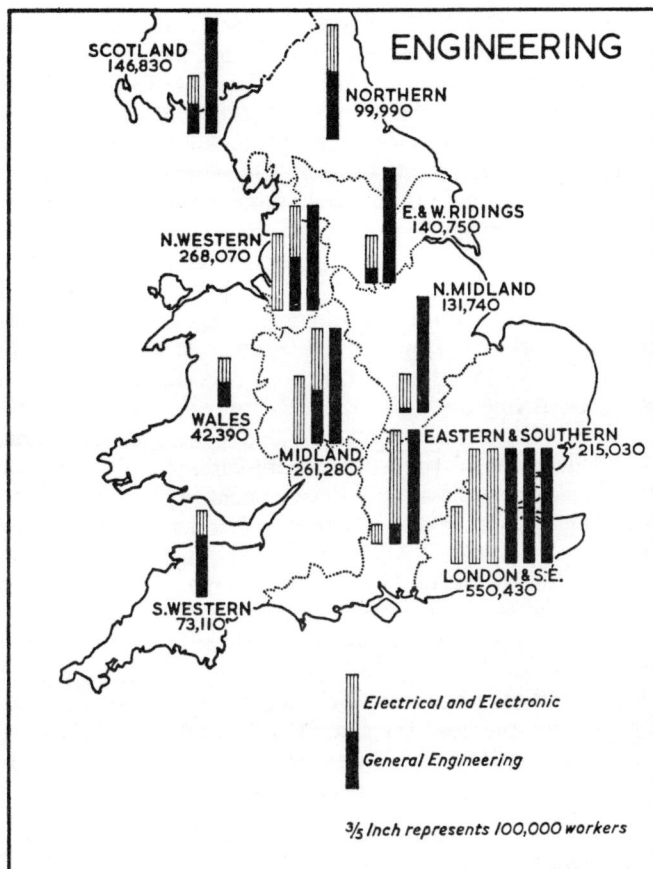

FIG. 12—THE ENGINEERING INDUSTRY: REGIONAL
DISTRIBUTION OF WORKERS, 1959

The Development of the Industry. As a separate 'industry'
engineering can roughly be said to date from the end of
the eighteenth century, when steam power first began to be
widely used. Since that time its evolution has been determined
partly from within, by a stream of new inventions, partly—

because of its role as a servant of industry in general—from without, by the changing needs of the time. Locomotive engineering and railway construction from the 1830s onwards, marine engineering in the second half of the nineteenth century, and the beginnings of motor-car production in the 1890's, all mark notable stages of its growth.

As the new inventions appeared, existing firms took them up and developed them. For example, the early motor-cars and motor-cycles were made mostly by bicycle firms and coach builders.

World War I and the period immediately following saw an important new stage in the development of the engineering industry. Until that time it had been concerned rather more with general engineering—with prime movers (i.e. all types of engines), boilers, textile machinery and ships. New inventions and further technical progress, in many cases stimulated by war needs, made possible a rapid development in the manufacture of aeroplanes, motor-cars, electrical machinery and apparatus and radio equipment. This side of the industry grew enormously in the 1920s and 1930s, and accompanied some relative decline in the importance of the older industrial areas (based on the coalfields) and the growth in importance of the London area and of parts of the Midlands.

World War II naturally provided a stimulus to engineering. Subsequently the need for new capital equipment and the export drive have led to further expansion, mainly on the lines of the inter-war years, except that the shipbuilding industry maintained a higher level of output.

Conditions Favouring Engineering. The first need of an engineering industry is a sufficient supply of technicians, skilled craftsmen and specialized workers. To make mass-production methods pay, there must be an adequate home demand; this will depend on a relatively high standard of living or at least the existence of many manufacturing industries requiring machinery. It is desirable, too, that there should be close contact with the steel industry. In many branches of engineering, *integration* (see Chapter VI) secures this contact.

Indeed, much modern engineering progress, particularly the production of high-speed motor-cars and jet-propulsion units, has depended on the development of suitable alloys; the engineer and the metallurgist work together. Engineering is, in short, the product of a closely-knit and well-developed economy; in this it differs from textiles, pottery, and miscellaneous manufacture, which can be comparatively easily started from scratch.

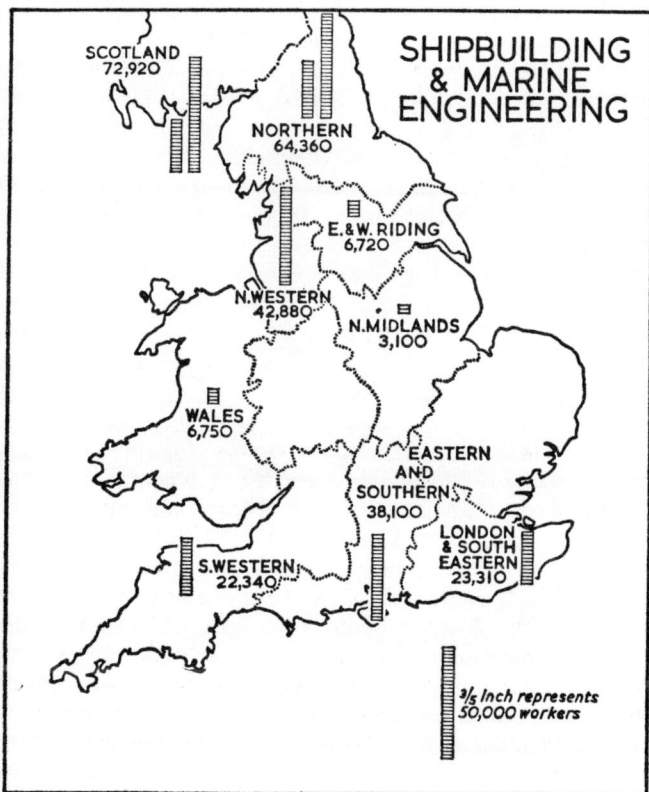

FIG. 13—THE SHIPBUILDING AND MARINE ENGINEERING
INDUSTRIES: REGIONAL DISTRIBUTION OF WORKERS, 1959

Shipbuilding. The predominance in shipbuilding held by Britain in the early years of this century was not established until 1850. This leadership was obtained partly as the result of the substitution of iron and steam for wood and sails, and partly by our free-trade policy, which both enabled us to acquire cheap raw materials for shipbuilding and stimulated our foreign trade, thus increasing the demand for shipping space. So great was the growth of the shipbuilding industry that in 1910–14 Great Britain was building 61 per cent of the total world tonnage of ships under construction.

This pre-war leadership was lost, however, and between the wars the industry suffered grievously. After 1921, unemployment never fell below 20 per cent of the total labour force until the end of the next decade, and the number of insured workers fell from 320,000 in 1924 to 265,000 in 1930. Between 1930 and 1933 unemployment rose to 60 per cent of the total labour force.

After 1937 there was some recovery, and World War II provided a powerful fillip to ship construction. This recovery was maintained for some years, partly as the result of the increased demand for oil tankers; but since 1957 there has been some contraction in the industry.

Booms and Slumps in 'Capital Goods' Industries. Industries producing capital goods are liable to bigger fluctuations in demand than are industries producing consumer goods. (This point is elaborated in Chapter XXII and elsewhere in this book.) The steel, engineering and—particularly—shipbuilding industries are more sensitive to the ups and downs of the trade cycle. A trade boom, or a war, will stimulate the demand for new ships and will lead to the fullest use of shipbuilding resources. Ships, however, have an average life of about twenty years; so when the initial increase in demand is satisfied, the industry is left with labour and capital equipment for which there is no immediate use. The construction of ships for stock would be prohibitively expensive; there are no alternative uses to which shipbuilding equipment can be put; and highly specialized shipbuilding labour cannot easily change its occupation. This constitutes a major economic problem to which at present no satisfactory solution has been found.

Electrical and Electronic Engineering. The manufacture of electrical goods tends to concentrate in the South-East, West Midlands and in Lancashire. In particular, the manufacture of electronic apparatus has a marked concentration in and around London; this is an example of the attraction of the consumers' market, mentioned on page 47.

The industry has expanded enormously in the last forty years, during which electricity has been relatively cheap and so has found more and more uses both in homes and in workshops and factories. Except for the war years the national consumption of electricity has steadily increased year by year. Similarly the development of radio broadcasting in the 1920s and of television in the 1950s has provided a powerful stimulus to the industry.

Like most kinds of engineering, the electrical side is concerned with the production of capital goods, e.g. generating equipment, cables and transformers; but in addition it has developed a vast field of production in consumer durables, i.e. radio and television sets, refrigerators, electric fires, record players and all the other electrical gadgets now commonly used in the home. Demand for consumer goods of this kind tends to be maintained at a more constant level than that for the heavier capital goods.

Population Growth and Industrialization. This list, of course, does not begin to exhaust the catalogue of British industries—as a glance at the table on page 61 will show. It has merely dealt briefly with the most important of the older staple industries and the most flourishing of the new ones. A study of history and geography is really needed to round out the picture; there is no room for that here. Something else is also needed, however, to put that picture in perspective; and that is a comparison of the size of population before and after Britain became industrialized. Between 1801 and 1901 the population of Great Britain increased from $10\frac{1}{2}$ millions to 37

millions; from 1901 to 1961 it went up by over $15\frac{1}{2}$ millions
more. (See Fig. 20, page 132.) Over 52 millions is an enormously
large population for these small islands. If it had to live on
what Britain's own soil and fisheries could produce, even with
every acre of moorland tilled like a window-box, it could
barely live at all. The only way we maintain our standard of
living—one of the half-dozen highest national standards in the
world—is by selling abroad the products of our industry, the
services of our ships and the abilities of our citizens, and receiving in return the food and raw materials which we have no
space, or no resources, to produce for ourselves. (There will be
more to say on this in Chapter VII.) The diagram below shows
how Britain's foreign trade was made up in 1961; the totals
tell their own story.

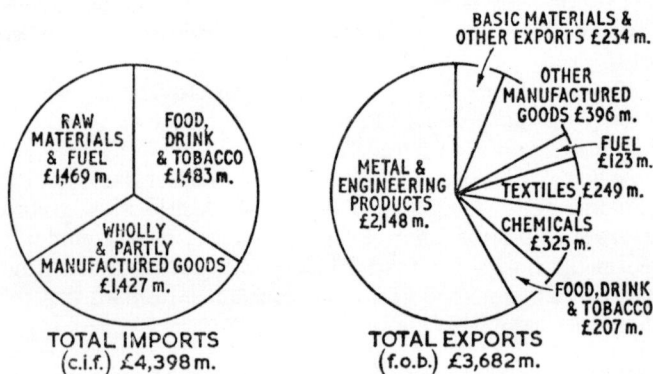

FIG. 14—FOREIGN TRADE OF U.K., 1961

The gap between total exports and total imports is not quite
as bad as it looks, because income and spending on 'invisibles'
—that is, shipping, insurance, financial services, the tourist
trade, and so on—are reckoned separately and show a balance
in our favour. In a normally good year this surplus on 'invisibles', together with income from overseas investments,
more than compensates for the deficit in 'visible' trade and
leaves a balance to strengthen reserves or to be invested abroad.

But ever since World War II it has been a constant struggle to come out all square. In the early post-war years we were only saved from disaster by help from abroad, especially Marshall Aid (of which more in Chapter XIX) and there were alarming setbacks in 1951, 1955 and again in 1961. Why these arose, and why they constantly threaten to recur, will become clearer when we have looked at the particular questions raised by international trade. No sensible person minds an occasional deficit—there are bound to be ups and downs in international trade—but a chronic bias towards running into the red is another story. Britain reached her present standard of living by specializing; she has got to go on making specialization pay, or see that standard come crumbling down.

CHAPTER VI

LARGE- AND SMALL-SCALE PRODUCTION

WE have seen that there is a great diversity in the size of British firms, whatever the type of production—primary, secondary or tertiary—in which they are engaged. In this chapter we shall see why this diversity exists; what are the influences which cause one firm to settle down at a small size, another to expand, and others again to join themselves together in still larger concerns. We shall be working, in fact, at what are called the *economies of scale*, technical or commercial.

What is a Firm? The word 'firm' needs a little explanation. Any of the organizations described in Chapter II may be a firm. It may consist of a single shop or office or factory; or it may own and control a number of separate factories or branch offices or a whole chain of retail shops. Or it may be a super-firm, like Unilevers or Imperial Chemical Industries, controlling a large number of subsidiary firms which themselves own and control a large number of branches. So it is as well to be clear whether, in any particular connection, one is talking about the unit of *control* or the unit of *production*. One could say a great deal about Unilever which would not make sense if one said it about a small trading post owned by the United Africa Company—a Unilever subsidiary—in the depths of the African jungle. Where technique is concerned, it is the unit of production which matters most; where commercial policies—buying and selling—are concerned, it is the unit of control which has to be considered; though the two things are, as we shall see, not entirely separate.

The Relative Importance of Large and Small Units. To get a general idea of how important are the various sizes of productive units—which may or may not be single firms—one can look at the following figures showing the percentage of employees working in 'establishments' of different sizes—an 'establishment' being a factory, works, mill or workshop engaged in production or repairs and employing more than ten people. (It should, of course, be noticed that this does not cover farming, mining, retail and wholesale trade, or other services; and that it leaves out the really tiny concern like the one-man cycle repair shop and others with *fewer* than ten workers.)

TABLE II—SIZE OF MANUFACTURING FIRMS IN GREAT BRITAIN
(*based on returns of employers in the 1958 Census*)

Number of Employees per Establishment	Percentage of Total Establishments	Percentage of Total Labour Force
More than 500	3%	48%
50–500	23%	40%
10–50	74%	12%

These figures suggest that a substantial proportion of the total output of goods is controlled by a relatively small number of big establishments, leaving only just over half the total output to be controlled by the overwhelming majority of smaller establishments. The biggest establishments—those in the 'over five hundred employees' group—include a large proportion of those engaged in iron and steel smelting and rolling, in shipbuilding, in engineering (marine, motor, cycle and electrical) and in the manufacture of chocolate, biscuits, glass, rayon, tobacco and tyres. It would seem, therefore, that in these lines of output large size gives a particular advantage. Cotton and woollen spinning and weaving, carpet making, boot and shoe manufacture, canning and preserving, furniture manufacture, pottery, are found predominantly in the smaller and medium group; here, one must suppose, large size either does not matter so much or is actually a disadvantage. It will become clearer as we go on why this is so.

The Forces of Growth: Monopoly. How do firms grow? How, in fact, have they grown in the past? Until the end of the nineteenth century the growth of individual firms, outside a very few industries such as steelmaking, was slow. During the last fifty years both firms (controlling units) and establishments (producing units) have increased very considerably in size. A firm can grow in two ways. It can increase its sales by pushing its products into new and wider markets; or it may increase the range of its products. Or a new, bigger firm may come into existence by the *amalgamation*, the joining together under a single control, of two or more smaller ones. All these kinds of expansion are aimed at improving the firm's capacity to make profits.

The advantages they bring are of two kinds: one is economy in the cost of production, the other, getting rid of competition. The first of these is an advantage to the public as well as to the firm; the other generally benefits the firm only, often at the public's expense. Competition, as was hinted in Chapter III, keeps prices down; for no customer will knowingly buy dear goods when equally good cheap ones are equally easily available, and the cheaper producer consequently gets the custom. For a business man working under competitive conditions the only way to make more profits is to produce more and to try to keep his costs low; raising prices, unless for reasons which are causing his rivals to do the same, merely means loss of custom, and the same applies to keeping prices high when his rivals lower theirs.

But if all the rivals can be brought together in one form or another of industrial combination, the picture changes: the business men controlling that combination now have a *monopoly*, they are the only suppliers of the goods concerned, and they can fix whatever price they like without fear of being undercut. Thus they may make what is called a *monopoly profit*. It may not be a big profit; in fact, possible monopoly profits in some products are so small that it is not worth while organizing a monopoly at all; but it may be very large indeed. It all depends on how people feel about the goods in question. If the product is something of which they absolutely must have a certain quantity, so that they will give up a great deal rather than have that quantity reduced, the monopolist can

raise his price a long way above the cheapest possible competitive level and still not lose custom. (Salt and matches are
examples of the kind of goods on which monopolists thrive.)
If, on the other hand, they can do without the product, or buy
much less of it, with comparatively little discomfort, if it gets too
dear for their liking, then raising the price above the competitive level loses more for the monopolist through reduced sales
than it gains for him by the larger profit on each item. (This
difference in the way buyers act in response to price changes is
called *elasticity of demand*, and we shall hear more of it later.)

Monopoly, therefore, does not always and invariably mean
higher prices; but it often does, and even where it does not
actually raise them it cuts off the main drive towards reducing
them; that is, the desire to get some of a rival's market and the
fear that a rival may encroach on one's own. Not having to
worry all the time about rivals is itself a comfort for business
men; so not only a positive desire for more profits but a mere
preference for peace and quiet may lead to combination. This
is particularly likely to happen in times of depression, when
firms with a lot of standing charges to pay (rent, interest on
bank loans and debentures, salaries, and so forth) are competing intensively to sell on a shrinking market even when every
sale means a loss—because not selling at all would mean a bigger loss still. Unless they reach some sort of agreement, the
result is a crop of bankruptcies—not always on the part of
those firms which would be least efficient in the long run. In
that case, the survivors are apt to buy up the victims cheap.
One way or another, by agreement or by forced purchase,
depression always encourages monopolistic combinations.

Forms of Industrial Combination. There are many different
kinds of combination. The tightest kind of all is actual *amalgamation*, when several firms sink their identity either in that
of the strongest among them or in that of an entirely new company. Amalgamation may link up firms producing the same
commodity—this is called *horizontal integration*—or it may
link up a sequence of processes, of steps in production, previously carried on by separate firms—this is *vertical integration*,

or *combination*. J. & P. Coats, Paton & Baldwin Ltd. and the
English Sewing Cotton Co., who between them control the
cotton-thread trade in Great Britain, were formed originally by
the integration of a number of different cotton-thread-making
firms; the Imperial Tobacco Company was similarly formed
by bringing together several tobacco and cigarette manufacturers; Tate and Lyle, the sugar manufacturers, are another
example. Vertical integration has linked together firms producing pig iron, steel, and ships, or newspaper firms and newsprint
manufacturers and lumbering concerns, or manufacturers and
retail outlets—as with H. E. Randall Ltd. or the Bata Shoe Co.
Thus the firm bringing about the amalgamation either gets control of its raw material supplies at one end, or control of a distributive organization at the other, or both. Often horizontal
and vertical integration occur together as a firm expands, and
then we find a giant organization like Imperial Chemical
Industries Ltd. or Unilever Ltd.

Trade Associations, Cartels and Holding Companies.
Short of amalgamation there are other ways of getting the commercial advantage of common action. Without any formal
agreement at all, the different firms in an industry may make it
a practice to follow the lead of the most powerful among them
in matters of price and to keep off one another's traditional
territory instead of competing all out all the time. Or they may,
by joining a trade association and agreeing to its rules, bind
themselves to avoid certain kinds of competition; to give no
more than a certain amount of credit, to make no special deals
with favoured customers, sometimes to keep their prices for a
certain period to a certain agreed figure. Or they may unite in
something a good deal tighter called a *cartel*, setting up a
central organization which decides on sales quotas, handles the
actual selling of goods at determined prices, and fines those
who exceed their quota or sell at cut prices outside the cartel
channel. The firms concerned keep their identity and the cartel
does not affect their internal management, but so far as market
policy goes they have effectively become part of a larger unit.

Experience shows that cartels are apt sooner or later to split up as the more efficient members get tired of hanging back and missing the opportunities of profit which lower prices and expanded sales would bring them. A more lasting kind of union is the *trust*, in which a special company or holding company is set up to acquire control of subsidiary firms by buying a majority holding in the latter's shares. Some wonderful pyramids of control have been built up in this way; a group of investors who owns 51 per cent of the shares of Company A, which owns 51 per cent of the shares of companies B, C, & D, each of which in turn has a number of subsidiaries, can control a whole economic empire by, as it were, sheer leverage. There is evidence, however, that this pyramiding is now less important than formerly and that the subsidiaries of the holding company are in most cases wholly owned by the parent company. This may be due to the inconvenience which minority share-holders can cause to the policy of the Group. This refers only to British conditions. The difference between the trust, as it has grown up in America, and the *holding company*, as formed in Great Britain, is a matter of legal detail; they are organized almost in the same way and for the same purpose. When the holding company or trust does not merely co-ordinate the buying and selling policies of the subsidiary firm, but actively reorganizes them and dove-tails their activities, it is virtually indistinguishable from an amalgamation.

So far, we have dealt with the size of the unit of control, with the commercial advantages gained by the large unit or combination, and with the different devices by which separate firms have tried to reap these advantages. Now it is time to look at the productive side, at the economies of scale as they affect the actual establishment, the 'plant'.

Technical Advantages of Large Scale. Many economies of scale are inherent in the principle of the division of labour; they are special cases of the advantages of specialization explained in Chapter IV. But specialization does not invariably mean large scale. There are technical influences which may be more or less important according to the kind of enterprise. Certain types of machinery and equipment cannot be used at all except on a large scale—for example, plant used in the manufacture of steel. One cannot run a pint-sized blast furnace any more than one can run a dinghy-sized ocean liner; up to a very large size indeed, the bigger the furnace the better the technical ration between fuel used and steel produced. Moreover, an establishment comprising several furnaces is a better proposition than a single furnace, because it can vary its output much more smoothly to meet peaks of demand. Then, too, the large establishment can make full use of expensive auxiliary machinery such as overhead cranes, which would not be profitable if they were idle half the time. And if establishments are vertically integrated (see page 85) so as to link successive processes, they can achieve valuable economies in transport and in fuel; as when pig iron is converted directly into steel without being allowed to cool. Taking together (1) the large minimum size of plant, (2) the advantages of having multiples of that plant to work with, (3) the need for a large through-put of work to keep expensive equipment occupied, and (4) the further gain which comes from vertical integration, it is obvious that steel manufacture is an industry where economies of scale are all-important.

All through manufacturing industry one can see similar influences at work, though not always so strongly. They may be completely outweighed, as we shall see, by influences working in a contrary sense; but the following advantages generally hold good:

Firstly, a large machine is apt to need no more men to work it than a smaller machine; so an establishment big enough to use large machines can enjoy lower labour costs and pay higher wages at the same time.

Secondly, what applies to high-powered machinery applies also to high-powered administrators and managers. In a small undertaking the manager must spend a certain amount of time doing work which could perfectly well be handled by employees of lesser ability—routine work and minor jobs which wastefully nibble into his energies, but of which there is just not enough to make it worth while to employ a full subordinate staff. In a large firm, that full subordinate staff can be fully

occupied, and the manager will be free to deal with the problems of policy and administration which are the proper business
of a man of first-class ability. Moreover, in a big firm management itself is divided up into departments, so that executives
with specialized abilities can concentrate on purchases, or on
sales, or on advertising, or on costing, or on technical direction. When a firm comprises a number of separate factories or
other productive units in different parts of the country, its
administration or management is often centralized at a head
office in London, so that all the chief executives are in close
contact and matters affecting the whole firm can be easily
discussed and decided.

Thirdly, a large organization can afford to spend considerable sums of money on research into better methods of production and better qualities of product; a laboratory and a team of
scientific research workers, even more than a big overhead
crane, is only an economic proposition if its costs can be spread
over a large output. The cost of such facilities per unit of a large
output is so small as to be outweighed many times over by the
resulting economies and improvements; per unit of a small output, such facilities are prohibitively expensive, so the small firm
has to do without them.

Fourthly, the large firm can usually borrow or raise fresh
capital more cheaply and easily than the small one. This is
because it is usually better known, it has bigger assets to serve
as security, and its name inspires confidence in the minds of the
public or the bankers.

Fifthly, the large firm scores both in the buying of fuel and
materials and the selling of products and by-products. Costs of
labour and transport are proportionately less for larger consignments of goods (think of the clerical work involved in shipping 100 separate one-ton consignments compared with that
needed for a single 100-ton load) and by-products will be
wasted altogether unless enough of them are produced to make
collection worth while. This gain in buying and selling is something quite distinct from the monopoly profit discussed earlier;
it is a genuine economy from everyone's point of view, not only
from that of the firm itself.

This list does not exhaust the advantages of large-scale production, but it helps to explain why the larger firm has come to play such a dominant part in certain industries.

The Limits of Growth. Why, if the larger firm has so many advantages, do we still find so many middle-sized and small firms? Why do some industries have no large firms at all? Why do firms on the whole run so much smaller in Britain than in the United States?

Limits of the Market. Partly, the answer lies in what was said in Chapter IV about the size of markets. Where that size is limited by high transport costs, or by tariff barriers and other artificial obstacles, or by considerable differences of taste among consumers, there is less scope for large-scale production. (The United States has a much bigger internal market than Great Britain—over three times the population and a higher purchasing power per head—and a market, moreover, in which people are much more ready to buy just what their neighbours buy.) It is easy to see that for some industries this limitation is so important that large-scale production is never likely to be profitable. It is possible to produce bricks very much more cheaply by using mass-production methods, with a great deal of expensive equipment, on the best brickfields; but then they have to be transported to wherever people want to build houses, and their weight is so great in proportion to their value that transport costs to any distant destination can more than swallow up the gain. Perishable commodities, like flowers and fruit, when they need disproportionately expensive handling and transportation to get them on sale quickly, obviously have a restricted market. Then, as was noticed in Chapter IV, the market may be limited by taste and need, as with such things as jewellery, scientific instruments and highly specialized equipment and, to a lesser degree, clothes and furniture.

Personal Attention. Size of markets apart, there are many kinds of goods and services where the 'personal touch' is appreciated. We have seen that it is appreciated in retail trade. It is appreciated even more in tailoring and dressmaking, where the customer wants not merely something different from what other people are wearing but the advantage of having the maker's skill directly concentrated on his or her individual personal requirements. The manufacturer who wants a special tool to meet a special technical requirement is, similarly, not merely one buyer in a necessarily small market, but a buyer who wants concentrated *personal* attention. It is much easier for the small firm to provide this than it is for the large firm. Sometimes the desire for the personal touch may have very little to do with the actual quality of services rendered—the car-owner with a temperamental engine may prefer to take his troubles to his own small local garage where he will get sympathy, rather than go to a larger establishment which will merely do the job and present the bill, even where the latter is better equipped to do it thoroughly. But the desire exists, and favours the small firm.

Shortage of Managerial Ability. Then there is a factor which is, in a way, the obverse of one of the advantages of scale discussed earlier; the big firm can make full use of first-rate managerial ability, but by the same token it *needs* first-rate managerial ability to run at all—and that ability is scarce. The general manager of a really big firm must be an exceptional man indeed; he must combine the ability to take in and assimilate a vast amount of information with powers of sound judgment, imagination and leadership. There are only so many men of this type born in every generation, and not all of them go into business; there are simply not enough to go round all the firms which could, if markets and technique were the only deciding factors, expand to maximum size.

Disadvantages of Large Scale: Internal Friction. Finally, it must not be forgotten that large size has positive *disadvantages* of its own—what can be called *diseconomies of scale*. Remember what was said in Chapter IV about the amount of organization which is needed to link up the different kinds of job evolved through the division of labour. To put the matter

in its simplest form, when there is a single boss who is production manager, sales manager, personnel manager and advertising manager all rolled into one, there is evidently no need for
him to call a conference in order to line up sales and advertising
policy, or to discuss the intake of new workers to cope with a
new order. He does not have to keep the peace between himself
in one role and himself in another; he does not find his orders
to himself misunderstood, or worry about putting suggestions
to himself in a tactful manner, or explaining a new idea to himself, or persuading himself not to go over to a competitor. All
these considerations take up a good deal of the time and
energy of the top executives in a large, highly-specialized establishment; they may take up so much time and energy as to
neutralize, or actually to outweigh, the advantages of specialization carried to its furthest point.

Industrial and Public Relations. Besides these relations
between different members of the managerial organization,
there are relations with workers and with customers. In the
smallest firm a worker with a grievance can have it out with the
boss, man to man; in the medium-sized firm the shop steward
can do likewise; in the very large firm there may be rank on
rank of authority between the workers and those who carry
final responsibility for settling the matters which those workers
feel strongly about—and with every lessening of personal contact there is more opportunity for mutual misunderstanding.
The story of the nationalized industries, particularly the highly
centralized coal industry, shows how important this weakness
may be in the really outsize organization. Red tape may be felt
to be just as much of an oppression as personal tyranny.

This applies to the customer too. Dealing with the smaller
firm, he deals either direct with the boss or with someone not
far removed from him; so if he has a query or a complaint, if
he wants a point stretched in his favour or a muddle cleared up,
the matter can be decided on the spot and on its merits. Dealing with the very large firm—or, still more, with a nationalized
industry or Government department—he has to deal with
subordinates, so remote from the final authority that they

cannot be given a free hand but must go by the rule book and the established practice. This is a very real disadvantage, as anyone who has had an argument with a railway (before or after nationalization) will realize.

Expensive internal organization; costly labour troubles; poor relations with the public; these are the *diseconomies of scale* which offset the advantages of the big firm. Of course the point at which economies and diseconomies balance varies with different circumstances and in different industries; think how much easier internal organization has become since the invention of the telephone, think how much simpler it is for the steel industry, where strikes are extremely rare, to maintain good industrial relations than for the coal industry with its bitter legacy of conflict. But this question of the point of balance is one about which not nearly enough is known; economists and social scientists generally need a great deal more information before they can say confidently (except in extreme cases): 'This industry is over-concentrated', or 'That industry is not concentrated enough'.

CHAPTER VII

MARKETS

So far we have used the word 'market' in a very general sense as the sum of sales possibilities open to a firm or industry. We have seen how scale of production and size of market are connected; we have seen what influences affect the size of the market itself. But we have not paid any attention so far to the way in which markets *work*; how prices are settled, how this process of price-settling differs from one kind of market to another. These questions will be our business in this and the following chapter.

What is a Market? If one is not thinking particularly about economics, or the sales prospects of a firm or industry, the word 'market' usually calls to mind the picture of some particular place—say the central square of a country town—where sellers gather on market day to meet buyers; a picture of rows of vegetable or fruit stalls, of cattle pens, and of buyers moving from one to another comparing prices and qualities and bargaining with the stall-keepers. This is the simplest and oldest kind of market, older than the retail shop, older indeed than money itself; but it is only one type among many. There is, in fact, an almost bewildering variety of markets of all kinds. But they all have this is common: they exist whenever and wherever goods, or services, are bought and sold.

Economists distinguish between *perfect* and *imperfect* markets. Perfect markets are rare, for reasons which will become clear as we see what is needed for perfection; but by looking at what happens in a perfect market one can see what forces are, in fact, at work, even when hampered by market imperfections, to settle prices and sort out goods between different buyers and sales between different sellers.

The 'Perfect Market'. In a perfect market, to quote the great economist Alfred Marshall, both buyers and sellers are 'all so keenly on the alert and so well acquainted with one another's affairs that the price of a commodity is always practically the same throughout the district'. The combination of such a degree of 'alertness' and such a close acquaintance with one another's affairs calls for a very special set of circumstances. The ordinary consumer has other things to think about than being 'alert' to all the prices charged by every possible seller of every possible thing he buys; even the most conscientious housewife has a limited amount of time and energy to spend on bargain-hunting; so that when retail prices are not fixed by official regulation or by agreement with manufacturers they may vary a good deal in practice even for the same goods sold in the same neighbourhood. Similarly, shopkeepers have other things to do besides keeping an eagle eye on one another's prices; they are more alert than the consumer, because such alertness is part of their business skill, but adjusting prices up or down from hour to hour, or even day to day, is a nuisance, so that, even where they are free to change, the change may be rather sluggish and uneven. Moreover, alertness is not enough in itself; it must be possible for the alert inquirer to find out what is being charged, and to find out, moreover, in time for the knowledge to be relevant to his particular deal. The person who buys a second-hand book at a local stall might perhaps have got a copy much more cheaply from another private individual who had had it for years and did not want it; but if they are not acquainted with one another the deal will not go through.

Perfect knowledge, perfectly free access, a perfect readiness to take advantage of both, are rather exceptional than otherwise. This is all the truer since knowledge of the prices being charged is very little use without knowledge of the goods they are being charged for—'value for money' may cover any number of combinations of quality and cheapness. The kind of buying and selling which makes a market 'perfect' is in fact a highly-skilled job; and about the only markets which are really 'perfect' in the economist's sense are those in which both buyers

and sellers are whole-time professional dealers whose business
keeps them in close and continuous contact with one another.

How the Single Price is Reached: Perfect Competition.
Nevertheless, one can see the forces at work to settle market
prices most clearly if one looks at the old and simple kind of
market in which reasonably alert and well-informed buyers
(say, experienced housewives) meet reasonably alert and well-
informed sellers (say, stall-holders with apples to sell). For
simplicity's sake one may assume that the apples are all of the
same size and quality; in practice, of course, both buyers and
sellers will allow for variations. Suppose that apples are plentiful, with the picking season in full swing. Looking at his own
well-filled stall and the well-filled stalls of his neighbours, each
seller will sensibly conclude that if he is going to get rid of all
these he will have to tempt the buyers with attractively cheap
prices. They probably will not, in the first place, all reach the
same conclusion as to what is a sufficiently attractive price; one
may scribble '6d.' on his board, another '7d.', a third, pessi-
mistically, '5d.'.

What, then, will happen? The buyers are wide awake, the
apples are all the same; there will be a crowd round the seller
with the lowest price and no buyers for the most expensive.
Each will think again. Naturally the cheapest seller would be
only too glad to get a higher price; realizing that the way
things are going, he could sell his stock twice over, he quickly
rubs out '5d.' and substitutes '6d.', judging that at that price he
will nicely clear his stall. The dearest seller can only lose by
sticking to a price at which he will fail to sell any apples at all;
he will mark down his price to '6d'. The stall-holder who
originally wrote up '6d.' will congratulate himself on his superior
judgment and leave his price as it was; and that (perhaps with
a little more fluctuation up and down as sales quicken or
slacken) will be the *market price* of the day. No seller will remain out of line for long; for a higher price will mean lost
custom and a lower price needlessly lost profits. *Competition,*
both between buyers and sellers, has produced that single
market price. (Why the single market price settles down at this

level rather than that, and what causes it to rise or to fall, is a question of the balance of supply and demand—to be looked at in more detail in the next chapter.)

Imperfect Competition. Competition, however, may either act sluggishly or be prevented, in one way or another, from acting at all. As we have seen, mere lack of knowledge or alertness respecting prices may account for variations in the same neighbourhood. A second reason for market imperfection is the growing practice of producing *branded* articles. Toothpaste, tea, salt, soap—in fact almost every manufactured commodity sold on the retail market—are sold under particular names, devised by makers who claim special distinguishing qualities for them. Any hoarding or paper or magazine is full of these claims. One is urged to buy this candy bar rather than that because its flavour is deliciously different, whereas hardly anyone could tell one from another blindfold; or to ride this bicycle rather than that for speed and comfort, whereas no engineer could find a ha'porth of difference between them; or to take this rather than that cough mixture, both having precisely the same chemical formula. A clever advertising campaign may wake possible buyers up to the existence of a new product or tell them of real advantages which otherwise they would not know about; in this way, advertising makes markets more perfect rather than less. But its more usual effect is to split up what would otherwise be a single market with a single price into a number of markets with different prices, where each product has only one seller.

This state of affairs is called *imperfect competition*—competition exists, since buyers will switch to the nearest substitute if prices diverge too much, but it is blunted by the effect of advertising in making the customer 'refuse all substitutes' for his preferred brand so long as the divergence is not too big and the claims for superiority not too absurd. And—this is important in practice—under imperfect competition the seller who wants to sell a bit more has an alternative to the lowering of prices, which is his only hope under perfect competition; he can simply expand his advertising, which is not nearly so much

H

in the public interest. Not only is price competition blunted by
the use of brand names backed by advertising, it may be actually prevented by one or another of the monopolistic agreements discussed in Chapter VI, or forbidden by Government
regulation, as described in Chapter III. In that case there will
certainly be a single price for the goods concerned—indeed, a
more certainly and reliably single price than in any but the
most perfectly competitive market; but it will not move
smoothly, like the price in our imaginary apple market, to clear
off abundant supplies or to choke off excessive demand.

At one extreme therefore is the market of perfect competition
where no one seller nor any one buyer can control the price; at
the other extreme is the monopolistic market where the price
is fixed by the one seller of the commodity. In between is a
large area of imperfect competition which gradually merges into
monopoly on one side and into perfect competition on the other.

Functions of the Market. To sum up, the function of a
market is to bring buyers and sellers together (whether personally or through long-distance communication) and also to
enable them to fix a price which will balance the amount of the
commodity demanded, day by day or season by season, with
the supplies forthcoming. All markets perform the first function; not all succeed in performing the second.

Types of Market. To describe all the different types of
market in the world, or even in Great Britain, would obviously
be impossible; as we have seen, the word 'market' sums up the
whole mechanism for the buying and selling of goods and services, and an encyclopaedia would hardly give enough room
for a complete discussion. Still, it will be helpful to look at the
main classes of market and their characteristics, rather more
realistically than we have done so far.

We have spoken of the 'market' of a manufacturer or producer as if the only people concerned were the final buyers who
consume his products; and that is justifiable enough when one
is thinking of the appeal of his goods, the advantages of scale,
and so forth. It is, however, very rare for producers of goods to

sell direct to the final consumer. Generally, the manufacturer of goods, or the importer of foreign products, or the farmer, sells to a factor or wholesaler dealing in large quantities; the latter sells to the retailer, and the retailer sells to the public. Even this is an over-simplified sketch, for the chain may be either longer or shorter; also, producers and manufacturers themselves buy, for trade purposes, from one another and through wholesalers.

The Retail Market. To begin with the retail market, with which we are all familiar: this consists of all the shopkeepers, large and small, private or co-operative, the stall-holders, the barrow-boys, the pedlars, who sell to the ordinary public those things needed for personal use and consumption. In this class should be also included those firms which advertise their goods in newspapers and periodicals for order and delivery by post. (This sort of firm is enormously more important in the United States, with its widely scattered farm population remote from shopping centres, than it is here. The 'mail order' firm of Sears Roebuck, Inc., is one of the biggest retailing concerns in the world.)

The Wholesale Market. A wholesaler, broadly speaking, is a dealer who sells goods in large consignments to other wholesalers, to producers, and to retailers, but not to the general public. Confining our attention to those wholesalers who act as links between producers and retailers, we find wholesale markets commonly used in the grocery, drapery, tobacco, confectionery, pharmacy, coal, greengrocery and ironmongery trades. Not all trade passes through the wholesaler's hands; some large retailers buy direct from producers, some producers (e.g. small market gardeners) sell direct to the public, and some wholesalers supply both the public and smaller retail traders. But this pattern—producer to wholesaler to retailer to public— is fairly representative.

The Wholesaler's Function. Why not, many people have wondered, shorten this distributive chain and save the wholesaler's share of the final cost? By and large, the answer is that where it is economic to by-pass the wholesaler, or for that matter the retailer too, producers have always been reasonably ready to do so. Under free enterprise, anyone who thinks he can make a profit by direct sale at a lower price is free to try—and if he can, by providing his own retail outlets, sell more cheaply to the public than his rivals whose goods pass through several different hands, the public will be equally free to turn to him in their millions and starve the middleman out.

When this does not happen it is because, on the whole, the policy of direct sales does not pay. The producer's business is making things or growing things and disposing of them as simply as possible, not packaging them up in small consignments and shipping them in single lots or storing them or displaying them. That is someone else's speciality. The 'distributive chain' is just one more example of the fruitful division of labour. The wholesaler generally caters for a local or regional market, buying goods in bulk and distributing them locally in the quantities needed by the various retailers. He employs salesmen who can advise the retailer about the products of a number of manufacturers, which saves time in interviewing, in inspecting samples, and in ordering. He may (as in the tea, tobacco and wine trades) do what is really a special kind of producer's job by making up blends of commodities to suit particular tastes. Finally, the actual holding of large stocks is itself a specialized job; someone has to do it, or the flow of goods would be impossibly jerky, and the retailer in particular is unlikely to have either enough capital to lock up in large reserves of goods or enough storage space to keep them in. In international trade, even more than elsewhere, the wholesaler has a particularly useful job as a source of information to importers on goods available and to exporters on market conditions and practice.

There is, of course, always the possibility that an elaborate chain of distribution from producer to consumer has, in some particular case, ceased to be necessary but is surviving through sheer force of habit, or because no one is willing to take the risk of trying new methods, or because the big well-established firms forming the links of the chain have a virtual monopoly of 'know-how'. In such cases a sharp break with the established practice—possibly by Government action—may conceivably offer a chance of real economy. But it by no means follows, because there is a long chain and a large mark-up from producer to consumer, that a shorter chain would, when all the necessary work had been done, make that mark-up less.

Commodity Markets. An important special type of market is the commodity or produce markets—dealing not in finished goods but in raw materials and staple foodstuffs. These are mainly organized markets, in the sense that actual transactions take place in a recognized building or area, according to well-defined rules and regulations, and only recognized buyers and sellers may take part, the general public being excluded. Metals, textile materials, rubber, and grains are dealt in on such markets; so are special services such as shipping freights and insurance. Specialized markets and exchanges of this kind have grown up in London—the world's greatest port —and in some of the main provincial towns where a particular commodity is important to local industry. London has its Rubber, Metal (tin, copper, lead and zinc), Wool, Fur and Tea Exchanges or Auction Centres; raw cotton is sold on the Liverpool Cotton Exchange which has replaced the former public board known as the Raw Cotton Commission. The principal grain markets in London are the Mark Lane and Baltic Exchanges—the latter, for historical reasons, also dealing in shipping freights. Most leading commerical countries have such exchanges; those of the United States, especially those dealing with wheat, maize, meat and cotton, are particularly important. Rules and procedures differ, partly for historical reasons, from country to country and from market to market, but professional expertise is common to all.

Function of the Commodity Market. When World War II broke out, many of the London and Liverpool Exchanges were closed and the buying and selling of the commodities concerned were taken over by the Government, so that the restricted supplies available could be most effectively and directly used in the war effort, and the import programme strategically matched to shipping possibilities. This was meant to be a temporary measure, but for various reasons, as we shall see, the return to normal was slow. With their close contacts, restricted numbers, and professional skill, these exchanges under normal conditions come very near to the economist's ideal 'perfect market', They provide a most delicate and responsive mechanism for ascertaining the prices which will balance supply and demand to-day, next week, three months or six months hence.

This delicacy and accuracy is made possible partly by the skill of the dealers, partly by the fact that many commodities, such as cotton and wheat, are standardized into grades so that buyers can make their purchases (if necessary through agents) without inspecting the commodities and in full confidence that they will get what they expect. Cotton, for instance, is graded as 'fair', 'good middling', 'middling', etc., for each of a number of types and lengths of staple. These grades are based on standards known to and accepted by everyone in the trade, and a purchaser is always entitled to have the grade of his consignment confirmed by sample.

Speculation. Another function which such markets perform is to even out price fluctuations. Agricultural crops, e.g. wheat and cotton, vary considerably in size from harvest to harvest, and of course stocks run down from just after one harvest to just before the next. The demands of manufacturers, on the other hand, are comparatively stable—their customers want bread, shirts, sheets and so forth, all the year round and year after year. Continuing demand and fluctuating supply, left to themselves, would mean sharp changes in price, with food and raw materials being used lavishly in time of temporary plenty and consequently not being available in time of temporary shortage. (This still happens in primitive countries, where the period just before harvest is apt to be a time of near-famine because the harvest plenty of last year has gone in earlier feasting.)

Where organized commodity markets exist, dealers buy

freely in time of glut, hold what they have bought for a time of shortage, and make their profit by selling when everybody most wants what they have to sell and are thus most willing to pay a high price. Thus, they act as buffers between producers and manufacturers, who would otherwise have to bear the full brunt of price changes. Producers can get their produce off their hands and get cash in exchange at the time when they need it; manufacturers can make contracts for future delivery at an agreed price, which gives them a firm basis on which to plan. Thus the burden of risk due to price movements is carried by the dealer, who is the better able to carry it since he is, precisely, a specialist in market forecasts. Moreover, these price movements are actually smoothed out, since in time of plenty the dealers' buying keeps prices higher, and in time of scarcity their selling keeps prices lower, than they would otherwise be.

The people carrying out this risk-bearing and smoothing-out function need not actually handle or move the goods concerned at all; they may merely buy and sell grain which remains in the elevators or wool which remains in the warehouses, and so be pure 'speculators'. This does not mean that their activities are wasteful. Unfortunately, however, this useful and indeed highly necessary kind of speculation is not the only kind. When a speculator makes it his business not so much to forecast market conditions as to mislead other people about them, or when the unskilled outsider takes a hand and leads or follows a stampede 'into' or 'out of' cocoa or wheat or rubber as the case may be, price fluctuations may be actually amplified instead of being smoothed down, and supplies spread less, instead of more, evenly over time. This is bad for producers, for consumers, for the unwary amateur speculators themselves, and indeed for everyone except the few unscrupulous individuals who make a speciality out of fishing in troubled waters.

Local Markets. Many towns throughout the country, particularly those in farming districts, have their own *local markets* dealing mainly, though not exclusively, with farm produce. Unlike the big commodity markets, they are open to any member of the public whether he wants to sell or to buy; but in practice it is usually only people concerned in the particular trade who take part. As we shall see, much of the trade in farm produce which used to pass through local markets is now channelled, by regulation, through official Boards and other public agencies.

Other Markets: Capital and Labour. So far, we have only discussed markets in which actual commodities are bought and sold; but there are also markets for capital, for labour services, and for property. The London Money Market, which comprises the banks and other leading institutions dealing in long- and short-term capital is so complex and important as to need a chapter to itself; moreover, it can hardly be understood unless one has learned something about money. It is described in Chapter XVI. We must note that it includes the *Stock Exchange*, which provides for the purchase and sale of shares and securities of all kinds. This, like the commodity exchanges, is a closed (i.e. professional) and highly organized market which approaches very closely to the ideal of a perfect market.

The market for different kinds of *labour services* is of a rather special kind; the two functions of a market—to bring buyers and sellers together, and to settle prices—are, in this case, completely separate. Buyers and sellers of labour—employers and employees—may be brought together by means of the Employment Exchanges controlled by the Ministry of Labour; or, where the labour is that of young people, by the Youth Employment Bureaux controlled by the education authorities; while numerous private agencies provide markets for the labour of teachers, secretaries, domestic servants, and theatrical artists. But the price at which that labour is bought, the wage or salary, is for the most part settled quite outside these institutions. Domestic servants, secretaries and actors may strike their own individual bargains and so do most salary-earners in business, but the greater part of wages are settled either by periodical negotiations between employers (private or public) and the Trade Unions into which wage-earners are organized, or by official bodies whose decisions have legal force, as in agricultural work and in catering.

Real Estate. The market for real estate or property, whether for sale or to let, is mainly in the hands of specialized agents mostly, for obvious reasons, confining their activities to their own neighbourhood. Here again prices are to some extent settled outside the market by official regulation. Although the rent of furnished accommodation and the selling price of houses is determined by the market forces of supply and demand, the rent of unfurnished houses, below a certain rate-able value, is controlled. The aim of this is to protect the consumer by *preventing* the market from fulfilling its function of balancing supply and demand. In this case, supply and demand left to themselves would bring about very high rents. As things are, where rents remain comparatively low, supply and demand remain out of balance.

Transport and the Size of the Market. Technical progress in the past hundred and fifty years has enormously increased the *geographical size* of markets—using the word 'market' in its widest sense as the sum of contacts between buyers and sellers of any commodity. Railways, steamships and air transport on the one hand, refrigeration and canning on the other, have made it possible to transport most kinds of goods to almost any part of the world at a comparatively low cost. Before their development, only the most valuable and easily transportable goods were worth shipping long distances—even if it were physically possible to do so. A little trade in grain, a more substantial (and indeed historically very important) trade in salt fish, and the famous trade in precious spices, comprised virtually the whole international movement of foodstuffs up to the early eighteenth century. Tea and cocoa, both luxuries by reason of transport costs, began to reach these islands late in the seventeenth century, but in staple foodstuffs Britain, like other countries, had no choice but to be virtually self-sufficient. Now, supplies of meat and wheat from the New World and the Antipodes make it possible for far more people to live in Britain than could be fed from British farmlands; and in return Britain's manufactures can be sent all over the world.

Not only has actual physical transport been improved, but *communications*, by telegraph, cable, telephone, have made it possible for information about supplies, prices and market requirements to be instantly transmitted between countries thousand of miles apart. In this way, price differences due to lack of up-to-date information are smoothed out, and the expression 'a world market' becomes a reality.

Break-up of the World Market. Unfortunately, other forces have worked the other way. We have had two world wars, both naturally breaking up the world market; we have had, as a result, a complete breakdown of the old system (to be discussed later) which used to keep the buying powers of different national currencies in step with one another and so made it easy and safe to buy and sell across national frontiers; we have had large-scale unemployment between the wars, and other economic changes. All these events have led governments in Britain and elsewhere, wisely or unwisely, to clamp down restrictions on the movement of goods, workers and money. Customs duties, and regulations limiting or forbidding various classes of imports, reduce the volume of trade between countries; fear of unemployment among their own citizens has caused almost all countries to limit the number of immigrants; the desire to keep capital at home or to prevent tax-dodging leads to measures limiting the flow of international credit. The picture is not entirely black. Since World War II restrictions on the free flow of world trade have been attacked in the International Monetary Fund and under the General Agreement on Tariffs and Trade. Such bodies as the Organization for European Economic Co-operation, and later the European Economic Community and the European Free Trade Association, have worked towards the removal of barriers to trade, mainly regional trade. But all these efforts have not yet greatly altered the picture: the world market in goods, labour and capital made possible by technical progress is still prevented from existing in practice.

Changes in Marketing. Very important changes in market-ing, particularly of agricultural produce, have come about over the last twenty years. These changes have been of two main kinds. In the first place, producers have banded themselves to-gether in associations for selling their produce; these are a particular instance of the selling associations mentioned on page 86. In the second place, Government departments have intervened in the market, either directly as buyers or sellers or by imposing controlled prices.

Farm Produce. Sellers' or marketing associations for the disposal of farm produce have been set up in Great Britain and in many other countries, most of them dating back to the years of deep trade depression following 1930, when the world prices of foodstuffs fell much more than the prices of other things and so caused very heavy losses to farmers. Even before the depres-sion, however, farmers were apt to find marketing arrange-ments unsatisfactory. The individual farmer, with his crop on his hands and an acute need to sell in order to clear his barns and replenish his bank account, was always in a weak bargain-ing position compared with the comparatively few dealers. At the local market the British farmer was apt to find the dealers banded together in a 'buyers' ring' to keep prices down; in the big organized markets such as the Chicago Wheat Pit in America the American farmer sometimes found his year's work at the mercy of the less-reputable sort of speculator. Few, work at the mercy of the less-reputable sort of speculator. Few farmers, if any, had the resources to hold off and wait for better

What a single farmer can hardly do, however, a large local or national organization can manage much more easily; particu-larly if, as in Great Britain, it is given power by law to compel would-be independent sellers to come in and abide by its rules. The association buys its members' crops and disposes of them to consumers (as with milk) or to manufacturers (as with hops). It may restrict production when a glut is feared or prices are chronically inadequate (hop acreage was restricted in Great Britain in the thirties; the United States had much more drastic Government enforced restrictions on a number of crops). It may vary standards of saleability (in a good potato year, small potatoes were compulsorily kept off the market and fed to stock; in a bad year they could go to the greengrocers). Thus the farmer's bargaining position was improved—on the general principle that unity is strength.

Marketing Boards. In some cases farmers have themselves taken the initiative in organizing their marketing, and have set up co-operative associations such as the various wool-growers' associations. The farmers' co-operatives of Denmark are famous all over the world for their achievements not only in improving their members' bargaining power but in raising standards of efficiency and in educating the countryside. In Britain, however, organization has been through Marketing Boards set up by Government action in the 1930s. The actual organization varied from Board to Board; but the object was everywhere the same, to guarantee the farmer a sale for his produce at a price which made production of the commodity worth while. ('Worth while' to whom? The best-placed and most efficient farmer, or the worst-placed and slackest? No one has satisfactorily decided where the line should be drawn.) From the farmer's point of view the Boards have been reasonably successful; but they have been responsible for some rises in price to the consumer. They now control marketing by buying and selling all home produced milk, eggs and wool: they also regulate farmers' production and sales of potatoes, hops, tomatoes and cucumbers. The Fatstock Marketing Corporation is a commercial company set up in 1954 by the National Farmers' Union as a new initiative. It is still mainly owned by farmers and is the biggest meat wholesaler in the country, handling a large percentage of the pigs marketed.

Government Trading, Price Fixing and Rationing. A second development, that is buying and selling and price regulation by Government departments, arose out of the needs of war, continued for several years after 1945, and, though mostly reversed after 1951, has left traces behind. A particularly important feature was the bulk purchase, by Government representa-

tives, of foodstuffs and other commodities. This began as a part
of national wartime strategy—food and raw materials being as
important to victory as weapons, and quite as hard to get
through the submarine blockade. It was continued thereafter
partly in the hope that the single official buying mission would
have better bargaining power than a number of competing
traders, partly in order to tie up purchasing deals with political
aims, such as strengthening Commonwealth links, and partly,
during the post-war Socialist Government's tenure of office,
through distrust of private enterprise.

Rationed home-produced foodstuffs were also marketed exclusively through official channels up to the moment when the
retailer took over, and he, of course, had no power to raise
prices or vary rations. Many unrationed goods were price-
controlled. The 'utility' scheme applied to clothing, shoes,
fabrics, furniture, and many other things, combined price control with control over specifications; this aimed at ensuring the
production of good sound articles in a limited number of
ranges—remember how standardization cuts down costs. All
these measures added up to the abolition, over a wide field, of
the normal market system. Almost none of them now remain.
However, the market in *housing* is still, as it has been ever since
World War I, affected by rent restriction and special privileges
for sitting tenants; hire-purchase terms are subject to government regulation; and when the trade in *home-produced staple
foods* returned to private channels there remained a complicated system of 'deficiency payments' and other subsidies to
farmers out of Exchequer funds.

CHAPTER VIII

PRICE

WE began the discussion of markets by showing how competition, given knowledge and alertness, and access of buyers to sellers and sellers to buyers, leads to a single price for a single commodity. The question of why that single price should be just what it is, no higher and no lower, was left over for special treatment; and that is what we shall now consider.

Price and Scarcity. This study of *price formation*, as it is called, is in a way at the very centre of economics. It arises from the central, all-important economic fact, the great obvious fact stated in the first Chapter of this book, that there is *not enough* of most of the goods and services which we want, or of the resources to produce them, for everyone to have just as much as they want of everything. Certain things, which economists call 'free goods', are available to everyone without effort —light and air, for instance. But food, clothing, shelter, all the thousands of different things which meet our needs and desires, are in the economic sense *scarce*—that is, we could all do with more of them than we have. (Economic scarcity is not the same thing as natural scarcity. A naturally scarce thing—say, a pebble of a particular odd shape—may have no economic scarcity because no one wants it. And a naturally very plentiful thing, like grass, may be economically scarce because farmers with cattle to feed could use more hay than is available.) All of us everywhere, even millionaires, have unfilled wants. The un-filled wants of the millionaire are generally unimportant, the unfilled wants of the very poor are sometimes very important indeed, but everyone, rich or poor, is constantly having to choose between satisfying *this* want or *that* want a little more adequately. Governments, acting on behalf of their citizens, have to choose in just the same way; more new houses, or more new power plants? More teachers, or more nurses? When a government rations food or other things in wartime, it is in effect doing the citizens' choosing for them.

If there were no division of labour the only way of filling the most urgent want would be to buckle down and set to work filling it by one's own labour—one might want to replace the leaky roof of one's hut, but choose to leave that urgent need unfilled because it was still more urgently necessary to pick and dry fruits while they were in season, and one had not time and energy for both jobs. Once the division of labour comes in there is an alternative: to induce someone else to fill that want for one, by offering him the means to fill *his* wants. And that, of course, is what we do when we go to a shop and induce the shopkeeper to satisfy our want for an ice-cream cornet, or a pair of socks, or a wireless set, by offering him money with which, in turn, he can get his own wants satisfied. Every time anyone buys anything, he is choosing between that thing and the other things which his money could buy.

Marginal Utility and Willingness to Buy. Now, the shorter we are of anything, the more important it is to us to get a bit more, and so the readier we are to choose that bit more rather than the other things our money would buy; the readier we are, in fact, to pay a high price for it. Anyone can realize how true this is by comparing the way he would feel about paying three and sixpence to go to the cinema once a week with the way he would feel about paying seventeen shillings and sixpence to go five times; or the value he would set on a handkerchief if he had none at all with the value he would set on more handkerchiefs if he had a dozen. Very few people who had been to the cinema four times in a week would be willing to give up anything at all to go a fifth time; and whereas the person with no handkerchief at all might feel, in some circumstances, that he would willingly do without his next meal in order to be relieved of his embarrassment, the person with a dozen might not give up even a penny for a thirteenth.

This private valuation which we set on the little bit extra, the last handkerchief or the last weekly cinema visit or, in general, the last unit of anything which we consume, is called in economic language its *marginal utility*; and the fact that a little more of any particular thing gets less and less important to us as we get more and more of it is called *diminishing marginal utility*. It is because of diminishing marginal utility that things fetch higher prices the scarcer they are, and lower prices the less scarce they are. All the buyers in a market are weighing up, more or less carefully, the importance to them of a bit more of what the sellers have to sell; all of them are willing to pay a higher price for the first bit more (as it might be the first handkerchief), than for the second or third or fourth.

If, therefore, there is a glut, if the commodity concerned is more plentiful than usual, prices will have to come down lower than usual in order to match the lesser value which the buyers set on the extra quantity and induce them to buy. If prices do not come down, the sellers will be left with some goods on their hands. If, on the other hand, there is a shortage, the sellers can put up their prices higher than usual, because the smaller supply will only fill the more urgent wants, and in order to get those wants filled people will be willing to pay the higher price. Low prices tempt buyers—both those who are not very keen and those (the poorer buyers) who have other very important claims on their money. High prices freeze off buyers, leaving only those who are very keen and those (the richer buyers) whose money will meet other claims without difficulty. In this way, prices share out scarce goods between different consumers, falling as scarcity diminishes, rising as it increases. (We assume, for the time being, that no controls are imposed to prevent sellers charging higher or lower prices according to the state of the market.)

Price as Incentive to the Supplier. Not only do prices share out the scarce goods which have come on to the market, by choking off or encouraging *demand*; they do a great deal to settle what goods shall come on to the market in future, by encouraging or discouraging *supply*. Any rise in price makes it more profitable for producers to grow or manufacture more of the commodity concerned; thus the supply is increased. Any fall in price makes it less profitable, and thus the supply is diminished. The sequence runs: special scarcity—higher marginal utility—higher price—higher profit chances—bigger production—bigger supply (so that the special scarcity is remedied by more resources being attracted towards meeting it); or special plenty—lower marginal utility—lower price—lower profits (or actual losses)—smaller production—smaller supply (so that resources which were being comparatively wasted on meeting less urgent needs are attracted to more important uses).

Demand and Supply: an Example. It is often helpful to use graphs to show the connections between the demand for a commodity and the price at which it is sold, and between that price and the supply. (Demand is, of course, not the same thing as need or desire; it is need or desire backed by money. A desperately urgent need with no money to back it has no effect on the market, whereas the most languid preference backed by money does have an effect—which is why the market cannot always be left to itself to share out really important and necessary goods like basic foodstuffs.)

A Graph of Demand. The diagram (Fig. 15) shows the amount of tomatoes (all of the same grade and quality) which might be sold in a week at different prices.[1]

Prices are plotted in shillings and pence along the vertical axis OY and quantities in thousands of pounds along the horizontal axis OX. At 3s. 6d. per lb. quite a lot of people cannot afford tomatoes at all—they need the money too badly for other things—and those

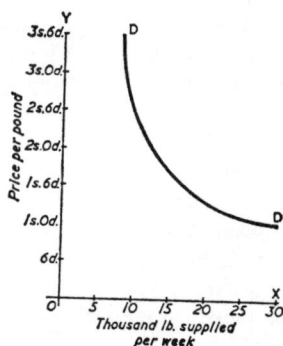

FIG. 15—DEMAND CURVE

---

[1] A *demand schedule*, showing prices in one column and the respective amounts of the commodity sold at each particular price in a parallel column, is sometimes drawn up to facilitate the plotting of the graph.

I

who do buy only get an odd half-pound or so to cheer up
their Sunday evening salad bowls. So only about 8,000 lb. are
bought. At 3s. there is not much difference—a few more people
are buying, but they still treat their tomatoes as a luxury.
Total demand now equals 8,300 lb. At 2s. 6d. more buyers
come in and the better-off buyers (or those keenest on tomatoes) start buying in rather larger quantities, eating tomatoes
twice a week perhaps instead of once for a treat. Demand now
stands at about 10,000 lb. At 2s. and at 1s. 6d. quite a number
more are tempted, and the demand, as people begin to buy
tomatoes for a second vegetable, for sandwiches, and for grilling
with the breakfast bacon, rises first to 12,500 lb. a week, then to
16,750 lb. a week. At 1s. practically everyone can afford some
tomatoes and most buyers can afford a lot. They are now a
really economical second vegetable; they go into soups and
stews; and thrifty housewives are buying them in large quantities for bottling. From 16,750 lb. the demand has leapt up to
30,000 lb.

This graph illustrates not what actually happens over a
season but what would happen, at a single time, *if* prices stood
at various possible levels. Over a period of time things can
change. People's tastes alter; in this particular example, there
are many more people willing to give up something—to pay a
price—in order to get hold of tomatoes than there would have
been (say) forty years ago, because the value of tomatoes for
health is better realized than it used to be. If one plotted the
prices and quantities before and after such a change in taste,
one would still find quantities increasing as prices fell, but for
each price the quantities at the later date would be bigger. The
demand curve, the line linking the points plotted on the graph,
would still run down from left to right, but the later one would
be bodily to the right of the earlier one. The same sort of thing
happens as people's income changes—a richer community
would buy more tomatoes at every price (except perhaps the
lowest of all), while a poorer community would buy less.

A Graph of Supply. It is possible to show in the same way
the relation between market price and the supplies offered.

Prices, once again, are plotted along the vertical axis OY and amounts offered along the horizontal axis OX (Fig. 16).

The curve S_1 indicates the amounts which might be offered at various prices in September. At 3s. 6d. there would be a tremendous profit margin for the lucky grower who had raised a crop on fertile ground handy to the market, a lesser but still handsome profit for the less conveniently placed grower whose crop had needed more fertilizer and carried heavier transport charges, a quite adequate profit, diminishing with distance, for the overseas grower, and, let us say, a just worth-while profit for the grower under glass with artificial heat. Taken together, they might send to market 25,000 lb. At 2s. 6d. hothouse production would not be quite so worth while and some greenhouse owners would grow something else instead; without their contribution, the supply is perhaps 21,800 lb. At 2s. the more distant

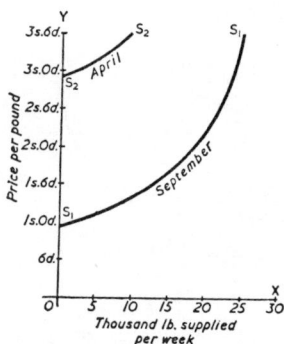

FIG. 16—SUPPLY CURVE

overseas growers drop out, and either sell their crops locally or grow something else. This brings supplies down to 18,500 lb. At 1s. 6d., only the home growers, with their lower transport costs, can make a profit; at 1s. production is only worth while for the most favoured and efficient of these, and only 3,000 lb. are available. (All these prices, of course, are those *expected* by the growers when they make their plans. Producing tomatoes, like producing practically anything else, takes time.)

It is even clearer with this second graph—or it should be— than with the first, that these prices represent possibilities at a given time, and not actual events over a period of time. Over a time—from season to season, in fact—the conditions of supply change. It is flatly impossible to grow tomatoes in the open, in Britain, for marketing in winter and spring; it is quite easy to do so for marketing in early autumn, as everyone knows who has a plant or two in his own back garden.

So, in fact, more tomatoes are attracted on to the market by a price of 1s. in September (curve S_1) than by a price of 3s. in April (Curve S_2). Taking one year with another, however, higher prices for tomatoes will attract more tomatoes at any given season, that is under given conditions of supply, than will lower prices.

The Balance of Supply and Demand. Now if one takes the first graph, showing the *demand curve*, the amounts which would be demanded at different prices, and the second graph showing the *supply curve*, the amounts which would be supplied at different prices, and puts them on top of one another (Fig. 17), one can see where the September price must in fact settle if no one controls it. It will be about 1s. 8d. a lb., a price just high enough to attract 15,000 lb. *into* the market and just low enough to tempt buyers to take 15,000 lb. *off* the market. That is what economists call the *equilibrium price*, the price which strikes an exact balance between supply and demand. A really exact equilibrium price is in practice rather rare. Prices of most goods do not alter to meet every shift of demand and every change in costs. Manufacturers fix prices at a figure which they think will be about right to ensure that their output is sold, and stick to those prices until it becomes obvious that they are really badly out of line, one way or another, with what customers are willing to spend. If the price proves a little too high, they will generally try to alter the conditions of demand by rousing people's appetite for their goods with an advertising campaign rather than immediately cut the price; if it proves a little too low, they will try to cut their costs rather than raise it. In fact, one cannot draw a supply curve for the sale of most manufactured goods where the price is fixed by the

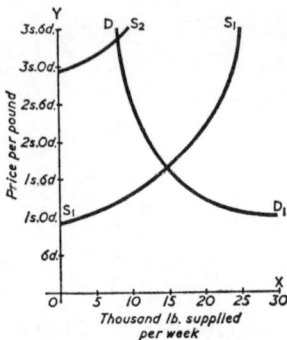

FIG. 17—SUPPLY AND
DEMAND CURVES

manufacturer. With the staple commodities which are traded in the produce markets described in Chapter VII, the position is different; there, prices do change from day to day and from hour to hour according to the latest picture of the supply-and-demand position. But for most things which the ordinary consumer buys, prices are adjusted at long intervals and by jerks.

Controlled Prices. When prices are not fixed by sellers but imposed by authority, they may never reach an equilibrium at all. Suppose, to go back to our tomatoes, that the price is controlled at 1s. That means that only those producers who can cover their costs at 1s. will send tomatoes to market at all, so that the supply is pulled down to 3,000 lb. a week; while the whole demand for 30,000 lb. a week will be turned loose on the market.[1] Obviously, since about one-tenth of the amount which people are willing to buy at that price is available, some other way will have to be found of sharing out the supply. Perhaps it will be first come first served—in other words, queues. Perhaps dealers will keep their tomatoes under the counter for favoured customers. Perhaps—though this is never likely to happen with tomatoes—the scarce goods will be *rationed* to an amount per head per week which will just add up to 3,000 lb. In that case, everyone can count on getting their share, regardless of whether or not they would be able and willing to spend more on getting more and regardless of their incomes.

Why Rationing is Imposed. Rationing and price control are essential in an emergency, a state of affairs, whether caused by wartime blockade or otherwise, where basic necessities are much scarcer than usual. For in these circumstances the rich can go on buying as much, or nearly as much, as ever— they can do so by giving up (by way of higher prices) things which matter comparatively little to them, and their demand will drive prices to a level which the poor, even by giving up absolutely everything else, simply cannot pay. As no civilized

[1] A situation in which demand widely exceeds supply at current prices is often called a 'sellers' market'.

country will allow mass starvation, rationing is used to keep down the demand of the rich or comparatively comfortable buyers. And even were all incomes exactly equal, so that everyone felt the pinch equally, it would be necessary to have rationing of foodstuffs in wartime just as it is necessary to have rationing of biscuits and water in a lifeboat—in order to spin supplies out over a dangerously uncertain future.

Disadvantages of Rationing. The arguments for rationing of necessities in wartime or other sharp emergency are in fact unanswerable. But the system has very serious drawbacks. With prices held down, there is no incentive to producers to turn out more goods and remedy the shortage; the natural sequence from the shortage to its remedy is broken. If the producers are given a subsidy, instead of a high market price, to encourage them, that means a heavy burden on the Exchequer and hence on the taxpayer, who thus pays for cheap food by way of high income tax or tobacco tax or purchase tax. If the artificial cheapness of the rationed commodity is not balanced in this way, then the money which consumers would have spent on it if the market were free gets spent on other things, unrationed things, driving up their prices and encouraging their production so that resources get used to remedy the less important shortages instead of the more important.

A large number of officials are needed to run the system and retailers have to spend time, or pay wages to extra employees, to deal with coupons and allocations. And there are always the 'wide boys' to run a black market for the less scrupulous buyers; not so many, fortunately, in Great Britain as in some other countries, but enough to make law-breaking seem a good deal less serious and more ordinary than it did before the war. Moreover, just as no civilized country will put up with mass starvation, so no free country really relishes restrictions on personal liberty. So altogether one must conclude that rationtioning is, economically speaking, at best a necessary evil. Where its 'necessity' begins and ends is, however, not a strictly economic question; because the answer depends on how much waste and loss one is willing to put up with for the sake of 'fair shares', once 'fair shares' have ceased to be a matter of life and death.

Elasticity of Demand. There is another important point which the supply-and-demand diagrams help to make clear. Plotting amounts demanded at various prices, we found lower prices always attracting a larger demand. (There are a very few exceptions to this rule, but they can be ignored.) But the amount of difference which a price reduction makes is not always the same, even for the same commodity. If one looks at the tomato demand curve, one sees that the first reduction, from 3s. 6d. to 3s., tempts comparatively little extra demand into the market: a fall in price of about 14 per cent increases demand only by a little under 4 per cent. The reduction from 2s. to 1s. 6d., that is a fall of 25 per cent, brings a much bigger layer of demand into action; the increase is from 12,500 to 16,500 lb. or 32 per cent. The fall in price of 33 per cent, from 1s. 6d. to 1s., nearly doubles the amound of the demand.

This relation between price movements and the changes in demand associated with them has a technical name, *the elasticity of demand.* This phrase makes one think of demand as held down compressed by price and as springing up, more or less vigorously, when the pressure lightens; which is quite a good way of looking at it. Marshall explained elasticity as follows: 'The elasticity of demand in a market is great or small according as the amount demanded increases much or little for a given fall in price, and diminishes much or little for a given rise in price.'

Suppose, for example, that the price of tomatoes falls from 2s. 6d. to 2s. per lb., and that this causes the total amount bought in a given period to increase from 10,000 lb. to 12,500 lb. In this instance the total amount spent on tomatoes (or what is called *consumers' outlay*) remains constant at £1,250, and the elasticity of demand for tomatoes over that particular price range is said to be *unity*. But suppose this same fall in price caused an increase in demand to more than 12,500 lb., then the demand would be said to be elastic—consumers' outlay would have expanded. Conversely, an increase to less than

12,500 lb. would signify that demand was *inelastic*—consumers' outlay would have contracted.[1]

The elasticity of demand varies for different kinds of goods because people's response to changes in their prices are different. It is a useful exercise to run over mentally some of the things one buys, or sees bought for one's household, and ask oneself: 'How much more of this would I buy in a week, or a month, or a year, if its price were a quarter less? halved? cut by two-thirds? How much less would I buy if its price went up by a quarter? a half?' and so on; and then to think of the things which are just too expensive, and reflect on which of them, if any, one would buy if *their* prices were cut; and then to take the speculation a little further, and consider how many people might be just on the verge of buying, only needing a small price reduction to bring them into the market, and how many would need a very big reduction before they were interested.

This sort of consideration is of the utmost practical importance to the business man—will a price cut increase sales enough to outweigh the smaller profit on each item? Will a price increase lose so much custom as to reduce his total income? It is equally important to governments thinking of raising or lowering the tax on a commodity. If the higher price made necessary by a higher tax chokes off a great deal of demand—if the demand for that commodity is highly elastic—then the yield of the tax will actually fall instead of rising; whereas where demand is inelastic the higher tax will leave total consumption little affected and the total yield will rise.

Elasticity and the Possibility of Substitution. It is usually found that the elasticity of demand for a commodity varies according to the possibility of finding an adequate substitute for it. When the only alternative to travelling by train is to

[1] The elasticity of demand for a commodity can also be explained, more precisely, as the ratio of the percentage change in demand to the percentage change in price, where the change in price is small. This can be expressed as a formula:

$$E = \frac{\text{percentage increase (or decrease) in quantity bought}}{\text{percentage decrease (or increase) in price}}$$

walk, fares can rise and rise and the only custom lost by the railway will be that of people who do not mind staying at home. When there is a bus service available, an increase in fares will result in travellers taking the bus unless they are especially hurried. Some things have plenty of substitutes; rayon and cotton, wood and plastics, cinema and theatre (to say nothing of dozens of different makes of wireless sets, motor cars, soap powders, and manufactured goods generally) can be substituted for one another without much of a pang even by people who have quite definite preferences. So the demand for any one item in these groups will be elastic over most of its range. Other things have practically no substitutes; pepper and salt, for instance, and tobacco or cigarettes. The influence of substitution works both ways; the demand for a commodity *which can be substituted for other things* will increase more rapidly, as its price falls, than the demand for one which has no alternative uses.

There are other reasons, too, which affect the elasticity of demand; readers may usefully work out for themselves the influence of the following: Necessity to life and health? Possibility of making the goods last longer? Level of the price per item in comparison with the average income? (Compare a car and a reel of cotton!) It must always be remembered that one can only talk sensibly about elasticity *in the neighbourhood of a given price*. The elasticity of demand for salt is, around the present price, small; no one would buy much more even if its price were halved, no one would buy much less even if its price were doubled. But if the price went up a thousandfold the picture would certainly be different; at that level, with nice-tasting potatoes a real luxury, demand would be highly sensitive. The elasticity of demand for colour photography is, around the present price, large; but if the price fell to, say, a penny a picture, so that practically anyone could buy almost as many colour films and prints as they wished, it is highly unlikely that a further fall to a halfpenny would sell many more films.

For any commodity, even a vital necessity, there must come a point where *higher* prices will make no further difference, because people's whole resources are going to buy that necessity anyway. This is, of course, a quite unreal situation, because, in the famines and sieges when it might theoretically arise, either the necessities are rationed or the strongest, not the richest, grabs what he can. And for any commodity, even one with myriads of uses, there must come a point where *lower* prices will make no further difference because everyone has as much as they want at—literally—any price.

Elasticity of Supply. Like demand, supply may be elastic or inelastic. If a small change in price produces a proportionately bigger change, in supply, either way supply is elastic; if the response is proportionately smaller, it is inelastic. Very similar influences affect elasticity of supply and elasticity of demand. If a thing can be readily switched from one use to another, then its supply, in either of those uses, will be more elastic than if it is difficult or impossible to adapt. If it is technically easy for producers to expand or contract their production, then its supply will be more elastic than if there are technical difficulties in varying output. If there are numbers of potential producers to whom a small price increase would offer a chance of profit, and a number of actual producers who can barely cover their costs at present prices, then its supply will be more elastic than if there are just so many producers, all with a comfortable profit margin, and no one else remotely qualified to join them. Readers may consider for themselves the effects on elasticity of supply of:

1. Production by means of very expensive, highly specialized equipment, or by unskilled labour using simple tools;

2. Limited, or widely spread, natural resources or inborn abilities;

3. Production by manufacture or production in the course of Nature;

4. Certainty or uncertainty of yield.

But here we are getting near the topic of Cost; and this needs a chapter to itself. Before considering costs, moreover, we must look at the things whose prices make up costs, the things which an enterprise must pay for in order to be able to produce; that is, the factors of production.

CHAPTER IX

THE FACTORS OF PRODUCTION

EVEN without having read the first seven chapters of this book, everyone knows that there is more needed for production than just human effort. For one thing, effort must be exerted *on* something—directly or indirectly, on the gifts of Nature; land, water, forests, minerals, For another, in almost every kind of production it has to be exerted *with* something— tools or machines, from the simplest to the most complicated. If one looks at the economic process from the point of view of the different ways in which human effort, the gifts of Nature, and man-made equipment are combined in different industries and in different communities, one can learn a number of essential things about the way it works.

Economists call these three necessary things the *factors of production; land* (short for 'all natural resources'), *labour* (all kinds of human effort), and *capital.* This last factor is a little more complicated to describe than the others; we will discuss it first so that the whole picture shall be reasonable clear.

What is Capital? When one sees or hears the word 'capital' one is apt to think of a sum of money, of cash or of a deposit in a bank. This is natural enough, because with money one can buy actual equipment and materials and necessities of production generally; so that someone who has 'a capital sum'—a good lump of money available—can start forthwith laying it out on what he needs in order to produce. But, of course, money by itself and in itself never built anything or grew anything or made anything or moved anything. Capital in the real sense consists of tools, machinery, buildings, ships, generating stations, railway lines and rolling stock, raw material stocks— in short, all those goods which do not *directly* satisfy our wants but which are used to produce those goods and services which do satisfy them. Capital goods, naturally, have themselves to be produced just like any others; and, moreover, they wear out or are used up—some in a continuous turnover, like the fuel in a blast furnace, some fairly quickly, like an aeroplane engine, some very slowly, like buildings and bridges.

Every business, and every community, has therefore to devote some of its resources to keeping its capital equipment in good trim and its stocks at a convenient level for smooth working. If this is not done, the process of production will be hampered and the output of consumer goods will fall off. Conversely, with more and better equipment, the output of consumer goods goes up—every worker using it can produce more. So capital must be *maintained* to preserve the standard of living, and *increased* if we want (as most of us do) to improve it.

Saving and Capital Goods. Money capital, the lump sums needed to buy capital goods, is created by *saving*; that is, by people refraining from spending the whole of their income, as it accrues, on consumer goods and services. The following diagram shows how people divide their money income, spending

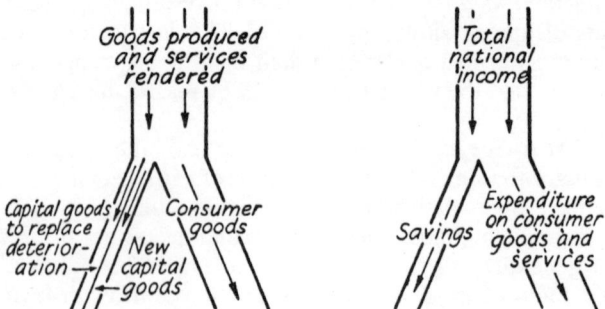

FIG. 18—SAVING, EXPENDITURE AND PRODUCTION

some of it now and saving some for the future. It also shows that this division of income corresponds to a division on the productive side—between the production of consumer goods to satisfy wants now and capital goods to satisfy future wants.

In the diagram, the different quantities exactly match—total national income and total national production (or gross national product) at current prices, total national savings and total output of capital goods for replacement and for net increase. In fact, they can and do get out of step, and then, as we shall see later, a number of extremely awkward things can happen. But discussion of these must wait until the national income itself has been discussed (Chapters XI and XXII).

Different Ways of Saving. When people save, they do not as a rule keep the actual money by them or hide it in secret places—a line of conduct which would not create capital or help production in any way. They may, as we saw in Chapter II, invest it—use it to buy shares of one sort or another, and so pass their savings straight into the hands of the business men who need a capital sum to launch or develop an enterprise.

They may similarly buy Government securities—bonds or Savings Certificates—and so provide the State with capital. Or they may deposit their money in a bank, or pay premiums on an insurance policy; in which case the bank or the insurance company does the investing, making loans or buying securities and thus getting the money, by one more stage, into the hands of the enterprises (private or public) which need capital. Thus these enterprises are provided with the means to pay for new factories or power stations or machinery; to meet their bills for materials and fuel and wages between the time work is begun and the time its product is sold; to replace and repair existing capital goods; and to keep enough cash in reserve for emergencies.

The Price of Money Capital. As it is only by getting hold of money capital that business men can do these things, and so run their businesses and make a profit, it is worth their while to pay something for the use of it out of the profits which they make. Money capital, in fact, has a price of its own—that is, interest. We shall study interest properly in Chapter XII. Meanwhile we merely notice that it is what lenders get for lending their capital—their savings—and that borrowers pay it because it is necessary and profitable for them to get capital into their businesses. Those people who prefer to buy shares rather than to buy debentures or Government bonds or to put their money in banks, get, it will be remembered, a dividend; that is, a direct share of the profits which their investment has made possible. We shall see later that expectations of profit, and the rate of interest paid on loans, and the way the national income is divided between spending and saving, and the way the national production is divided between capital and consumer goods, all hang together in a rather complicated way—a way which, frankly, even the best economists do not yet altogether understand.

The Savings of Businesses. Of course a good deal of saving is done by firms themselves. A firm which did not 'save' out of its yearly revenue at least enough to pay for repairs and replacements, and to allow for the fact that its machinery may be out of date before it wears out, would very soon be in trouble. One can put off actually spending on these things for a while, which is more than one can do with spending on wages and fuel, but the money must be there for the time when that spending is really needed. Most firms, however, do more than this; they put by part of their profits not merely for maintenance but also for expansion, so that when they want to build a new works, take a bigger office or employ more staff, they can do so without issuing more shares or going to a bank. This is called 'ploughing back profits'.

A Simple Example of Capital Creation. Indeed, one can see this process of capital creation going on, quite apart from banks and stocks and shares and business organization generally, wherever people turn from supplying to-day's wants to work on something which will yield bigger fruits next week or next year. Take, for example, a primitive village with no water supply except for what can be fetched daily in buckets from a stream half a mile away. Carrying water is a tedious and time-consuming job and a bucketful does not go far anyway. If a pipe or conduit of some kind were built, even of the very simplest sort made of hollowed logs laid end to end, the village would not only get much more water but the time and labour spent on water-carrying could be used for other purposes, say, in cultivating gardens better, and so the standard of living of the village could be raised.

Only, of course, making the conduit would itself mean much more work, while it was going on, than the daily bucket-carrying; which would in turn mean less time and energy for doing other daily jobs. *Some* extra work now means *much* work saved later; *some* goods not produced, and enjoyed, now, means many *more* goods produced, and enjoyed, later; there is an obvious gain, but however big it may be it will not be worth while if—to take the extreme case—the village actually starves to death because everyone is too busy laying pipes to do anything about the crops. The pipe-laying plan, with all its future advantages, can only go forward if and when the villagers' production of daily necessities shows a margin over daily needs; a margin big enough to allow for the drop in the production of 'consumer goods' caused by a proportion of the village workers leaving their normal work to construct the pipe-line. This margin, which the villagers could take out in better current living, but which they have chosen to use for still better living in the future, is, in effect, their savings. The man who, with an income of £500 and the option, therefore, of living at the rate of £500 a year, chooses instead to spend only £450 and to save the rest, is making exactly the same decision as those villagers.

The Power to Save. When one looks at the matter this way it becomes pretty clear why different communities in different parts of the world do such very different amounts of investment in capital equipment. For investment, there must be saving; for saving, there must be a margin between income and needs. Of course, 'needs' is a very vague term. One finds some people, with very modest ideas of what is a 'need', steadily saving away on an income on which other people simply cannot manage to make ends meet. But for all that, some needs must be met to keep people alive at all, however unambitious their tastes may be; and a very large part of the world's population (as, for instance, in China and India) produces no more than just barely enough to meet those needs, and so cannot save—or, consequently invest—at all. (It might be a good thing, at this point, to glance back at Chapter IV.)

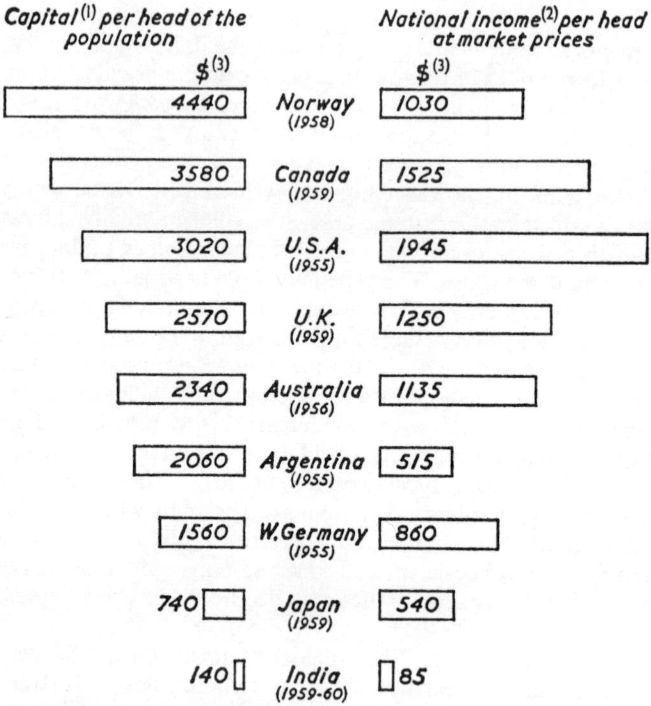

Capital [1] *per head of the population*		*National income* [2] *per head at market prices*
$[3]		$[3]
4440	Norway (1958)	1030
3580	Canada (1959)	1525
3020	U.S.A. (1955)	1945
2570	U.K. (1959)	1250
2340	Australia (1956)	1135
2060	Argentina (1955)	515
1560	W. Germany (1955)	860
740	Japan (1959)	540
140	India (1959-60)	85

FIG. 19—CAPITAL AND NATIONAL INCOME PER HEAD

NOTES

(1) Capital here excludes land, residences and consumer durables.

(2) National income equals consumption plus net investment (i.e. investment after deduction of depreciation on past investment).

(3) The figures, derived from Colin Clark, *Growthmanship* (Institute of Economic Affairs), are in U.S. dollars at 1950 purchasing power.

Very often this inability to save is found in regions where, if only saving were possible, all kinds of resources could be developed; in these circumstances the situation may be transformed by loans from abroad, loans made out of the savings of other people who do have a margin. During the last hundred years such *international lending* has taken place on a very large scale. Up to World War I Great Britain lent abroad more freely than any other nation (the long industrial start referred to in Chapter V made this possible), and the yield on the capital lent came back to her in the form of a flow of imports. These were part of the extra products which the equipment bought with that capital had enabled the borrowing countries countries to produce. (The opening up of the Canadian prairies and the Argentine pampas by British-financed railways, and the ensuing flow of wheat and meat to Britain, are cases in point.) Today the United States is the biggest foreign lender; and the whole process of international lending has changed in a way to be discussed later.

Relation Between Capital and Income. Expectations that a large supply of capital equipment per head goes with a large income per head will find some support from Fig. 19, but clearly no simple arithmetic ratio between capital and income is revealed by the figures. This is not surprising: a country with rich natural resources and a hard-working ingenious population would seem likely to produce more using a given quantity of capital than a country where resources are few and the population idle. Again, if two countries with the same standard of living have populations of the same size but spread thinly in one case and closely concentrated in the other, the former will almost certainly have to have more capital invested in such things as transport and communications facilities. Capital-intensive industry, i.e. industry requiring a high proportion of capital to labour employed, is of greater importance in some countries than in others. Also, a larger proportion of consumption in richer communities is likely to be enjoyed in the form of spending on services which, unlike consumer goods, do not demand the use of considerable capital resources. The

K

reader should be cautious in basing conclusions on the statistics in Fig. 19, for all are not equally reliable and statistics of capital invested are particularly hard to come by. We can, however, conclude that capital per head is no more than a rough guide to relative income and therefore that rises in the standard of living cannot be expected to keep exactly in step with increases in capital invested.

Land and Natural Resources. It is not easy to draw a perfectly clear dividing line between the factor of production 'capital' and the factor of production 'land'. What about a field which has been hedged, drained, and fertilized? Hedging and draining are every bit as much capital investment as the conduit pipe in our imaginary village; but one can hardly distinguish, in a settled country, between the original land and the improvements which have been made in it. Still, broadly speaking, the division exists and has some practical importance.

Natural Resources are Fixed Geographically. In the first place, natural resources are fixed by Nature—by geology, climate, and so forth—in one place or another, and are unequally distributed over the earth. Human labour and capital equipment can be moved from places where they are abundant to places where they are scarce. But one cannot shift a coal-mine, or a climate, or a fertile plain. It is only the *products* of natural resources, not the resources themselves, which can be moved. This unequal distribution of different kinds of natural wealth provides a motive for trade between regions and between nations; it also, of course, helps to explain why some countries have a greater productive capacity than others.

Natural Resources are Fixed in Total. In the second place, the total natural resources of the world cannot be increased. Humanity must make do with what it has got. So many square miles of cultivable land; so much coal and oil and iron hidden below the earth's surface; so much potential water-power; so much standing timber; these resources may be more intensively used than they are now, resources as yet unworked or undiscovered may be laid bare, but the 'estate of man' is, essentially, 'given'.

Natural Resources are 'Given'. In the third place, natural resources are 'given' in another sense; man did not make them—he found them. In a settled country this distinction hardly matters; whatever each new generation finds ready to work on or with is equally 'given' whether it was originally a natural resource, like the river Thames, or capital equipment, like the docks of the Port of London; and it is equally not 'free' since it belongs to someone, whether private person or public authority, and its use must be paid for one way or another. In a new country, however, there is a real distinction; a settler on the American or Canadian prairies in the last century found a naked land where nothing existed but what Nature had provided, and that land often cost him nothing at all. These three considerations make it desirable to treat land and natural resources generally, as a separate factor. Their importance will show up more clearly when we come to discuss *rent* in Chapter XII.

Labour. Labour includes all kinds of human effort, whether physical or mental, skilled or unskilled. The amount of human effort available depends, in the first place, on how many people there are to exert it—that is, on the size of the population; with given total numbers there will be a considerable difference according to how many, out of that total, are of working age and how many are too young or too old. If a country contains a large proportion of children under fifteen or of people over sixty or so, then it will have a smaller effective labour force than one in which the non-working age groups are proportionately less.

Size of Population. The total size of a country's population depends on the past balance of birth-rates and death-rates and of emigration and immigration. The population of Great Britain in 1700 stood at between 5 and 6 millions; now it is over 52 millions. What changes in the four factors mentioned above have caused this increase? Neither immigration nor emigration have counted for much; on balance, there has indeed been more movement of emigrants *from* Britain than of immigrants *into* Britain. Over a large part of the period—the eighty or ninety years before World War II—the birth-rate fell uninterruptedly. What has happened to cause the increase has been a tremendous fall in the death-rate, particularly the death-rate among young children. Although large families were customary until, roughly, the present century, in the old days most of their members died before growing up. With the eighteenth and nineteenth centuries the picture changed; more and more children survived and grew up to have families of their own. In our own time, many fewer children are born to each family, but the death-rate is a fraction of what it was even a hundred years ago; and not only do more people grow up, more people grow old.

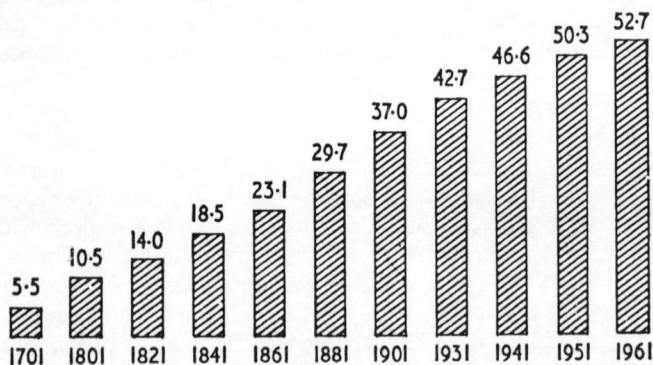

FIG. 20—GROWTH OF POPULATION OF GREAT BRITAIN
SINCE 1701

There are three main reasons for this decline in the death-rate; the advance in medical science which, over the last two centuries, has mastered the worst traditional killing diseases—typhus, smallpox, plague—and gone far towards mastering others, such as tuberculosis; the improvement in standards of cleanliness, hygiene and sanitation; and better food, the result both of higher living standards and greater knowledge. (When one reads accounts of the way babies were fed in the seventeenth century one wonders how any of them survived at all.)

Age Distribution. Age distribution, which, as we saw on page 131, is important to the productive efficiency of the population, also depends on this past balance of birth-rates, death-rates, emigration and immigration. One obvious result of a falling death-rate (unless birth-rates are actually rising too) is an increase in the proportionate number of old people. The effects of the falling death-rate in Great Britain, coupled with the falling birth-rate (until the 1940s), are shown in the diagrams (Fig. 21) on the opposite page, which are taken from the Report of the Royal Commission on Population (1949).

The state of affairs shown in these diagrams has its awkward side from the economic point of view, particularly as the trends which they illustrate seem likely to continue. A growing proportion of old people means a growing proportion of people past work; people who, whether by drawing on their own savings or by virtue of retirement pensions and other forms of public provision for the old, absorb an increasingly large part of the national product to which they are no longer contributing anything. The more non-producers, the less product to go round.

The problem is not new; many primitive tribes have solved it, particularly in times of famine, by simply knocking their grandfathers and grandmothers on the head and, sometimes, eating them. This solution, however, would hardly do for us.

Health and Working Capacity. Apart from total size and age distribution, there are other reasons affecting the ability of a population to produce. One very obvious reason is *health*— how many working days are lost in a year through illness? How widespread are the ailments which drag a worker down and make him listless and feeble? Even in Britain loss of working time through sickness rises into millions of man-days a year; in tropical countries where malaria and parasitical diseases really never relax their grip, only a fraction of the human effort which a healthy population could put forth is available.

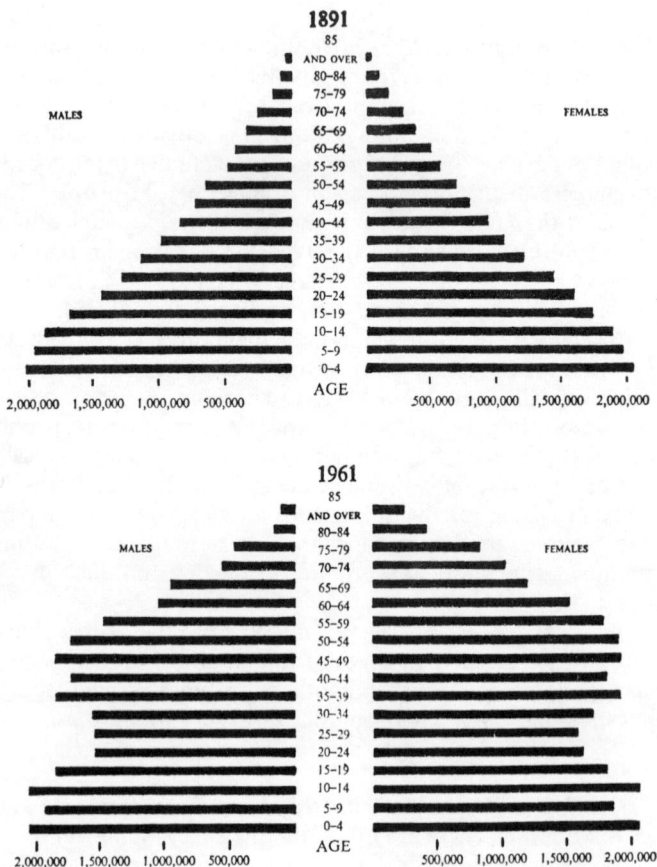

FIG. 21—AGE PYRAMIDS FOR GREAT BRITAIN, 1891 AND 1961. (*Reproduced by permission of H.M.S.O.*)

Education and Training. But perhaps most important of all, in determining economic effectiveness, is the standard of education, technical skill, and training among the people; economic progress demands first-rate administrators, scientists and technicians—and, it should be added, intelligent and level-headed citizens.

Proportion between the Factors of Production. We have now looked at all these factors of production separately; it is time to look at them together. It is true enough to say that a bigger population generally disposes of more labour power than a smaller population, but that does not necessarily mean that it will produce more *per head*, which is what matters from the point of view of the standard of living. Product per head depends not on the single factor of production, labour, but on the combination of all three factors. A population disposing of plenty of labour power but desperately short of land and capital will find that that labour power yields it very little return. Overpopulation—that is, too many people in relation to natural resources and capital—means poverty. And it should be remembered that while total capital can be increased, total natural resources cannot.

Malthus's Theory of Population. In the early nineteenth century, when the population of Great Britain was increasing very fast indeed, an eminent economist named T. R. Malthus wrote an exceedingly depressing book called *An Essay on the Principle of Population as it affects the Future Improvement of Society.* He argued that whenever the standard of living was raised by better farming methods providing a better food supply, people would marry earlier, have bigger families, succeed in rearing more of their children to maturity, and within a generation produce so many extra mouths to consume that extra produce that the standard would go right back to where it had started from. Of course, the extra hands belonging to the extra mouths would produce something extra to eat, and one could expect technique to improve, too, as time went on; but the land they had to work on was limited, and so it would, he thought, be wildly optimistic to expect production to keep abreast of the kind of population increase which he saw going on in Britain—an increase which temporarily higher standards would always automatically bring about.

Malthus was perfectly right in arguing that natural resources set a limit to the growth of population, but so far as Great Britain was concerned his dismal prophecies did not come true. For one thing, it turned out that a higher standard did not invariably induce people to marry earlier and have larger families; on balance, it worked just the other way—given a reasonable prospect of living better, people took a longer view and became more cautious about the size of their families. For another thing, all sorts of possibilities opened up, in the years after Malthus wrote, of which he had no idea; to him, or to any of his contemporaries, it would have seemed absurd to suppose that Great Britain might feed a doubled and trebled population by exchanging an enormously increased volume of manufactured goods for vast quantities of food from the New World and Australia.

Population Pressure To-day. Many scientists and economists of the present day are wondering whether Malthus was not, after all, a true prophet who merely got some of his dates and facts wrong. For the total population of the world is growing at the rate of some 20 millions a year—in the last sixty years it has grown from about 1,600 millions to about 2,800 millions—and there are no more New Worlds to be opened up to feed them. There are other ways of increasing food supplies—irrigation, improved crop and animal strains, better cultivation and herd management, the conquest of plant and animal diseases—but these take more time to produce their effects, and, meanwhile, every three weeks over a million extra mouths appear to claim their share. Will the growth slow down in time for a really serious food shortage to be avoided? No one knows.

The Optimum Population. How does this argument about the *dangers* of population increase link up with what was said in Chapter IV about the *advantages* of a big population, providing a large market and full scope for specialization?

The answer is that these two forces—the decrease in natural resources per head as the number of mouths grows, and the increase in possibilities of specialization as the number of hands grows—work in opposite directions. If the greater specialization makes it possible to get a greater product even out of lesser resources per head, then population increase is an advantage; if the shortage of resources per head is so acute that its effects outweigh the advantages of greater specialization, then population increase is a disadvantage.

At the point where—with given technical knowledge—these two forces just balance, the population reaches what economists call the *optimum* or best—the size, that is, at which production per head is as high as it can be. Naturally, changes in technical knowledge are tremendously important influences. If steam transport, for instance, had not been discovered, Britain's optimum population would be a fraction of what it now is.

Mobility of Labour. When some countries or regions have less than their optimum population and others have more, both kinds benefit by *migration*, the movement of workers from where natural resources and capital are short to where they are plentiful. Nineteenth-century Europe, where population on the whole tended to run past the optimum, benefited enormously by the fact that the surplus could find new opportunities in the New World, particularly the United States; and the New World also benefited equally by the fact that these new migrants raised the population to a level where fuller advantage could be taken of the natural resources available.

On a smaller scale, each region benefits when, within a country, people move from where labour is over-plentiful compared with natural resources and capital to where it is scarce. The demand for labour in different places is constantly varying. Old industries decline—remember the worked-out coalfields mentioned in Chapter V—and new ones expand. The more smoothly and readily people change their jobs to match these changes in demand—the greater, that is, the *mobility of labour*—the better for the standard of living.

Unfortunately from the economic point of view, most workers like to stay put. People dislike forsaking jobs which they have learned and grown used to over, perhaps, most of a lifetime, and they dislike still more leaving their familiar neighbourhood and friends to move to some other district or to a foreign country. There are always the rolling stones who enjoy change for its own sake, but they are a minority.

Obstacles to Mobility. Moreover, even when workers are quite *willing* to move, they may not be *able*. Since the war, the housing shortage in particular has checked the mobility of labour. This is one reason (others are mentioned on page 47) for the policy of bringing the work to the people instead of trying to get them to move to the work. Another reason for immobility is lack of knowledge about the existing opportunities for better-paid or more agreeable work. Labour Exchanges and Youth Employment Bureaux help to fill this lack, but cannot do so entirely.

Combining the Factors in Business. This same question of the best proportion of labour to capital and natural resources appears, on a smaller scale, in every business undertaking—with the difference that the business man can decide for himself how much of each factor of production he will use, whereas no one can decide what the total population of a country shall be.

Some of each factor will always be needed, but there is usually, for each type of enterprise, a certain range over which it is possible to vary the amount of labour, or equipment, or land employed. A farmer with a certain number of acres to cultivate may weigh the advantages of taking on an extra man (or men) or buying another tractor, and an industrialist may choose between taking on additional hands or installing a more automatic kind of machinery.

An elementary example will show the sort of calculation involved. A farmer, let us say, wants to increase his output of wheat. His land is a fixed quantity; so, let us assume, for the present, is his capital equipment. How many workers should he employ in order to get the biggest yield? (This 'biggest yield' may be calculated as yield per man or as yield per acre, and the practical decision depends a good deal on which is regarded as the more important; but that question can wait.) Taking into account the state of technique at the time—remember the workers with sickles and the combine-harvester in Chapter IV —one can draw up a table showing how output will vary with changes in the numbers of workers, thus:

TABLE III—RELATIONSHIP OF OUTPUT TO LABOUR FORCE
(*Figures are hypothetical*)

Number of Workers	Total Return in Bushels	Average Return per Man	Return Added by Last Man
1	500	500	500
2	2,000	1,000	1,500
3	6,000	2,000	4,000
4	9,600	2,400	3,600
5	12,000	2,400	2,400
6	13,800	2,300	1,800
7	15,000	2,143	1,200
8	16,000	2,000	1,000
9	16,700	1,855	700

The Law of Diminishing Returns. This table shows several significant things. So long as the farm is seriously under-manned, each extra worker not only raises the total yield and the average yield, but what is technically known as the *marginal return*, the extra amount gained by employing one more pair of hands. Up to that point, obviously, the more the merrier on any calculation. In this table it comes where three men are employed. After that point, though the *average* return continues to rise, the marginal return starts to drop off.[1] In this table, the

[1] A simple way of keeping marginal and average returns straight in one's mind is to think of cricket scores. A batsman scores in successive matches 26, 36, 42, and 100 runs: average 204÷4, or 51. In the fifth match he does less well than in the fourth, scoring 66 runs instead of a century. But his average is nevertheless improved; instead of 51 it is now 270÷5 or 54.

point of maximum average return comes when four or five
men are employed. With more than five, the fall in the marginal return gets steeper and the average begins to drop;
though, of course, the *total* yield goes on rising and would
continue to rise until so many men were milling about in the
fields that each extra man hindered more than he helped.

TABLE IV—RELATIONSHIP OF OUTPUT OF MAIZE
TO QUANTITY OF FERTILIZER USED

Nitrogen in lb.	Total Yield in Bushels per Acre	Additional Maize for every 10 lb. of Fertilizer
0	12·4	—
10	26·5	14·1
20	31·0	4·5
30	34·0	3·0
40	36·1	2·1
50	37·7	1·6
60	39·0	1·2
70	40·0	1·0
80	40·7	0·7
90	41·2	0·6
100	41·6	0·4

SOURCE: Woodworth, R. C. and Brooks, O. L., *Economics of Fertilizer Use on North Georgia Farms*, unpublished MS., Dept. of Agricultural Economics, University of Georgia, Athens, Ga., quoted in *Economic Analysis of Fertilizer Use*. Data, edited by Baum, F. L., Heady Earl, O., and Blackmore, John, The Iowa State College Press.

The fact which these tables illustrate—the fact that, when the
quantity of a single factor of production is increased while the
others remain unchanged, its yield will after a certain point
begin to fall off—is called the *Law of Diminishing Returns*. It
may sound rather theoretical and unreal, but it is only a sum-
marized way of putting the very practical matters discussed in
the last few pages. Instead of a single farm, think of all the
cultivated land available; instead of a dozen or so possible
workers, think of the world's population; and it becomes fairly
clear why Malthus worried about the future.

Of course, one must remember that any particular table

shows the possibilities as they exist in a given state of technique and organization. Alter these, and the possibilities alter too. Suppose some of the labour involved to be turned to technical improvements—to equipping farms with tractors and grain dryers, to developing and producing weedkillers and insecticides, to improving strains of plants or beasts; suppose that better transport and commercial arrangements make it possible for farmers to specialize more according to soil and climate; then all the figures will change for the better. In practical terms, that means that a given amount of land will yield a living, directly or indirectly, to many more people. Our old friend specialization, the division of labour, works to counter the effect of diminishing returns. It works more obviously and strongly in industry than in agriculture, so much so that people have been known to associate increasing returns entirely with the former and diminishing returns entirely with the latter; but this is just confused thinking. There is no essential difference.

For *any* sort of enterprise, the returns to *any* factor of production will vary as its quantity is increased in proportion to the others; starting from the least quantity which will let the enterprise function at all, the returns will rise at first, then level off, and then fall away. An essential part of the business man's job is to know where to expect these turning points, and to decide his production policy accordingly. (This decision is closely bound up with the question of *scale*, discussed in Chapter VII; in some industries technical factors make it impossible to get the best proportions unless the scale is large.)

Combination Depends on Cost: Economizing in Labour. Naturally, the way these decisions go will depend very largely on the comparative *costs* of the different factors. When labour is cheap, it pays the employer better to employ more men than to buy expensive machinery. There can be no doubt that the prevalence, for thousands of years, of slavery or of some form of serfdom prevented employers of labour from exploring the possibilities of gain through the use of labour-saving capital equipment. One does not bother to 'save' what is dirt cheap anyway.

When, on the other hand, labour is scarce in relation to other factors, only those jobs offering good wages will attract it, and so employers have to do their level best to see that whatever labour they do get has plenty of equipment, to make its yield high and make those wages profitable. In the 'new countries', like the United States, Canada, Australia and New Zealand, labour tended from the beginning to be scarce in comparison with natural resources; so wages in these countries ran correspondingly higher than elsewhere. Hence it is not surprising that so many labour-saving inventions and technical improvements, such as the combined reaper and binder, the mechanical coal-cutter, the sewing machine and the typewriter, should have been developed in the United States. (Why the United States rather than, say, New Zealand? Because of the big United States market—see Chapter IV.) Trade-union pressure, by raising wages beyond what many businesses could carry with their existing methods of production, has had much the same effect; one economizes in what is expensive.

Economizing Land. Similar arguments apply to land. It, too, is used lavishly or sparingly according to how scarce, or how expensive, it may be. Land at the centre of a big town is scarce and expensive, so many-storied buildings representing a great deal of capital and housing a great deal of labour are the rule, and only those enterprises are carried on which need very little actual physical space in proportion to labour and equipment—such as trading and financial and professional activities. In smaller towns and suburbs it is less expensive, and it is possible to carry on enterprises whose technique calls for a bigger proportion of land, such as manufacture in general. In the open country, where it is plentiful and cheap, it is within the reach of those enterprises which have to use it on a large scale—that is, particularly, farming.

And the more plentiful and cheap it is, the more extensive can be the type of farming. It would be wasteful to run sheep on land for which market gardeners are willing to pay a good price because it is handy to their market, just as it would be wasteful to have market gardens on the shopping sites around

Piccadilly Circus. The price paid for different kinds of land, whether by sale or by lease, sorts it out between extensive and intensive uses, just as the price of labour sorts out labour between different occupations.

CHAPTER X

COSTS

WE saw in Chapter VIII how prices sort out scarce goods among different buyers and how price movements, reflecting changes in supply or in demand, or both, normally ensure that these are kept in balance or, as economists say, in *equilibrium*. We saw that when prices fail to reflect these changes there is failure to reach equilibrium; with prices too high, goods flow into the market faster than consumers will take them off, and unsold stocks pile up, while with prices too low there are queues and waiting lists, and would-be buyers are constantly told: 'It's on order, but——'. Price, then, is determined by supply and demand; but how are supply and demand themselves determined?

Costs and Price Determine Supply. We have seen that what lies behind *demand* is the choice which consumers make between this and that way of spending their money—a choice which depends partly on the amount of the goods in question which they are already enjoying, partly on their incomes, and partly on their characters and tastes, a matter of psychology whose study lies outside the field of economics. But what lies behind *supply*? Why do sellers offer so much, and no more, of each of the types of goods on the market?

One very simple and obvious answer is that they bring just as much as, and no more than, they expect to be able to sell profitably at the ruling price; this is true enough. But this answer gets us nowhere at all; it merely brings us smartly back to where we started from. We must look further. *What settles the amount which sellers think they will be able to sell profitably at the ruling price?*

144

This is the point at which we find ourselves studying *costs*, the prices which producers pay for the factors of production which they use. For it is the *cost* to each producer of the goods which he is offering which determines whether, at the ruling price, he will make a big profit, or just enough profit to stay in business, or a loss. In the tomato market example, the cost of hothouse production was too high for hothouse tomatoes to be produced when the market price fell below 2s. 0d. a lb., the cost of long-distance importation was too high for Canary tomatoes to be produced when the market price fell below 1s. 6d. a lb., and so on.

One can say, to put it in a nutshell, that with a given demand curve—that is, a given set of sales possibilities at different prices—it is the amount on the market to-day which settles the price, but *it is the price which settles what will be brought to market to-morrow*, or next week, or whenever producers have managed to adjust their plans, because it is the price which settles whether producers will have got a big, small, or negative net return over their costs.

How Costs and Price Interact. Now we can go one step further. *It is the price which settles what costs shall be incurred.* For at a high price it is worth paying out a lot in costs, and at a low price it is not worth paying out so much, and at a still lower price it is not worth incurring any at all. Since some producers can generally produce more cheaply than others (we have seen, for instance, what a big spread in costs there is in the coal industry) not all will react to price changes in the same way; one enterprise will thrive where another merely struggles along, failing to pay dividends and drawing on reserves, or actually goes out of business. But taking all firms together, the amount of costs which they can profitably shoulder, and therefore *will* shoulder, depends on the price they get for their product.

This sounds a little odd. One generally sees the matter the other way round, with price depending on cost. 'This gadget cannot be sold for less than 10s., because it costs 10s. to produce it.' Of course, it is quite true that no firm will go on

L

indefinitely producing gadgets at a cost of 10s. each to sell at 7s. 6d. each; but if they have been so mistaken as to spend 10s. a gadget, while the public is only willing to buy that number at 7s. 6d. each, they have no option but to accept 7s. 6d. and so recover at least some of what they have spent—since they cannot unspend it. In the long run, people who make that sort of mistake too often go out of business, and no one makes more mistakes than he can help; and so, in the long run, costs do decide how big a supply will come on to the market and thus where the price will settle. Rising costs squeeze out the weaker producers, reduce supply, and so raise prices; falling costs make production profitable for more producers, increase supply, and so lower prices. In equilibrium, the weakest producer in business can just hang on, no extra producer is tempted to come in, and supply is stable.

Taking the long run and the short run together, we see that costs and prices, supply and demand, all hang together and influence one another; one can no more say that 'cost settles prices' or that 'demand settles prices' that one can say that the upper or lower blade of a pair of scissors does the cutting. One or another blade may be more obviously moving—as when a change in taste pushes up the demand for a product or a special natural shortage pushes up its cost—but neither could cut without the other.

Connection Between Costs and Prices of Different Goods. Even this rather complicated way of putting it gives far too simple a picture. For different commodities are not produced, or consumed, quite independently of one another. Some cannot be produced without automatically producing others at the same time—like coke and gas, or mutton and wool, or wheat and straw. Others cannot be consumed without automatically leading to the consumption of others—like motor cars and petrol, or pens and ink, or bricks and mortar. Some are close competitors on the market, like natural and synthetic rubber others are closely competitive users of the same factors of production, like wheat, barley and oats (all competitive users of approximately the same sort of land) or motor-cars and ship (both competitive users of steel). So any change in supply, or in demand, for a single commodity is likely indirectly to affect the supply, or the demand, for many others. Every economic event —a new invention, the discovery of a new material, the spread of a plant disease, a shift in fashion, a rumour of war or a slackening of international tension—sets repercussions going which have not died away before a new series has begun.

This, however, is merely a warning that an elementary explanation of how economic affairs work cannot tell the whole story or make the reader able to predict just how any particular economic event is going to turn out. Even the best economists find economic prediction a very tricky and uncertain business. But if one has got the elements in mind one can at least avoid the worst kinds of misunderstanding.

Costs Settled Indirectly by Consumers' Demand. Now to look at the various kinds of costs—for obviously costs are very differently made up in different industries and different enterprises. They all have this much in common; they are the prices business men pay for the factors of production which they use, the prices of different kinds of natural resources, human labour, and capital equipment or stocks. In a firm's accounts they appear as the amounts spent on raw materials, fuel, lubricants, lighting, on wages and salaries, on interest on the capital invested in plant or buildings, on making good depreciation, possibly on rent and rates.

All these factors of production have been acquired from previous owners, owners who have set a price on them; we are back in the market again, the market for land, for building materials, for this or that kind of equipment, for this or that kind of raw material, for this or that kind of labour, with supply and demand in every case settling the price. Obviously, one could go on, back and back and back, without ever finding a price which was given once for all as the data of physical science are given. One can say, 'The temperature of boiling water at sea-level is 100° Centigrade', and know that that will always be true; one cannot say, 'The cost of this grade of coal is £5 a ton', and know that *that* will always be true.

Still, one can say of this matter of costs, as the poet Pope said of mankind: 'A mighty maze, but not without a plan.' Every time an enterprise appears in the market as a competitive buyer of some factor of production, it is doing so in order, directly or indirectly, to satisfy a consumer demand. The more pressing the demand, the higher the price, and the higher, therefore, the price which it is worth offering for the factor of production in order to secure it; in the last resort, it is the business man's judgment of how consumers feel about his product which settles whether he will go on buying the factors of production up to a high price or drop out at a lower one.

Indirectly, through the actions of business men, *it is consumer demand which pulls the factors of production from one use into another.* When the pull in one direction is weak, and the price offered correspondingly low, the factors of production will turn to where the price is higher because the pull is stronger. Making due allowance for the immobilities mentioned in Chapter IX, workers will go to those enterprises where wages for their trade are highest, and encourage their sons to enter those trades which command the highest wage. Land will be leased or sold to those enterprises which, because their profit prospects are brightest, can afford to pay the highest rent or purchase price. Capital will be lent to those enterprises which again because their profit prospects are brightest, are willing to offer the highest interest. Demand for the factors of production, then, *is consumer demand at one or more removes.*

The Supply of the Factors of Production. And what about supply? On the most general lines, the answer is to be found in the last chapter; natural scarcity and historical development between them have decided, in every community, what land of various types shall be available, what population shall provide a labour force and what shall be its skill, what savings have been made and how they have been embodied. Within these general classes, particular kinds of labour, or of capital, or of mature and exploitable natural resources, are relatively plentiful or scarce according to how the pull of consumer demand has been exerted on them in the past. (The increase in demand for television sets and television programmes and the decrease in demand for cinema seats has resulted in a shift of factors of production from the services of the cinema to the services of television. Readers should try to think of other examples of this kind.)

Distribution of Costs in Different Industries. For any particular enterprise, these wide considerations are far outside the picture. To the board of management deciding whether or not to rent more factory space, raise more capital, and take on more labour, the price they must pay—that is, the costs —are 'given', i.e. beyond their control. Different kinds of cost are more important to different kinds of enterprise.

TABLE V—DISTRIBUTION OF COSTS IN CERTAIN INDUSTRIES
(*Based on Board of Trade Census of Production Reports for* 1958)

	COAL MINING £ *million*	COKE OVENS AND BY-PRODUCTS £ *million*	POTTERY £ *million*	IRON AND STEEL £ *million*
Materials and Fuel	195·5	164·6	41·0	123·3
Wages and Salaries	528·5	15·1	42·2	34·2

Notice how much more significant a change in wages must be to the coal industry than to the coke-oven or iron and steel industries; we saw in Chapter V how the close connection between miners' wages and coal prices has led in the past to wage disputes. On the other hand, changes in the cost of raw material or of fuel are sharply reflected in the price of coke or of steel sheets. In wholesale trading enterprises, neither wages nor raw materials are nearly so important as the rate of interest on capital; for the business of a wholesale trade is to carry stocks, and hold them until sold, and the wholesaler's main cost is the sums he must pay for the use of the money capital which is tied up during this waiting period.

Prime Costs and Overhead Costs: Heavy Industry. It is not only in their sensitiveness to changes in particular kinds of cost that enterprises differ. They also differ, with very great practical results, in the extent to which they are free to alter the amount of costs which they incur. This is because certain items of cost are apt to be relatively constant whatever the level of output, while others can be expanded or reduced simply by producing more or less. Here, let us say, is a steelworks. It has an enormous capital investment in blast furnaces, rolling mills, and heavy accessory equipment. None of these things are any use for any other purpose—unless perhaps as scrap iron. Once they are erected, the capital invested in them is sunk for good. No alternative pull on it can have any effect; it is completely specific to steel production. The firm also has a labour force, some of it highly skilled technically, with valuable particular knowledge of the firm's particular products; some of it highly skilled administratively, forming an indispensable managerial team; some of it comparatively unskilled and unspecialized, labourers and routine office workers. It uses fuel and raw materials at the rate of so many tons a day; it pays transport charges inwards or outwards; it pays advertisers, accountants, legal and technical advisers. All these are costs.

Now suppose that steel prices fall to a level at which these costs are no longer covered. What can the firm do about it? —assuming that there is no slack to be taken up in the way of inefficient practices open to improvement. Curtail production? Certainly that will reduce the total cost of raw material, fuel, transport, the wages of unskilled labour, what are generally called *prime costs*; but it will do absolutely nothing to reduce the burden of interest on fixed capital—and it is no use trying to sell that fixed capital for use in another, more profitable line, because it is hopelessly specific to steelmaking.

Nor will it do much to reduce the cost of wages and salaries paid to key workers and managerial staff; if one lets a good man go in slack times one may not get him back, or find anyone equally good, when one needs him again. Since all these *fixed costs* or, to use the usual term, *overhead costs*, go on just the same whether production is large or small, each item in a

smaller output has to be debited with a larger share of them—
so each is actually more expensive to produce. The loss involved in cutting down production is, in such enterprises, often
actually heavier than the loss involved in producing, full steam
ahead, to sell at less than cost price.

Prime Costs and Overhead Costs: Light Industry. For
contrast, look at a small building firm. Its fixed capital consists
of a yard, a small office, some sheds, half a dozen ladders and
some scaffolding, a certain number of trowels, plumb-lines,
spades, shovels and other simple tools. Practically all these
things could serve in other uses. There is, again, a nucleus
of skilled workers forming a working team which might be
hard to bring together again if it were dispersed, and a larger
fringe of extras, skilled and unskilled, who would be easier to
dispense with. There are stocks of rapidly turned-over raw
materials, replaced or added to as needed; there are, again,
transport charges, light and heat for office premises or workshops, some advertising, the telephone, and so forth.

Suppose this firm is confronted with the same situation as the
steel works—a fall in the price of houses such that total costs
are no longer covered. It can adapt itself far more smoothly.
Interest on fixed capital is a negligible part of its budget; it is
unlikely to have any long-term, unbreakable contracts with
suppliers; its biggest cost items are materials and labour, and
both (apart from the small nucleus of valued old hands) can be
reduced in exact proportion to output. At the worst, the team
can be disbanded, the workshops closed down, and the firm
can go into a sort of hibernation till things look up, leasing its
premises to someone who can use them profitably for some
other purpose, and paying its minute fixed charges out of the
proceeds.

Growing Importance of Overhead Costs. According, then,
to whether prime costs or overhead costs are more important to
a firm, its response to price changes will be more or less swift
and smooth. Now the more advanced a community is economically, the more capital equipment it uses, and the more special-

ized and therefore unadaptable that equipment becomes; and so the heavier is the proportionate burden of overhead costs, and the more difficult it is for those enterprises whose products are less valued by the consumer to shrink, and so to release resources to produce what is more valued.

With economic progress, there does come a certain lumpiness and rigidity. When economic activity is expanding so fast that *every* industry has to expand, this hardly matters; those producing the most-demanded products expand faster than others producing what is less demanded, and that is all. But when the rate of expansion is less—when the population, for instance, stops growing or starts to shrink—it is practically certain that some industries will have to contract. The same is true when new technical methods are successfully introduced; think, for instance, of the present railway system which, owing to new methods of transport, is involved in scrapping miles of track, stations and equipment. Then these lumpinesses and rigidities become really serious. We shall meet with this question again, in all its practical awkwardness, when (in Chapter XXII) we come to consider full employment and the obstacles to achieving it.

CHAPTER XI

THE NATIONAL INCOME

THE proof of the pudding is in the eating; the proof of the way in which a nation's economic affairs are arranged is in the livelihood which its citizens enjoy—the standard of living. There is no absolutely satisfactory way of measuring this standard; for one thing tastes differ, and change in course of time; for another a good many things which are obviously important to the standard of living (such as good home cooking) do not enter into the ordinary economic field at all, since they are not paid for; and for another the only common measure for all the different goods and services making up the standard is their money value, and that measure, as we shall see later, is itself highly variable.

Nevertheless, if one leaves changing tastes out of account, and reckons that the 'non-economic' ingredients of the standard remain much the same, and makes allowances for changes in the value of money itself (see Chapter XVII) the way *national money income* is changing gives at least a rough guide to the way national standards of living are changing. Moreover, knowledge of the total national money income and of the way it is divided up between different income-groups and different income types (e.g. wages, salaries, profits) is very valuable to the Chancellor of the Exchequer when he comes to draw up his annual budget (see Chapter XXI) and to the Government generally when it is making decisions on economic policy. So in recent years it has become the practice of the British Government and of many others, to issue an annual statement of the amount of the national income.

Calculating the National Income. To do this is by no means a simple business. Ignoring for the moment people like old-age pensioners, invalids and the dependent members of families, we can say that all the individuals in the nation draw money incomes in return for their contribution to the production of money's worth. They may contribute labour, or business judgment, or the services of capital or land of which they are owners. The whole yield of the factors of production (see Chapter IX) and the whole return to the people directly or indirectly providing them, should come to the same figure; they are two sides of the same thing. So one should be able to calculate the national income either by simply totting up all the incomes received by economically independent individuals or by totting up all the separate values, at current prices, of the net production of goods and services, and get the same result.

In practice, the people making these calculations run up against two kinds of difficulty. One is simply the difficulty of collecting figures. A great many incomes are given, straight away, in income-tax returns; but even apart from the margin of error to be allowed for returns made with an eye to tax-dodging (and in some countries this error is stupendous), this source of information dries up below income-tax level. For a great mass of small incomes, one has to rely on known wage-rates and correct the results, rather shakily, for short time and overtime. The other difficulty is more fundamental: it is the logical difficulty of avoiding double counting. Not only State pensions but also National Debt interest payments have to be deducted from the national income total; because people receiving them are really living on other people's incomes, just as dependent children are.

On the other hand, some incomes which do correspond to a contribution to production never get into the hands of individuals at all—like the net incomes of public enterprises such as the National Coal Board, or that part of the profits of companies which is paid as a direct tax to the Inland Revenue. These amounts have to be *added* to the individual incomes total to get a true picture. Then, looking at the matter from the national product side, the total which one gets by simply totting up values at current prices must be corrected to allow for the taxes on some things and the subsidies on others; obviously one would get a very wrong picture if the national product appeared to rise every time a penny was added to the tobacco tax or a penny taken off the subsidy on a pint of milk. So all indirect taxation has to be deducted and all subsidies added. That is comparatively easy—all the figures are there; and it is also fairly easy to allow, as one must, for net inflows and outflows from abroad. But deciding what ought to be deducted from *gross* output in order to get a figure net of depreciation is quite another matter. The true national product is quite different according to whether stocks are being kept up and machinery, buildings, roads, rolling-stock and the fertility of land maintained or whether stocks are being run down and equipment and farmland allowed to deteriorate. During the war the apparent national product was much bigger than the real national product for this reason.

Uses of the National Income Total. When the total has been calculated as accurately as is humanly possible, it can be used to help answer a number of important questions. How does it compare with last year's total?—with that of five years, or ten years, ago? With certain modifications for changes in the price level, these comparisons will show whether the nation is prospering or depressed. (Would we know this anyway, without statistics? In extreme cases, yes, certainly; but when some trades or places are prospering and others are not, only a comprehensive picture will tell the truth.) They thus give a standard by which to judge past policy and estimate the size of current problems.

Then, how does it compare with the incomes of other countries? Suppose a Government is sharing in an expensive international project. The size of the national incomes of the various countries taking part is the only reliable guide (though even so, a very rough one) to the proportion of the joint burden which each should carry.

Then, too, important conclusions about monetary and taxation policy can be drawn from any discrepancy between the 'national product' total and the 'national income' total. These are, indeed, perhaps the most important of all—but they cannot be properly discussed until we have studied the monetary and banking system and the Budget itself. It must be enough for the moment to say that the national income statistics are as essential to a government trying to keep employment high and stable as a clinical thermometer is to a doctor.

Distribution of the National Income: Types of Income. A number of other important facts about the nation's economic life come to light when the total is split up according to the *size of income* of different individuals and according to the *type of income* composing it. We have seen that goods and services are produced by the co-operation of the factors of production. Owners of these factors draw incomes in return for their use. How do the different factors fare as income-getters? We can give an answer in general terms, from general principles which earlier chapters should have made clear; the scarcer (in relation to demand) any factor is in comparison with the others, the more valuable each unit of that factor will be and the bigger the share of the total product which its owner will consequently draw. One cannot, however, deduce the actual distribution of the national income from general principles. It is better to look at the statistics and see what conclusions can be drawn from them.

Wages, salaries, and payment to the Armed Forces all really belong to the same type; they are payments to employees for work done. One may want to study them separately, for various reasons, just as one may want to study separately the wages of workers in different industries, but they are all earned by the same factor of production—labour. Farming incomes are different; they are certainly in part a return for work done by the farmer, but they also include a profit on the capital invested in his farm and (if he is an owner and not a tenant) the rent of his land. Professional earnings, those of the independent or 'self-employed' majority of doctors, lawyers, chartered accountants, and so forth, are also obviously a return to labour, but the fact that the self-employed professional generally has a 'practice', a body of regular clients, whose existence is a definite asset to him and which he may actually have purchased with a capital sum, brings in an element of profit. The profits of traders are another mixed class of income, made up of the return on the trader's capital and the return on his own labour in his business. Rents, dividends and interest, which need to be considered separately for some purposes, are all incomes from property—the returns from land and buildings, investment in shares, or money loans. (Transfer incomes may, from this point of view, be regarded either as coming originally from labour—like retirement pensions—or from money loans—like interest on Government securities. It is only when one is trying to see what the national income amounts to in real total spending terms that they have to be reckoned separately.)

Here, according to the Preliminary Estimates of National Income and Expenditure 1956 to 1962, is how personal incomes were distributed between different types in 1962:

TABLE VI—DISTRIBUTION OF NATIONAL INCOME BETWEEN
FACTORS OF PRODUCTION

	£ million
Wages and salaries	15,370
Pay in cash and kind of the Forces	395
Employers' contributions	
National insurance and health	559
Others	685
Professional persons	372
Farmers	528
Other sole traders and partnerships	1,287
Rents,[1] dividends and interest	2,573
National insurance benefits and other current	
grants from public authorities	1,983
Total of personal incomes	23,752

Distribution of the National Income: Sizes of Incomes. Very broadly speaking, the table shows that about two-thirds of the national income (prior to tax) is a return to labour of various kinds, and one-third is a return to property whether in land, capital equipment, or money. This distribution, it should

[1] 'Rent' is used in the everyday use of the word, not in the economic sense.

be noticed, is not necessarily the same thing as the distribution between rich and poor. Whether an individual income is large or small depends not on what type of income it belongs to, but on how valuable is the particular work, or the particular property, to which it is a return.

As different sorts of work are of very different value, and as property is very unevenly distributed, incomes from either can be very unequal. The labour of a fifteen-year-old school-leaver may be worth no more than £3 or £4 a week; that of an un-skilled railway worker £10 or so; that of a skilled face-worker in a coalmine £20 or £25, and that of a really high-powered popular entertainer, a Danny Kaye, £2,000. The return on no property at all (not counting clothes and furniture and so on) is obviously nothing, and the return on £20 or so in the Post Office only 10s. a year; and a great many people have no more property than that. The return on £1,000,000, even if it is in-vested in low-yielding Government securities, is over £30,000 a year—and some people, though naturally very few, are mil-lionaires several times over. When one remembers that high property incomes and high earned incomes often go together, both because a property-owner can work with his own capital and because high property incomes make it possible to train for the best-paid jobs, it becomes obvious that there is scope for very great inequality indeed. In 1962 the Report of the Commissioners of Inland Revenue showed the distribution of incomes *after* deduction of direct taxation given in Table VII.

What these figures represent in terms of the standard of life obviously depends very much on whether the income of say £150 a year is that of a disabled pensioner with no relatives to help out, or that of a boy living at home with a father earning £950, a brother earning £200, and a sister earning £175; and a 'middle income' of £600 may represent ease or poverty accord-ing to whether the person drawing it has no family or six or seven children below working age. One has to be careful in drawing deductions about social conditions from bare figures of income.

Before tax, of course, the inequality would be enormously greater. Taxation makes much more difference than it used to, for in the last thirty years (and particularly after World War II) it has been deliberately used to reduce inequality, to take from the rich for the benefit of the poor. The proceeds of the heavy taxes on large incomes are used to provide cash incomes for the poorest of all and benefits in kind (the social services) from which the poor are the greatest gainers.

TABLE VII—DISTRIBUTION OF INCOME BETWEEN INCOME
GROUPS (1960–61)

NET INCOME (after deduction of Income Tax and Surtax)	NUMBER OF PEOPLE (thousands)
£6,000 and over	4
£4,000 to £5,999	34
£2,000 to £3,999	297
£1,000 to £1,999	2,493
£750 to £999	4,400
£500 to £799	6,672
£250 to £499	6,292
£180 to £249	1,407

(The lower income groups include adolescents and part-time workers)

Causes of Inequality between Incomes. If one asks oneself 'Why is A so much richer than B?' the answer may be 'Because A is a successful sales executive and B is a junior clerk', or 'Because A has a lot of money property and B has none', or 'Because A is a shrewd business man who knows how to take advantage of his opportunities, and B, who started with the same property, has no business judgment'. And those answers lead on to the following questions: Why is a top-flight sales executive's work better paid than that of a junior clerk? Why does money property yield an income—and what causes the income from a given amount of property to vary? Why does property yield an extra return in some people's hands? In other words, what are the causes determining the levels of wages (and salaries), interest, and profits?

Why Earnings Vary. Obviously, the worker who does more work at a *given wage rate* (working longer hours when paid by time, turning out more products when paid by the piece) will earn a bigger income than the worker who, at the same rate, does less. So what is said about wage rates cannot be applied unchanged to earnings. This elementary points has to be stressed because people very often do confuse the two. Wage rates may be stable and yet wage-earners' incomes may be rising because of better overtime opportunities and improved equipment or organization making better piecework output possible; or, even, with improved wage rates, wage-earners' incomes may be the same or smaller because short time, or industrial disputes holding up production, have cut down the amount of work they can do. This being understood, what about wage rates themselves? What settles them?

Demand for Labour. In the broadest way, it is demand and supply. The demand comes from employers; in the labour market, they are the buyers. As in any other market, the price the buyers will be willing to pay depends on how keenly they need the services which the thing they are buying will render them. In this particular case, the buyer's keenness depends partly on how much they reckon the public will pay for the goods for whose production the labour is necessary, and partly on how well supplied they already are with that particular kind of labour. However skilled and clever a person may be, he will not find employment at a high wage or salary if there is very little demand for the things he produces; the best of our modern poets earn less by their craft than do the best of our film actors, because the public is less willing to spend money on good poetry than on good films (or, for that matter, very bad ones).

However skilled and clever a person may be, moreover, he will not find employment at a high wage or salary if all his potential employers are so well supplied already with labour of his type that it hardly matters to them whether they take on any more or not. In a seriously understaffed office an extra typist may be worth her weight in gold and the staff controller will go round the agencies offering higher and higher wages to attract one; a second extra typist would be very useful, but could be dispensed with if she were too expensive; a third would be welcome if she were cheap, but not otherwise. Or think of a market gardener hiring workers to cultivate five acres of ground, or a builder taking on labourers—their keenness to secure the *necessary minimum* of labour is far greater than their keenness to secure the *extra* labour which, though useful, is not absolutely essential, and the wages they are prepared to pay vary accordingly. Underneath all the regulation of wages by collective bargaining or by State action—to be discussed later—there lies the inescapable fact that employers will only employ labour when they will not lose by doing so; when the amount which a man's work adds to the value of their total output is, *in the long run*, not less than the amount which they have to pay for that work. In technical language, wages are limited by the *marginal productivity* of the labour concerned; the amount which is added to the total value of the product when an extra man is taken on, or lost when he is dismissed or leaves.

Supply of Labour: Differences in Scarcity. So much for demand; what about supply? As one might suppose, the greater the scarcity of any particular kind of labour in relation to demand, the higher its price or wage. Some kinds of labour are extremely scarce by *nature*—very few people, in each generation, are born with the natural gifts needed to make a first-rate entertainer or a great surgeon. So, being scarce, these natural gifts command a very high price. Apart from this basic, unavoidable natural scarcity, there is scarcity of *trained* ability; a man may have natural gifts which have remained undeveloped because he, or more probably his parents, could not afford a long and expensive training period with nothing coming in. Since ability to afford long and expensive training has in the past been pretty closely confined to the minority who are already comfortably off, the supply of qualified workers in those fields which require it—the professions, and to a lesser extent the skilled trades—has been limited, and the price of that supply

M

correspondingly high. This limitation is gradually being reduced as free secondary and higher education is made available
to more and more young people, and professional and skilled
rates of pay (for this and other reasons) are falling in comparison
with the rates of pay for less skilled occupations; but since no
amount of training will do away with the scarcity of high
natural gifts, whether of general intelligence or special aptitude,
the skilled professions and trades are always likely to carry
some scarcity rates of pay.

Artificial Scarcities in Supply of Labour. Moreover, there
are artificial scarcities as well as scarcities arising from shortage
of gifted individuals and limited training opportunities. In
some occupations those already established keep up their own
scarcity value by denying entry to more than a strictly limited
number of newcomers. If this limit is set by pitching the qualifications for entry so high that only the most gifted and best-
trained applicants can succeed, it ensures high professional
standards—in medicine and law, for instance, this is essential.
If it is set mechanically—only so many apprentices in proportion to so many craftsmen in such and such a trade, only so
many training facilities to be provided in such and such a pro-
fession—or if the established group insist on a training period
much longer than is needed to produce a qualified worker, then
the only effect of the limitation is to maintain a privileged professional or trade group in the enjoyment of an artificial scarcity value, while keeping the equally able unprivileged out of
the fields where they could most usefully serve the community.

Trade Unions and Wages. This is one reason why the
highly organized, fully unionized occupations have generally
been better paid than the unorganized. Workers in these occupations have kept themselves scarce and so valuable, and those
whom they have excluded have added to the numbers, and so
reduced the value, of the unskilled. It is not, however, the only
reason. Even where trade unionism does not limit the total
supply of labour in a trade, it tends to make wages higher than
they would otherwise be by improving the workers' *bargaining*

power in the labour market. An employer may pay a very high wage rather than not get the labour he needs; but if he can get it for less he will, and it may be a long time before the competition of other employers forces up the market rate to the full value of what the worker produces. Meanwhile, any individual worker is apt (except in times of extreme labour shortage) to need a job more than the employer needs his services; what is a matter of minor inconvenience to his employer is a matter of daily bread to him. So competition of workers for jobs is, in the absence of trade unionism, more reliably at work to keep wages down than the competition of employers for workers is to keep them up.

Trade unionism changes all that. If the labour which an employer loses by failing to pay the full value of his workers' work is not that of a single, dispensable worker but that of a whole labour force gone on strike, he will be much less apt to refuse; and when faced with a situation in which he must reduce his costs in order to avoid loss, he will regard a wage cut as the very last resort instead of as the easiest way out. If the trade union can win its members' loyalty so that they will put up with almost any hardship rather than take work at a 'blackleg's' (i.e. sub-standard) wage, and if it can build up funds out of which to give strike pay and out-of-work allowances where necessary, it does away with competition between workers altogether.

Limits of Trade Union Action. But of course there are limits. A trade union which tries to force wages higher than the figure at which all its members can be profitably employed may succeed in doing so by well-timed strikes and threats to strike, but the result will be that the least urgently needed workers, those whose work is worth less to a prospective employer than the standard wage, simply will not find jobs and will remain unemployed. Where the product is one which the public would rather pay more for than see diminish in quantity, the higher wage cost may merely push prices up with very little fall in output and employment; but where the demand for the product is *elastic*, where (see Chapter VIII) a small increase in price will shut out a great deal of buying, the workers as a whole may find themselves actually worse off than at a lower wage.

Other Causes of Inequality: (i) *Women's Wages.* These considerations do not quite account for all the differences to be found in the wages paid for different jobs. Some of these, like the enormously complicated gradations of rates to be found in the engineering trade, are survivals of a long and complicated history of bargaining and would probably never come into existence if suitable rates had to be decided here and now from scratch. Others, like the less complicated but still very minute gradations for different jobs on the railways, are more marks of status than anything else—they are badges of relative standing and authority and seniority rather than exact equivalents of any extra or lesser value in the work done.

The difference between men's and women's wages, in the same or closely similar work, is again very much a matter of tradition. Although tradition is breaking down here, it is still felt proper that men, the traditional bread-winners, should get more than women, the traditional dependants, and since both employers and (on the whole) women employees accept this, the lower wage is the 'done thing', and a really well-established 'done thing' is proof against a lot of economic pressure—or agitation against injustice. Tradition, however, is not the whole story here. Because so few women qualify for the more skilled jobs, they are more plentiful, and hence cheaper, in the relatively unskilled ones. Because so many of them only spend a few years, between school and marriage, in the labour market, they generally cannot be bothered to organize in unions. And —an important point in business jobs where one 'trains on' from one position to the next—a worker who may dash off and get married at any time is not worth so much to an employer as one who can be counted on to stay, even if their *present* work is of equal value.

(ii) *Mobility between Jobs.* Other differences between rates of pay in jobs which, in the face of it, should be worth the same are accounted for by the lack of *mobility*: even withou difficulties of training, or artificial restrictions, moving from job to job, and still more, from place to place, may be difficult and is often disliked. It is lack of mobility, too, which has in the past kept workers in jobs which were disagreeable or extra strenuous or dangerous in themselves, even where the pay was no higher, or actually lower, than that given for pleasanter occupations. Coalmining is very much a case in point. Clerking is—in just the opposite sense—another. The dirty, arduous and dangerous job of the miner used twenty years ago to carry lower wages, although it was skilled and although the miners were unionized, than the comparatively clean, comfortable and easy job of the clerk, though routine clerking is less skilled and very few clerks belonged to a union. With greater mobility, the routine 'white-collar' jobs are increasingly easy to fill, and the dirty and arduous shirt-sleeve jobs increasingly difficult to fill; so that the clerk's salary lags, while the miner's wage rises.

Effect of Capital Equipment. Finally, it must not be forgotten that the factors of production work *together*; if a worker's wage depends on his productivity, his productivity in turn depends overwhelmingly on the equipment with which he works. The American factory worker is, on the whole, no more highly skilled than the British, and he works no longer hours; but because he has more mechanical assistance, he produces more goods and gets more wages. The two men on the combine harvester mentioned in Chapter IV produce more than if they had only an old-fashioned horse-drawn reaping machine, and very much more than if they were working with scythes; so the farmer can afford to pay them more.

Real Wages and Money Wages. When comparing earnings over a period, one must remember the possibility that the general trend of prices, or cost of living, may have changed. This question of general price changes is a large subject, discussed separately in Chapter XVII; at this stage, a simple and rough example is enough to keep the reader straight. If in a certain year a man earned £12 a week, and five years later is earning £24 a week, his money earnings (or money wages) have doubled. If, however, prices have risen over those five years, so that goods and services cost on the average about twice as much as they did, the man's real earnings (or real wages) have remained the same. Thus money wages are what is earned in terms of £ s. d., whereas real wages are measured in terms of what earnings will buy.

Methods of Wage Payment: Time Rates. When one looks at actual wages and the way they are calculated, one finds that they fall into two broad classes: time wages and piece wages. Time wages are paid by the hour, day or week (salaries are 'time wages' reckoned by the year); piece wages are paid according to the number of items which a worker, or gang of workers, actually turns out. In some occupations time rates are obviously the only possible form of payment—one cannot pay a signalman, or a clerk, or a bus conductor by the piece, for what would the 'piece' be? Even where the 'piece' can be comparatively easily identified and credited to a particular worker, time rates remain popular because they ensure that each worker can count on a definite sum of money at the end of each week, unless actual short time is being worked. Such a system of payment is easy to understand and makes collective bargaining easier.

Piece Rates and Bonus Schemes. Piece rates are usually favoured by employers when the workers' output can be physically identified and measured, because a worker on piece rates has an incentive to work harder and produce more in a day. Higher total production from a given amount of equipment means lower costs per unit (remember Chapter X) and therefore higher profit. Sometimes piece rates take the form of a straightforward payment of so much for so many units produced, as in fruit- or hop-picking. In industry, one also finds payment according to some kind of bonus scheme, e.g. a standard time is fixed, by negotiation between management and union, for a given task, and an extra payment proportionate to the time saved is made to workers who get through that task in less than the standard time.

In spite of the opportunities for better earnings, the trade unions have often mistrusted these schemes, because, unless union officials were extremely vigilant, the standard time has tended to be that of the most efficient worker, and so the less able have been unable to earn a bonus even when uncomfortably speeded up. Also, short-sighted or unscrupulous employers have sometimes not been above raising the standard again and again whenever they found that the workers' extra exertions were increasing their earnings. Skilled craftsmen also dislike the idea of work being scamped by workers in a hurry to earn their bonus; and no one, skilled or unskilled, likes a helter-skelter, devil-take-the-hindmost atmosphere in the works. Not even the employer likes it in the long run—nervous strain breeds bad feeling and lightning strikes.

Thus, the problem of *incentives*, of making it worth the workers' while to work hard and co-operatively rather than slackly and grudgingly, is not a simple one. The urgent need for increased output during the war and post-war years led to the devising of new incentive schemes designed to stimulate production and at the same time to yield a fair reward to the worker and to favour the teamwork which made a 'happy ship'. Memories of unemployment during the pre-war slump years caused some opposition to these schemes—workers were afraid of 'working themselves out of a job'—but on the whole, when properly worked out and applied, they were very successful. In some industries where they operated productivity increased by amounts varying from 20 to 100 per cent and earnings by 20 to 65 per cent.

The Machinery of Wage Negotiation. The time has long passed when wages were generally settled by individual bargaining between employees and employers. Some wages are still settled in this way—the wages of domestic servants, for instance, and a good many salaries, particularly in the higher ranges. But over the main range of the labour market wages are fixed through negotiations between recognized bodies of employers and employees—each, of course, guided by their knowledge of the state of supply and demand. Sometimes it is left to

the employers' associations and the unions concerned to see
that a wage agreement is honoured by all concerned, sometimes there may be legal compulsion. Broadly speaking, we can
distinguish three separate forms of wage-fixing machinery:
(1) negotiations between trade unions and employers' associations, (2) Joint Industrial Councils, and (3) Wages Councils.

1. *Negotiations between Unions and Employers' Associa-
ations*. The wages and conditions of work of more than 60 per
cent of the wage earners of Great Britain are decided in this
way. It is a method suited to industries where unions have
been long and firmly established. Most of these industries have
worked out their own procedure for discussing wage claims and
need no outside machinery to help them. Agreements cover not
only wages but the entire field of labour conditions and relations, including hours, overtime, holidays, disciplinary procedure, the handling of complaints, the distribution of work,
apprenticeship, and, to an increasing extent, redundancy.

2. *Joint Industrial Councils*. These councils were originally
formed as the result of the Whitley Report of 1916 on Relations
between Employers and Employed, which urged that machinery
be provided for the discussion of wages and all matters of joint
concern in a number of industries where there was no securely
established procedure for joint negotiation. Of the hundred or
so Councils set up on a national and local scale, just after
World War I, less than a half survived the inter-war years; but
during World War II, and subsequently, the need for close
collaboration between employers and employed brought about
a vigorous revival.

3. *Wages Councils*. In some trades and industries, trade
unions and employers' associations have never existed or
never been effective, either because the trade was made up of a
very large number of widely scattered units (e.g. catering), or
because the workers did their work at home, as in the 'sweated'
East London trade of matchbox-making in the early years of
this century. It was to improve the appallingly low wages in the

'sweated' home-work industries that the Trade Boards were set up in 1909. These consisted of an equal number of employers and employees, together with some impartial outsiders, and they fixed a minimum wage which—unlike the rates decided on by direct negotiation or by Joint Industrial Councils—was legally enforceable once it had been approved by the Board of Trade. By a series of Acts from 1945 to 1959 the scope and the powers of these Boards were enlarged and their names changed to Wages Councils. They were empowered not only to fix minimum wages with the authority of the Ministry of Labour, but to deal with problems of training, recruitment and working conditions—all the normal topics, in fact, of industrial negotiation.

Farm wages are controlled by the Agricultural Wages Board which is administered by the Ministry of Agriculture.

CHAPTER XII

CAPITAL, PROFIT AND RENT

THE connection between labour and the payment of wages or salaries is a simple one; the relation between capital and the payment of interest is not quite so straightforward. Interest is the return paid for the use of a loan of money—so much is clear: but why does the borrower of £100 have, at the end of a year, to pay back not merely the original £100 but an extra £4 or £5 as well? The lender has his money back; why should he get more? Public opinion and the law have, at various times in history, answered quite simply: 'He shouldn't.' In the Middle Ages the Church condemned the taking of interest as sin; it was usury, a taking advantage of other people's misfortune. (This is why the Jews, who as non-Christians were not subject to the Canon Law, had a clear field as money-lenders.)

However, the Church itself modified its views in the course of time, taking the view that the lender had a right to get something in return for the risk of default, and also as recompense for any inconvenience or loss suffered through not having his money ready to hand when wanted; and the law of the land followed suit. Once the principle that interest was justified had been conceded, it became all the harder to enforce laws limiting the rate to what was considered proper; and as commerce and industry developed, with traders and industrialists clamouring for credit and willing to pay for it, these laws fell into disuse and were repealed. Even to-day, however, the private money-lender who lends not to business men needing capital, but to private persons in difficulties, may incur penalties if he charges an 'unconscionable' rate of interest.

Interest the Price of the Lump Sum. The fact is that in a great many circumstances a lump sum is more valuable to the person disposing of it than a trickle of income amounting, over a period, to the same figure. To take a very small and simple example, a boy just starting his first job may need a bicycle to get from home to work and back again. Getting the job depends on owning the bicycle. His wages over a few weeks will pay for it easily; but he needs it now and what is wanted to buy it is a lump sum now. It is worth his while, since he wants the job, to pay more for that lump sum than the cash price would come to if spread over those weeks in which he would be earning it; and that is precisely what he does when he gets credit from the dealer and pays something extra for hire-purchase terms.

What is true of the boy with his bicycle is true of all kinds of business enterprise. Money is needed to pay for what has to be done *before* returns from the enterprise come in. When a house or factory is built, money is *needed* to buy materials to pay workmen, long before money can be *received* for the finished building. When a shipload of wheat is imported from overseas, money is *needed* to pay the growers, the shipping charges and the insurance, long before money can be *received* for the sale of the wheat. And the same holds good for stocks of goods in shops, bought to-day, sold next week or next month; and for films made over a period of months and paid for by audiences over a period of months more; and for practically every kind of economic activity one cares to consider. And, of course, the more capital equipment is used in an enterprise, the bigger the lump sum needed to buy that capital equipment and launch the enterprise.

Lump sums, then—money capital—are essential to enterprise. Anyone conducting an enterprise needs capital. The more he has, the bigger the enterprise he can conduct and the more profit he can hope to make. The demand for capital arises from the business man's expectation of profit to be won by using it. Essentially, this is also true of non-profit-making public enterprise; Governments demand capital because, whatever they do, capital will enable them to do it better. (Think of the capital needed to equip a mechanized army, build a nuclear power station or to project a man into space.)

The Provision of Capital. If the only capital available for business enterprise were the capital which business men happened personally to own, economic development would be most desperately handicapped. But fortunately there is a further supply, the savings of those who are not business men. An essential part of every modern economic community is the credit machinery by which these savings are brought into the hands of business men and made available to increase the productiveness of enterprise. This credit machinery, consisting of the banks, the money market, the issuing houses, the building societies and insurance companies, provides hundreds of million pounds' worth of capital every year; some to borrowers who need it for only a few days or weeks before repayment, some for months, some for years. As we shall see in Chapters XIV and XVI, the credit machinery and its workings are decidedly complicated, and it does a good deal more than merely make A's and B's and C's savings available for X and Y and Z to use. At present we merely note that, thanks to the existence of banks and so forth, there is an organized market for capital, doing the essential market job of striking a balance between supply and demand by way of a price—the rate of interest.

Demand and Supply of Capital. As we have seen, *demand* for capital depends on business men's expectation of profit from using the equipment and stocks which it will buy. That, in turn, depends on two other things: first, on how much difference a bit more equipment, or a larger scale of enterprise, will make to their prospective profit (obviously there will be an extra demand for capital when a new invention looks like opening up new productive possibilities, or when existing equipment is especially short because of wartime destruction or for any other reason); and secondly, on how good the sales prospects are for the things that equipment produces. (In times of all-round depression, when no one is buying anything which they can possibly do without, sales prospects obviously will not tempt business men to increase production by borrowing more capital.) These two considerations between them settle how much capital will be demanded at any given price, that is, at any given rate of interest.

The *supply* of capital depends, in the last resort, on what people are willing to save. ('In the last resort'—the qualification is needed because, as we shall see later, the banking system can expand that supply far beyond the actual cash which the public puts in.) Willingness to save depends in turn on a number of things. It depends, as we saw in Chapter IX, on how well off the people are; a big margin over what they regard as the necessary minimum for their current needs makes a large savings programme possible, a small margin or no margin at all cuts possible savings down to little or nothing. It depends, too, on their attitude to the future—their thriftiness. People who think more of present enjoyment than of bettering themselves or of providing for a rainy day save less, out of any given income, than people who take a longer view and are willing to give up some present enjoyment so that they or their children may be better off in the future. And it depends, too, on how keen people are to have their wealth in a handy form where they can use it at once when wanted—cash in one's wallet is obviously handier than shares in an enterprise, which one cannot be sure of being able to sell for a good price.

The keener people are on this handiness or, as economists say, *liquidity*, in their assets, the harder it will be to tempt those assets out of their hands on to the capital market. These three considerations—the size of the margin over current needs, the attitude to the future, and the strength of the desire for liquidity—between them settle the *supply* of savings which will be forthcoming at any given rate of interest. (The reader is warned that this is all very broadly speaking. A full explanation of what makes the rate of interest move up or down over periods of time would be far too complex for this book and is a matter for more advanced study.)

The Structure of Interest Rates: Risk. With the supply and demand for capital balanced at any level, there will be different rates for different kinds of loans, according to *risk* and to the *length of time* for which the money concerned is tied up. Everyone who lends money runs some risk that the borrower will default; so the standing and reputation of the borrower makes a difference to the rate of interest which he must offer to attract capital. The greater the risk, the bigger the inducement needed to get lenders to run that risk. British Government securities are generally felt to be the safest form of loan available; so rates of interest on money invested in such securities are always the lowest. Loans to Dominion Governments are at slightly higher rates, and the interest on debenture stock raised by reputable joint-stock companies higher still. A loan to a foreign government which is looked upon as politically shaky may only be forthcoming at 8 per cent or more; and the loans made by private money-lenders on 'your note of hand alone', as their advertisements say, may carry interest rates of 20 or 30 or even 50 per cent, without being condemned as 'unconscionable', because the risk of default is so high.

The Structure of Interest Rates: Repayment Dates. The rate of interest also varies with the length of time which is due to elapse from the negotiation of the loan to the agreed date of repayment; the shorter the period, the lower the rate. This is because of the 'liquidity' preference mentioned above. However people may be feeling at any given time about liquidity in general, there is less sacrifice of liquidity when money is lent for a week or a month, or on the understanding that the lender can get it back whenever he asks for it, than when the borrower has the right to keep it for years. A long loan may be reasonably liquid for the lender if he can sell his claim to repayment— say, a debenture or a Government bond—to someone else; but the market price of that claim at the time the lender wants cash for it may be less than its face value. National Savings Certificates, on the contrary, are highly liquid, because they can be exchanged for cash at a known price at any time. The British Government can generally obtain three-month loans, by the offer of what are called Treasury Bills (that is, documents pledging the Treasury to pay so much at a date three months ahead), from the banks at a little below bank rate; the banks also lend to traders on the security of Bills of Exchange (see

Chapter XIII) for up to six months at between 5 and 6 per cent. The rates on ordinary long-term Government loans, due for repayment after five or ten or twenty years, vary between about 5 and 6 per cent.

Profit. The term 'Profit' is used to denote the return which the owner or part-owner of an enterprise (in a joint-stock company, the shareholders) obtain on the capital which they have invested. Note that this investment is different from lending. The risk on a loan is merely the risk of actual default, since so long as the borrower is not actually bankrupt he is legally bound, however much he has lost on the transaction, to repay the sum borrowed and the agreed interest. Short of bankruptcy, the creditor gets his return, win or lose. The risk on investment of the owner's own capital is the risk of the firm's profit expectations turning out to be mistaken; if they do, the owners of the invested capital must grin and bear their loss—no one else will bear it for them. For every firm that goes bankrupt and so causes loss to its creditors, there are hundreds which fail to make the expected profits and so cause loss to their shareholders.

'Pure Profit.' Economists, however, distinguish between profit in this sense of a total return (net of costs) on invested capital, and 'pure' profit. The difference in meaning can be illustrated by a simplified example of the annual profit-and-loss account of a grocery business owned and managed by one man.

Dr.	£	Cr.	£
To Salaries and Wages	2,000	By Gross profit (i.e. difference between cost	3,800
Rates	120	of purchases and	
Lighting and Heating	60	receipts from sales)	
Stationery and telephone	30		
Miscellaneous expenses	100		
Balance in hand	1,490		
(i.e. commercial profit, not pure economic profit)			
	£3,800		£3,800

Why is not the balance in hand, the £1,490, pure profit? Because it allows nothing for the value of the work the owner-manager has done himself—work having a definite market value, measured by the size of the salary he could have earned as manager of a similar store for some other owner. Also, it allows nothing for the interest on the capital which he must have invested in his stock-in-trade and fitments—capital with which he might, instead, have bought Government securities yielding say 5 per cent. Finally, it allows nothing for the rent of the premises which he owns, and from which he could draw an income by letting them, at the rate than ruling in the real-estate market, to someone else. Suppose that the grocer could have earned £1,000 a year as manager of a branch of a chain store; that he has invested £1,000 in stock and fitments, which would yield him £50 a year if loaned to the Government; and that at current letting values his premises would, if rented to another person, bring him in £200 a year—then his *pure* economic profit is £1,490 less £1,250 or only £240 a year. This pure profit is the return neither to labour nor to capital, nor to real estate—all these are accounted for—but to the grocer's willingness to shoulder his own risks and take his own responsibilities; to his *enterprise*.

Profit the Result of Business Ability or Enterprise. Willingness is, of course, not enough. To make a pure profit, a profit in the economic sense, there must be *ability*, of the special business kind which consists in a knack of judging whether this or that risk is not worth taking for the expected return. This is very different from the technical skill which makes a good workman, or the professional skill which makes a good lawyer or teacher, or the artistic gifts which make a good novelist, singer or actor. A great many good workmen, who put their savings or a windfall into a little business of their own, lose their capital and have to go back to wage-earning for want of this specific business ability; many good teachers have come to grief when they set up as owner-headmasters of private schools; and the numbers of gifted writers who have failed as publishers, and of actors who have failed as theatrical managers, are only less considerable because fewer have tried. Business ability, like other kinds of special ability, is scarce.

Every kind of business calls for some measure of special business ability, but some kinds call for more than others because they have to do with more uncertain conditions of demand or of supply—they are, in short, riskier. There is always some risk, because conditions in the economic system are constantly changing and no one can calculate for certain just what the changes will be; so that there is always room for judgment and for errors of judgment. For example, a business man will suffer loss when prices unexpectedly fall and leave him holding large stocks of goods bought at the old price, which must now be sold for less than he had counted on. That loss has arisen because he misjudged the future course of prices; better judges may have judged better and run their stocks down beforehand, but no one can be right every time.

Again, fashions and tastes change, leaving commodities previously in popular demand as drugs on the market. (The trade in women's wear is much riskier, from this point of view, than that in men's wear.) Entirely new commodities arise and supersede old ones, as the car superseded the horse-drawn carriage; entirely new methods of production do the same as technical knowledge improves. Yet no one can say for certain, at any moment, that this or that novelty will catch on and become a major feature of daily life or that this or that new method will be successful.

Judging this sort of uncertain situation calls for business ability; economists call it the function of *enterprise*. The really gifted and successful *entrepreneur*, or business man, is the one who can pick out, among all the uncertainties surrounding his business, the really important trends, backing his judgment as to their direction, and as to how far they will go, by using his working capacity, and his capital, and his credit-worthiness which enables him to borrow more, to produce what he judges will be the most wanted in future by the methods which he judges will prove cheapest. Notice that the 'business man' in this sense, the man who chooses, among all possible alterna-

N

tives, the best method of using the factors of production and the best uses to put them to, need not be working for his own profit; he may be a planner in the public service, taking a chance on behalf of the whole community. The whole community will reap the benefit or bear the loss of the outcome of a Government choice between investing in more roads, more houses, more electric power stations or more schools. And even in private enterprise the man who takes a chance may quite often be a managing director who, though also a part-owner of the company which he manages, relies much less on his income from his shares than on his salary as a company executive.

But whether the man using business ability to judge uncertainty gets the resulting profits for himself personally or not, it is business ability which produces those profits. Business ability is essential so long as uncertainty exists—and that means always. Even if all changes of taste and technique were ruled out by an absolutely cast-iron standstill order imposed on a completely regimented world, there would still be unpredictably good and bad harvests, greater or less returns to extractive industry, technical hitches and strokes of luck in production. In a world where people are free to change the way they spend their incomes—and they way they earn them—and in which science is constantly opening up new but uncertain possibilities, business ability is needed all the more. And as it is scarce, those having it can reap gains which those lacking it cannot make.

Profit and Loss Sift Business Ability. Who has it, and who lacks it, is not always clear because so many people never get a chance to use and develop business ability through lack of capital, and because others who have very little business ability can, in normally prosperous times, rub along without disaster by sticking to a well-worn rut where judgment, as apart from routine competence, is not much needed. But the test of personal profit and loss does constantly work to weed out the less able (in this special sense) from the ranks of active business men, and send them instead into salaried employment of a kind not requiring special business ability. At the same time, it

works to promote the more able (again in this special sense) to
the control of more and more important enterprises. One of
the big problems confronting public enterprise, in which personal profit and loss do not affect those making business decisions, is how to find an equally reliable way of weeding out the
less able (always in this special sense) before they have done
much harm and getting the most able to those key positions
where they will do most good.

Rent. Economists use the word 'rent' just as they do 'profit',
in a sense rather different from its everyday meaning. Payment
for the use of a gas cooker or a dress suit or a deck chair is not
rent in the economic sense; nor, except in a very partial way, is
the rent of a house. In the strictest economic sense, rent is the
price paid for the use of natural resources, i.e. 'land', as defined in
Chapter IX, though what can be said of rent in this narrowest
sense also applies, over an appropriate period, to the payments
made for the use of anything whose supply cannot be readily
increased.

Special Characteristics of Rent. How does this distinguishing feature—the impossibility of increasing the supply of
the things paid for during the period being considered—affect
rent, the price of land, and make it different from wages, the price
of labour, and interest, the price of capital? If one looks back at
the account of how prices in general are settled (in Chapter VIII),
the answer should be fairly clear: with other things, an increase
in price brings about an increase in total supply, a decrease
brings about a falling off, so that both blades of the supply-and
demand scissors move; here, only one can move—demand—
since the supply is 'given' and cannot change at all.

This means that the owners of that fixed supply can exact a
higher and higher price as demand rises, without any possibility of seeing their position undermined by fresh competitors
coming in. They may 'compete' among themselves—no landowner can ask more rent for a farm than other landowners are
asking for similar farms in the neighbourhood—but taken together they are in clover for as long as the pressure of demand

increases. This is particularly important where the purest and most completely 'given' natural resource—sheer site value—is concerned. The 'supply' of farm land can be 'increased', in every sense that matters economically, by drainage and ferti- lizers, to a point where the 'original and indestructible powers of the soil', as the old economists called them, are unimportant compared with the additional powers bestowed by capital; but the supply of sites along a river bank, or around a railway ter- minus, or within so many miles of a city centre, is fixed by pure geometry. Whether the price goes up or down, the total acreage available will be just so much and no more.

'Windfall Gains' in Site Values. Now, as population in- creases, sheer space is bound to get more valuable, simply because there is less of it per head—it is scarcer—and scarcity, as we know, means high prices. So there is an historical tendency, which at some periods has worked very strongly indeed, for windfall gains to accrue to those who happen to be landowners or to those who, seeing how things were going, have bought land in the expectation of a rise. (There is plenty of scope here for business judgment and misjudgment, as the fortunes won and lost in 'real estate booms' testify.) The spectacle of these wind- fall gains going to people who (on the face of it at least) were neither rendering any active service for them nor making any sacrifice, has prompted the idea that the community as a whole rather than the fortunate landowners ought to reap the benefit of higher land values, and that these ought to bear a special tax.

In Britain this idea bore fruit after World War II in the *development charge* imposed when land was converted from a less valuable to a more valuable use. It was no use buying farm land to sell for building plots at ten times the price later; no one would pay ten times the price because the development charges would swallow the profit. The trouble with any tax, or development charge, so heavy that it takes all the profit out of buying land for its potential future value, is that it drastic- ally weakens the market forces which (see Chapter X) sort out sites between different uses, according to their particular suitability for the needs of different users. But the trouble with those market forces, in turn, was that they produced in practice, as time went on, such a revolting hotch-potch of residential and factory building, such a straggling mess of 'ribbon development' over the countryside, as no economist could defend even on purely economic grounds, let alone on social ones. So the sorting out of sites between different uses has been very largely taken out of the hands of private business and the sphere of private judgment and turned over to specialist town and country planning authorities. The post-war development charge, however, was scrapped in 1952.

The Brake on Rent. The tendency for landowners to reap windfall gains as population and economic activity increase has also been held up, and in Britain occasionally reversed, by other influences. It is held up by the fact that rent agreements are generally drawn up for a long term of years, so that at any given moment a great many landowners will be getting rents lower than they could ask for if they were free to negotiate new leases. When prices in general are rising fast, as they have done since 1939, this lag owing to long-term contracts means an actual and possibly violent shrinkage in land rents as a share of the national income. When farm land is concerned, habit and custom, and long-standing personal relations between landlord and tenant, are also apt to have a braking effect on rents. And the steep rise in rents which, nevertheless, took place in Britain in the early nineteenth century, when a rapidly growing population was having to be fed entirely off its limited home acres, was reversed with a vengeance in the last quarter of the century when first cheap grain, and then cheap refrigerated meat, began pouring in from overseas. Just as the landowner *need* do nothing in order to see his rents rise when the demand for land increases, so he *can* do nothing to prevent their falling when the demand for land decreases.

Other Windfall Gains and Losses. What is true of land, whether over a long or short period, is true for the short period of other factors of production too. During whatever time is

needed to produce more of them, an increase in the demand for
them means windfall gains to their owners[1]; during whatever
time is needed for the existing supply to wear out or be converted to other uses, a decrease in the demand means windfall
losses. For example, a sudden and considerable increase in the
demand for steel, such as arises in time of war, cannot at once
bring about a corresponding increase in the supply; steel production, as we know, calls for elaborate plant taking a long
time to produce. So until that new plant can be built, steel will
have a special scarcity value, a value like that of a unique land
site, and the price will rise in the short run far above what is
needed to make the new plant profitable.

This sharp difference, between the short-run emergency price
of a temporarily scarce necessity, and the long-run price which
will be enough to keep extra supplies rolling in, is the justifica-
tion for emergency *price controls*. The extra steep price rise
which the controls prevent would bring no extra supplies into
the market; it would represent windfall gain to suppliers, windfall loss to users. As windfall gains and losses upset business, and
as in wartime it is the Government, and hence the taxpayer,
who takes the windfall losses, there is much to be said for controls, even apart from the feeling that windfalls 'aren't fair'.
There is this much to be said, from the economist's point of view,
against controls: that when everyone expects a controlled price
to be slapped on to any especially scarce commodity, there is
less incentive for people with foresight and business judgment
to provide against that scarcity in advance; the knowledge that
no special profit can be expected if the scarcity does materialize
and make their goods more valuable will deter them from taking the chance of its *not* materializing, and so when it does come
it will be all the worse for lack of the supplies which they might
have provided. This argument hardly applies to wars and
earthquakes, but in any circumstance where business foresight
can make a big difference to the degree of eventual scarcity,
where 'windfalls' are not in fact pure windfalls at all, it is
important.

[1] The term 'quasi-rent' is used to denote gains of this kind. (Latin *quasi*
='as if')

XII]   CAPITAL, PROFIT AND RENT   183

'*Rent of Ability.*' One can even, by a stretch, apply the idea of economic rent to the earnings of especially gifted and irreplaceable people. One cannot make a silk purse out of a sow's ear; no amount of training facilities will turn ordinary competent run-of-the-mill lawyers, or actors, or surgeons, into first-rate, topflight stars of their professions. So, no matter how high the price set on the first-raters' services, the supply of those services cannot be increased to pull the price down again. Their earnings depend, like the rent of land, on demand and demand alone. There is a difference, however; the supply of land does not fall off as rents fall, but the supply of first-rate professional ability may very well fall off if its reward is cut to a point where the first-rate professional prefers more leisure and less concert-pitch activity. Moreover, land cannot be moved from where it is to where it would be worth more; human beings can, at a pinch, emigrate. This is a point of which we shall see more in the chapter on Taxation.

CHAPTER XIII

MONEY AND THE MEANS OF PAYMENT

EARLIER chapters have described the division of labour by which mankind meets its needs. To say that production is carried on by the division of labour is the same thing as to say that we are all, more or less closely, specialists. In a modern community no one, not even the farmer, produces more than a very small part of the goods or services which he and his family need. Instead, every worker specializes in producing something—goods or services—which he or the firm for which he works sells to the public through a market. Wherever the division of labour is established a market must be established too[1]; for otherwise the specialized worker would have no means of getting the things which he needs but which, being a specialist, he does not himself produce.

Division of Labour makes Money almost Essential. Division of labour, then, depends on the existence of a market. But the existence of a market, in any but the very simplest form corresponding to a very rough division of labour indeed, depends on the existence of something else: that is, *money.* Without money, the only possibility is to swap goods directly for one another; to *barter* them. And though barter is better than no exchange at all, it is enormously inconvenient. For one thing, the person who has the thing we want may not want the thing that we have, but something else altogether; for another thing, even supposing that all the would-be swappers could be neatly brought together in pairs, there would remain the difficulty of deciding how much of one thing is worth so much of another—the rates of exchange, that is, between goods.

[1] Except in a completely authoritarian organization like an army, a monastic institution, or a prison.

Some pairs of swaps are almost impossible to arrange without money—swaps, for instance, between a large commodity like a house and the mass of small commodities, food, clothes, and so forth, which the builder would want in exchange. And, without money to reckon in, every exchange whether simple or difficult involves the most time-wasting higgling and haggling over terms. Nor is this all; without money it is impossible for certain producers—particularly those producing perishable foodstuffs—to store or save wealth at all. And, finally, without money it is impossible for anyone to make more than a rough guess at whether he is getting richer or poorer, whether this or that line of activity is 'paying' or not; none of the fine calculations concerning costs and prices, described in earlier chapters, can be made at all.

Commodity Money. These difficulties of barter have been obvious to all but the most extremely primitive societies; and money in some form has been in use since history began. (History begins with the keeping of records, and any society advanced enough to keep records is too advanced to be content with barter.) Until quite lately, what has been used for money has been some particular commodity, chosen or gradually winning its special position out of the whole range of commodities produced, because of its high value, its convenience for the special purpose of exchange, and the consequent readiness of everyone to accept it in a deal.

Different parts of the world have at one time or another chosen to use different commodities for this special purpose, and very queer some of them have been: feathers of rare birds, particular kinds of sea shell, dogfish or shark-teeth, knives, cooking pots. But wherever civilization has reached a certain level and the division of labour has got beyond a rather rudimentary stage, the chosen commodity—the money commodity —has been a precious metal, gold or silver, minted into coins which everyone could recognize, and which everyone knew would keep their value because of the preciousness of the rare materials of which they were made. Money which everyone can recognize, and which everyone trusts to preserve its value, is money which everyone will accept; and this *general accepta-bility* is the essential characteristic of money. The precious metals had the further advantage that as they were precious —since a very little gold or silver was worth a very great deal of anything else—the coins into which they were minted could be of a convenient size for carrying about and handling.[1]

Functions of Money. General acceptability, the fact that anyone with goods or services to offer will accept money in return for them, at once gets over the biggest barter difficulty; it provides a *medium of exchange*. But providing a medium of exchange is not the whole story, as we have seen; for exchange of any complex sort to be possible, there must be a *measure of value*, and to keep track of complex exchanges and calculate gain or loss there must be a *unit of account*. Once the recog-nized, generally accepted money commodity is minted into standard sizes and weights, into coins of warranted fineness, it provides both; and a real, accurate pricing system becomes possible. Moreover, it provides something essential for econo-mic stability and progress—a *store of value*, which makes it possible for everyone to save and provide for the future, even if what he himself produces is highly perishable.

Finally, coined money made of metal of recognized weight and quality can provide a yardstick or standard for other, sub-sidiary means of exchange. Just as the Board of Trade provides a standard yard which does not stretch or shrink and to which the inches and feet on the measuring instruments used by sur-veyors and drapers and so on must conform, so the monetary authority has in the past established a standard coin, contain-ing a fixed weight of metal (usually gold) of given quality, to which all other coins bear a fixed relation. For example, in England the pound sterling from 1821 to 1914, and from 1925 to 1931, contained $113\frac{1}{623}$ grains of gold, and the subsidiary

---

[1] The minting of five shilling pieces in Britain has long been discon-tinued because they were too large. (Anyone who has seen a 1951 Festival Souvenir, or Coronation, five shilling piece, will realize how awkward a pocketful would be.) Silver threepenny pieces have also been abandoned because they were too small.

coinage (pennies, shillings and so forth) bore a fixed ratio to the pound sterling.

Precious Metals as Guarantee of Stable Buying Power. Thus, provided that the metal from which the standard coin is minted does not vary in its exchange value, the value of the coinage system will not vary either. The value—the buying power of money, in whatever form people happen to be holding it, will remain constant. This is important, because if that buying power varies it makes money untrustworthy as a unit of account and as a store of value. People holding it make windfall gains or windfall losses, in terms of real wealth, according to whether its value is rising or falling; and business accounts no longer give a truthful picture of profit and loss, since when the value of money is falling a 'paper profit' shown in the accounts may leave a firm with less real buying power than it started with, and when the value of money is rising a transaction which had increased the firm's real buying power may show up as a 'paper loss' in its books. This is a great handicap to trade and industry. So the more stable is the value of the standard money, the better. As we shall see, no standard money can give absolute stability like that of the standard yard and the standard ounce; but gold, in the past, has come nearer to doing so than any other standard.

Disappearance of Commodity Money. None of this sounds much like our present-day monetary system. Very few readers of this book will have so much as set eyes on a gold sovereign; no one who is under middle age to-day has ever paid for things in gold as a matter of course. The 'silver' coins in our pockets are not silver at all (except perhaps for a few old ones) but cupro-nickel; the 'copper' coins are of bronze. For everything but small change we use paper notes which, so far from being made of an especially precious substance, are in themselves worth nothing at all; and for large transactions business men and others use cheques, which (though banks prefer a proper form) can be made out on anything. How has this change come about?

Money in Nineteenth-Century Britain. Let us begin by looking at the monetary system of Great Britain as it existed during most of the nineteenth century and up to 1914. The standard unit of currency was the golden sovereign, containing a weight of gold equal to its face value—that is, it would be worth just as much simply as melted-down metal. For this reason the sovereign and the half-sovereign were known as 'full-bodied coins'. The silver and copper coins constituted a subsidiary coinage, necessary because a piece of gold small enough to buy pennyworths would be inconveniently tiny. The silver coins were minted from a silver alloy containing $92\frac{1}{2}$ per cent pure silver; the copper coins contained less than their face value of copper. But owing to long-established custom and use, the public freely accepted these 'token' coins.

Convertible Notes. During this period, notes were not issued in any denomination lower than £5. The Bank of England issued notes for £5, £10, £20, £50, £100, £500 and £1,000; and anyone who had a Bank of England note was legally entitled, if he liked, to take it to the Bank and get gold sovereigns or gold bullion equal in value to the sum stated on the note. The note was, in fact, literally what the writing on its face said it was: a promise to pay solid gold on demand. When such a promise must be legally honoured, the notes concerned are called 'convertible'.

The Bank Act of 1844. In order to make sure that the promises on Bank of England notes always could be honoured, the law (in Robert Peel's Bank Charter Act of 1844) provided that the Bank of England must always keep the total value of notes issued down to the quantity of actual gold which it had at its disposal, except for a small (£14 millions) 'fiduciary issue' of notes, which were covered not by gold but by Government securities. ('Fiduciary' means 'on trust'.) As there was no likelihood that all the holders of Bank of England notes would ever choose the same time to exercise their right to exchange them for gold, it was quite safe to leave this £14 millions uncovered. Thus the Bank's gold went a little further, as backing for the note issue, than it would have done in active circulation.

The Bank Act, however, kept the total note issue closely in step with the Bank's gold holdings. So long as it was in force, there could be no big increase in the note issue, and consequently no massive *inflation*, i.e. no large excess of money which people try to spend on an unchanged amount of goods and services, so driving up prices all round. (This is the same thing as a fall in the value of money; see Chapter XVII.)

Cheques and Bills of Exchange. A substantial proportion of business transactions were, as they are to-day, settled not by a direct transfer of cash, whether notes or gold, but by *credit instruments.* Of these the most familiar to us is the *cheque,* which is not money but an order to a banker, by a person having funds in that banker's custody, to pay a stated sum to a third party. Another, which the ordinary person not engaged in commerce is less likely to meet with, is the *bill of exchange,* which is like a cheque in that it is a written order to pay a stated sum to a third party, but which need not be addressed to a banker. Bills of exchange are of two kinds, *inland* and *foreign.* The former kind had greatly diminished in importance before 1914, having been largely superseded by the cheque. The latter was used, right up to World War II, as the chief means of settling accounts between traders in different countries.

A merchant exporting goods from England to France, for instance, would draw a bill for the value of the goods 'on' (that is, addressed to) the French importer. The latter on receiving the bill would 'accept' it (that is, indicate his willingness to pay) by writing 'accepted' and his name across the bill. The bill might be drawn 'at sight', meaning that it was payable as soon as it was accepted, or more probably at three months' notice from the date of acceptance. The bill would then be returned to the English exporter, who could get cash for it by selling it to one of the financial houses which handle such transactions (see Chapter XVI); he would get the full cash value, less a small handling charge, on a 'sight' bill or at its maturity on a three-months' bill, and a lesser amount, depending on the current rate of interest, on a three-months' bill for whose maturity he did not want to wait. The French importer, meanwhile, would pay into his bank enough to meet the bill when presented; and the financial houses in London and Paris respectively would square things up between themselves in a way to be described in Chapter XIX. The point to notice now is that neither the French nor the English trader has to remit any actual money abroad; and that while a bill is maturing it is an asset which, though it will not pass freely among the general public as coins and notes do, will be accepted in commercial circles where the acceptor's credit-worthiness can be assessed and is thus worth a definite sum in hard cash to its holder.

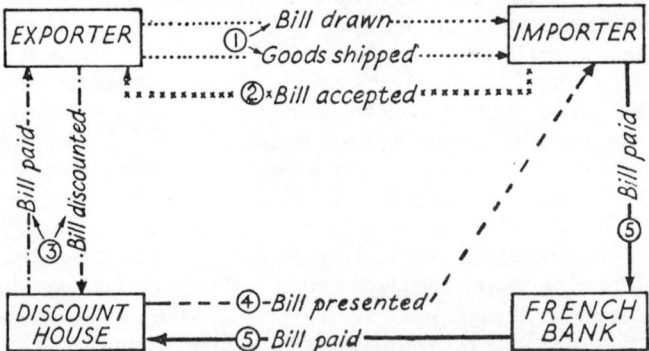

FIG. 22—BILL OF EXCHANGE

(*For an explanation of the work of the Discount Houses, see pp. 221–22*)

Money Orders and Postal Orders. Another, much less important form of credit instrument consisted before 1914 (and still consists) of Money Orders and Postal Orders. Like cheques and Bills of Exchange, they are orders to pay a stated sum to a third party; but they are drawn not on bankers or private traders but on the Post Office. They provide a safe and speedy means of sending small sums from place to place, but their use is restricted (they are frequently payable, for instance, only at a stated post office) and they are not widely transferable.

The Crisis of 1914. When war broke out in 1914 the Bank of England stopped issuing sovereigns and half-sovereigns and withdrew from circulation all those coming into its hands. At the same time the Bank Act of 1844 was suspended, releasing the Bank from its legal obligation to redeem notes in gold. These measures were taken in order to secure the biggest possible centrally-held stock of gold with which to purchase essential supplies from abroad. The gold coins were replaced (and much more than replaced) by an issue of 10s. and £1 Treasury Notes; in effect, the fiduciary issue was progressively expanded.

The Gold Bullion Standard. From 1914 to 1925 the British monetary system remained entirely detached from gold; the amount of money in circulation depended merely on Government policy. In 1925 Britain went 'back to gold', but with a difference. Bank of England notes were made convertible again, but only into gold bullion in 400-oz. bars; that is to say, at about £1,700 apiece. No gold coins were minted; so no more gold left the Bank than was wanted by the comparatively few people needing it for large special transactions. Its use was virtually restricted to foreign trade. (We shall see that in some circumstances it may pay better to settle with an overseas creditor in gold than to use the normal Bill-of-Exchange mechanism.) This 'bullion standard', then, had the advantage of economizing in the use of gold while still ensuring that the pound sterling was kept equal in value to the gold content of the (imaginary) sovereign.

In 1928 the title of 'Treasury Note' was dropped and the Bank of England took over the job of issuing 10s. and £1 notes on the same footing as those of higher denominations.

The End of the Gold Standard. The gold bullion standard did not last long. In 1931, with depression and crisis spreading from the United States to Europe and causing a universal demand for cash, Great Britain was forced to 'go off gold' again, abandoning convertibility as she had done in 1914 (see Chapter XX). The quantity of notes issued no longer depended on the gold holdings of the Bank of England; it had, however, an upper limit of £260 million, set by Act of Parliament, and depended in the last resort on the policy decided, on general economic grounds, by the Treasury and the Bank. During World War II the note issue was expanded to £1,350 million and has subsequently expanded to over £2,000 million, for reasons explained in Chapter XVII.

Post-War Changes. Soon after World War II the Bank of England stopped issuing notes of a higher denomination than £5. This was done partly to check black-marketeers (who preferred cash to cheques for obvious reasons, and so found big notes particularly handy) and partly because the general use of cheques had made them unnecessary in normal business. The *token coinage* system has undergone two main changes since 1914. In 1920 the silver content of the silver coins was reduced to a half, because with the rising price of silver as a raw metal the shilling had become worth 1s. 4d. and had ceased to be a 'token'. In 1946 a still steeper rise in the value of silver, together with the fact that the British Government had undertaken to repay a large amount of that metal lent by the United States during the war, led to its abandonment for monetary purposes for the first time in British history. Hence our present cupronickel sixpences, shillings, florins and half-crowns. *Cheques* are much more generally used than they used to be, because a much greater proportion of the public have a bank account. Only a few firms still use the *inland Bill of Exchange*. The *foreign Bill of Exchange* now takes second place, as a means of settling international trading debts, to the direct transfer of funds from one bank account to another; part of this decline dates back to the wartime and post-war practice of inter-Governmental bulk trading, which was financed by direct inter-Governmental payments. Another reason is the uncertainty whether a trader, although having accepted a Bill, has complied with all the exchange control regulations. Direct transfer of funds between banks obviates this difficulty. Thirdly, *Export Credits*, provided by the Banks, under the Board of Trade's guarantee have in part taken the place of Discount and Acceptance Houses (Chapter XVI) in financing foreign trade.

Legal Tender. As stated earlier, money in the basic sense is limited to notes and coins. These are the only forms of money which people can be legally compelled to accept in payment of a debt; which are, in the technical phrase, *legal tender*. (Bank of England notes are legal tender up to any amount; silver, threepenny bits and copper coins are legal tender only up to sums of £2, 2s. and 1s. respectively.) Creditors, however, rarely insist on legal tender; if they always did, in fact, our monetary system would break down, for there would not be nearly enough notes to cover all the transactions now carried out, by common consent, by means of cheques and bills of exchange.

'Emergency Money.' Just as a means of payment may be acceptable by common consent, without legal tender status, so legal tender money may fail to be acceptable in practice, whatever the law may say, if people do not in fact trust it. This has often happened (though never, so far, in Great Britain) when a national money has been rapidly losing value owing to post-war or post-revolutionary inflation; when, that is to say, money received to-day is likely to buy fewer goods to-morrow and still fewer the day after. With prices rising steeply, everyone wants goods rather than prospectively worthless money, and prefers barter transactions, in spite of all their inconvenience, to the risk of finding that they have parted with their wares for virtually nothing. In Germany after World War II a highly unofficial 'full-bodied money' replaced the crumbling official currency; that 'money' consisted of cigarettes, willingly accepted even by non-smokers because they knew they could use them, in turn, to make their own purchases.

The essential quality of money, in fact, is *acceptability*. Acceptability may be helped by the beauty and durability of the money material, or by its status as legal tender; but in the last resort it depends on public confidence that any given sum will buy about as much, in goods and services, in the future as at present.

O

THE COMMERCIAL BANKS

As the last chapter showed, a great deal of the business of any modern society is transacted by means not of cash but of cheques. As Chapter XII showed, a great part of modern production depends on borrowed money. It is the banking system which both provides the facilities used by those who draw or receive cheques, and supplies firms with day-to-day liquid capital. The banking system as a whole comprises the commercial banks, of which the best known are the 'Big Five'—Barclays, Lloyds, the Midland, the National Provincial, and the Westminster; the Bank of England; and a number of specialist financial houses (Discount and Acceptance Houses). Only the commercial banks normally do business with the ordinary public, and this chapter will deal exclusively with them.

Current Accounts. The most obvious function of a commercial banker is to look after his customer's deposits. These may be in a *current account*, which enables the customer whenever he pleases to order the banker to make payments from that account up to whatever amount the sum standing to his credit will cover. (That, of course, is what cheques are for.) Current accounts earn no interest. On the contrary, bankers usually charge the customer a small sum for keeping them, in order to cover the cost of the work done in handling cheques. Another method of payment is the *credit transfer*, widely used on the Continent and introduced in this country in the early 1960s. Using a special form, any person, whether or not he is a regular customer of a bank, can (provided he makes the money available!) request a bank to transfer a sum of money to the bank account of a third person.

Deposit Accounts. The other type of account is a *deposit account*, which does earn a small rate of interest. This is not used for drawing on by cheque. The customer is not expected to make frequent withdrawals, and should give notice of whatever withdrawals he does make. A customer can, of course, have accounts of both types, at one or more banks; or he may find it convenient to have more than one current account and use them for different purposes. Of total deposits held by the banks, about one-third are on deposit account and two-thirds on current account.

The Clearing House. As banks are constantly receiving from their customers, either for cash or to be credited to their accounts, cheques drawn on other banking firms, they have evolved the *Clearing House* system by which sums owed and owing by each bank to the others are set off against one another daily. Each commercial bank, moreover, itself has an account with the Bank of England, and any balances owing or owed when the Clearing House offsets are finished is made up by payment from the account of the debtor bank to that of the creditor bank.

Lending Policy: Security and the Length of Loans. Banks do not leave the money deposited with them to lie idle. They lend it to other customers, and charge interest on the loans (see Chapter XII). Thus they cover their own business costs and make profits for their shareholders. They would not, however, either make profits or even preserve their own and their customers' money if they lent indiscriminately to all and sundry. Before granting loans, therefore, they make certain that both the borrower and the purpose for which he wants money measure up to the standard which experience has shown to be necessary for sound banking practice.

The first things a banker considers when a customer approaches him for a loan are the nature of the *security* which that customer can offer and the *length of time* for which the loan is required. The security must be adequate to guard the bank against loss should the borrower fail to repay the loan at the agreed time and should the bank not wish to renew it. Bankers accept many types of security; Government bonds, shares, insurance policies, the assets of a firm (fixed property or goods), personal guarantees or house property. To be acceptable to a banker, the security must be *liquid*, that is, capable of being easily realized and turned into cash. To allow for the fact that it might not, when realized, fetch its present market value (see page 231), the banker generally lends less than that market value. For example, if a customer wanted to borrow £500 from his bank and offered as security 3 per cent Savings Bonds whose current market value was 95, he would have to provide more than £500 worth of those Bonds, in order to cover the possibility that they might have fallen to 90 or 85 if and when they had to be realized.

The longer the loan is to run, obviously, the wider the safety margin must be between the amount of the loan and the market value of the security. Bankers prefer to lend for short (i.e. under twelve months) and strictly-defined periods, renewing loans, if desired, at their discretion. They do occasionally lend for longer periods, even for several years, but experience shows that it is unwise for them to tie up much of their capital in this way.

Loans and Overdrafts. A borrower from a bank may get either a *loan* or an *overdraft*. A loan gives him the right to a sum of money for a fixed time, and he pays interest on the full amount for the whole period. An overdraft is a kind of intermittent loan; it gives the borrower the right to overdraw his account (that is, to order the banker to pay out more money than that account contains) up to an agreed amount. He need not avail himself of this right to draw extra money except when he actually needs it; and he pays interest only on the amount actually overdrawn and for the time that the overdraft lasts. This is merely a difference in form to suit the borrower's convenience; there is no real difference in principle—an overdraft is only a particular kind of loan.

An important thing about bankers' loans and investments is that every addition to their volume adds to the volume of deposits. This may seem too obvious to mention when one is thinking only of the first stage of the transaction, the stage at which Brown & Co., the borrowing firm, find themselves provided with a deposit increasing their original account at the lending bank. But when they use up that deposit, by drawing cheques against it, the *total* of bank deposits does not, as one might think at first sight, diminish accordingly. Those cheques, drawn in favour (let us say) of their suppliers, White & Co. and of Black & Co., are duly paid into those firms' respective bank accounts and go to increase *their* deposits. Bank deposits, or, as most economists call them, 'bank money', circulate in fact just as cash does, without losing buying power as they pass from account to account. We shall see later what limits the power of the banks to create 'bank money' by giving loans. (Even now, readers may be able to deduce some of these limiting influences.) Meanwhile, we must examine the nature and purposes of the loans themselves.

Types of Loans: Discount. Borrowers from banks may be broadly divided into three classes: (1) business firms and private individuals, (2) the British Government, and (3) the 'Money Market'—discount houses and stockbrokers.

Credit may be provided to industrialists and traders by discounting Bills of Exchange (i.e. as described in the last chapter buying them at face value less a *discount* depending on the rate of interest) although this kind of transaction is more usually handled by the specialist *discount houses*. Here, the security is fundamentally the goods in respect of whose sale the bill is drawn; this kind of loan is sometimes called *self-liquidating*, because the single transaction or set of transactions with which it is concerned provides the funds for repayment. (But see pp. 222–24 for the role of specialized *acceptance houses*.)

Loans on Goods in Process. A more typical transaction occurs when a firm wishes to buy a large consignment of goods the seller of which (e.g. a farmer) requires immediate payment, but which will not bring in a return to the firm until they have been worked up, distributed, and sold either to the next link in the distribution chain (see Chapter VII) or to the public.

If the firm is unable or unwilling to tie up sufficient liquid capital in this purchase it can go to the bank, which will lend the necessary sum on the security (if judged sufficient) of the goods; another self-liquidating loan. This is the sort of loan which bankers prefer, both because it is self-liquidating and because it is short-term.

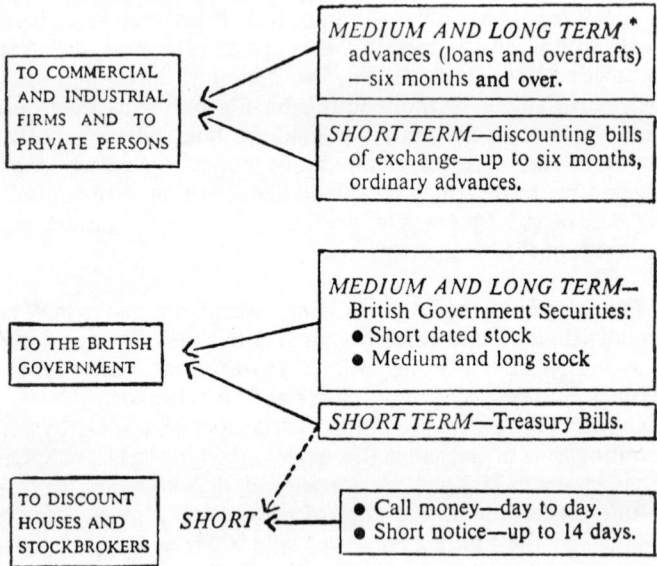

FIG. 23—BANK LOANS

* A comparatively small proportion of advances to commerce and industry is for periods of over a year.

Loans on Fixed Assets. Nevertheless, the banks often help firms, especially small firms unable to raise capital on the Stock Exchange, to extend their premises, plant or equipment, accepting the firm's assets as security and counting on repayment out of the proceeds of the extra trade brought about by the firm's expansion. A small shopkeeper wishing to move into larger premises or to install self-service equipment, or a

farmer buying a combine harvester, would turn to his bank.
Loans of this kind are sometimes made for a period of several
years.

Loans on Private Property. Private individuals may also
get loans (or, more probably, overdrafts) to meet periods of
special expense, by depositing as security insurance policies,
the title-deeds of real estate, or share certificates.

Loans to the Government: Short Term. A substantial proportion of bank loans are made to the Government. These are
of two kinds: short term and long term. Short-term loans are
made against *Treasury Bills.* They are highly liquid, and usually
run for three months. The historical reason for the incurring of
these debts (known, in total, as the 'Floating Debt') is that the
Treasury's revenue from taxation and Treasury disbursements
through the spending department and on the service of Government bonds, have never exactly coincided in time; there are
often periods when expenditure heavily outruns revenue, even
when over the whole year they come to the same amount.
Treasury Bills (like their rather clumsy and unpopular prede-
cessors, Exchequer Bills) began as a means of tiding over these
temporary deficits, just as a private trader's bills tide him over
the period of a transaction.

Later, and particularly during World War I, they developed
into a permanent though constantly revolving mass of short-
term credit, whose size still fluctuates seasonally, but which
never gets entirely, or even mostly, paid off. They are now an
important factor in monetary regulation. The Treasury may
issue them by tender[1]; this means that they are put up to a kind
of auction, going to whoever offers nearest their face value.
For instance, application may be made for a batch of three-
month Bills at a rate of £99 5s. 8d., and at the end of ninety-one

[1] In practice, it is by convention the Discount Houses which, on behalf
of the Commercial Banks, tender (in competition with various commercial
and industrial concerns and others) for Treasury Bills; the banks in turn
then buy bills from them in quantities which depend on their own supplies
of short-term money.

days the Treasury redeems them at their full face value of £100. Or they may be issued 'through the tap'; this means that the Treasury offers them at a fixed rate, in larger or smaller quantities at its discretion. 'Tap' bills are mostly taken up by Government Departments having spare balances at their disposal. The proportions in which these two methods are used depend on market technicalities too detailed for this book.

Loans to the Government: Long Term. Treasury Bills are a highly liquid form of loan, whereas the long-term loans made by the Banks to the Government are not liquid at all in the usual sense. They are mostly made on a 'long-dated' or 'medium-dated' stock with some years to run before 'redemption', that is, the date on which the Treasury becomes obliged to repay them at *par*, or face, value. One may instance War Loan, Funding Loan, Victory Bonds, etc. Not only the banks but also insurance companies, charitable and other institutions, and the general public, hold these securities, so although they are not 'liquid' in the sense of giving ground for cash payment by the debtor at short notice, they are freely marketable, and the banks can always vary their holdings according to the needs of their balance sheets.

Loans to Discount Houses and Stockbrokers. Finally, the commercial banks lend money at 'call' or at 'short notice' (i.e. for up to fourteen days) to discount houses and to stockbrokers. The amount which they lend in this way at any time depends on what ready funds they have available, as decided each day at head office. According to whether they are making additional loans, or calling existing loans in, money is said in the City to be 'easy' or 'tight'.

Foreign Exchange Transactions, The third function of the commercial bank is to exchange British money for foreign currency—and vice versa—for their clients, to meet their needs. 'Exchange control' (that is, Government regulation of the amount of foreign currencies bought and sold, and of the rates paid for them in pounds) still sets some limits upon this function, but the regulations, which from 1939 to the late 1950s concentrated the control of foreign exchange transactions in the hands of the Bank of England, have now been greatly relaxed.

Other Functions. The bankers also do for their clients a number of odd jobs which are, strictly speaking, not banking jobs at all. They act as trustees, advise on investments and on tax problems, collect dividends, and assist in the making and execution of wills. It is easy to see how these activities arose from the confidential relations of bank managers to their clients.

Meaning of a Balance Sheet. The functions of the commercial banks, as described above, can be more clearly understood by studying a simplified statement of accounts such as that of Lloyds Bank on page 203. This also illustrates something which a banker must always have in mind—namely, the correct proportion between the different types of assets held.

Liabilities. The sums owed by a banker to shareholders and customers are known as his 'liabilities'. He counts on never having to meet all these liabilities at the same time—A will be paying in while B is drawing out; and it is this certainty which gives him scope for profitable lending. He is, however, constantly having to meet a proportion of his liabilities, so he must take care to have enough cash in hand to meet day-to-day demands. The proportion now regarded as adequate is one-twelfth of total deposits. Over-optimism about the size of this necessary holding of liquid assets was the downfall of many banks—and their depositors—in the early days of banking. Early nineteenth-century records abound in thrilling stories of small banks running short of cash and desperately paying out in sixpences to stave off disaster, while the life-saving bullion was brought, full gallop across a railway-less land, by post-chaise from London. (The record for this kind of last-minute rescue was set up, during the financial crisis of 1825, with a London-to-Birmingham sprint of eight hours.) Nowadays banks are larger and wiser; there has not been a major bank failure in Britain since 1878; but bankers still have to make adequate cash their first consideration.

A bank's *capital* is provided by shareholders just as in any other joint-stock company, and constitutes a debt to them. Similarly reserves, held to meet contingencies, and undivided profits, are both liabilities (that is, debts) to the shareholders.

Deposit and current accounts, as already explained, represent the money deposited with the bank by its customers and are a liability to them.

The *acceptance* of a bill of exchange by a banker is a guarantee that the bank will pay the value of the bill when due; thus the banker assumes an obligation to meet a debt, and incurs a liability to the drawer of the bill. This is not, of course, the same thing as discounting a bill, a process which yields an asset and not a liability. The banker accepts the bill, and so shoulders the liability, for the benefit of the person on whom it is drawn, and is paid for doing so. It is worth getting the bank to act as acceptor because, with a big well-known, creditworthy name on the bill, it can be discounted more cheaply. (Interest rates, as will be remembered from Chapter XII, depend partly on the standing of the borrower.)

The Balance Sheet: Assets. The various *assets* of the bank, making up the wealth it owns and balancing the liabilities just listed, are arranged here in order of liquidity. First, obviously, comes *cash*—universally acceptable legal-tender money, ready to hand—either held by Lloyds Bank itself or available in its account at the Bank of England.

Money at call and short notice comprises loans, mainly to discount houses and stockbrokers, for periods up to fourteen days but often much less, sometimes merely overnight. Such short loans made to such safe borrowers are nearly as liquid as cash. On the other hand, the rate of interest is low—somewhere between 2 and 4 per cent in 1963.

STATEMENT OF ACCOUNTS AS AT 30th JUNE, 1962

LIABILITIES

CAPITAL:
Authorized £74,000,000

Issued:
48,733,308 shares of £1 each, fully paid .. 48,733,308
4,873,330 shares of £1 each, 10s. paid .. 2,436,665
£51,169,973

Reserve Fund:
Share Premium Account .. 2,436,665
General Reserve .. 26,000,000
28,436,665

Current, Deposit, and other Accounts, including Contingency Accounts .. 1,359,201,648
Balances in Account with Subsidiary Companies .. 2,339,542
1,361,541,190

Notes in Circulation (Isle of Man) (see Note II) .. 1,487
Acceptances 6,933,112

£1,448,082,427

NOTES.
I. Market value on the 30th June 1962 of the Investments in British Government Securities and Other Investments was greater than the figures quoted on this Statement.
II. Securities totalling £3,000 nominal are lodged for the Note Issue in the Isle of Man.
III. There are contracts running for the sale and purchase of foreign currencies amounting to £303,301,924.

ASSETS

		Ratio to Current, Deposit & other accounts %
Cash in hand and with Bank of England Balances with, and Cheques in course of collection on, other Banks in the United Kingdom and Ireland ..	£114,701,451	8·4
Money at Call and Short Notice ..	75,632,092	5·6
British Government Treasury Bills .. £172,135,000	95,330,551	7·0
British Bill of Exchange .. 14,172,970		
Dominion, Colonial and Foreign Bills and Refinanceable Credits .. 21,337,017		
Special Deposit with Bank of England ..	207,644,987	15·2
Investments (see Notes I and II):		
Securities of, or guaranteed by, the British Govt. ..	26,200,000	1·9
Other Investments, including Securities of Dominion and Colonial Governments, British Public Boards and British Municipal Corporations } quoted	201,876,494	14·8
unquoted	8,243,602	·6
	6,304,744	·5
Loans and Advances after deducting provision for Bad and Doubtful Accounts ..	613,693,606	45·1
Items in Transit ..	28,182,783	
	1,377,810,310	
Trade Investments:		
Subsidiary Companies:		
Lloyds Bank (Foreign) Limited, 24,000 Shares of £50 each, fully paid, at £50 per Share ..	1,200,000	
Lloyds Bank Executor and Trustee Company (Channel Islands) Limited, 100,000 Shares of £1 each, fully paid, at cost ..	100,000	
Other Trade Investments, at cost ..	36,242,153	2·7
NOTE. There is a contingent liability for uncalled Capital in respect of these Investments.		
Other Assets and Accounts (including sundry Properties at cost, less amounts written off) ..	7,342,588	
Bank Premises, at cost, less amounts written off ..	18,454,264	
Liabilities of Customers for Acceptances, as per contra ..	6,933,112	
	£1,448,082,427	

FIG. 24—A BANK BALANCE SHEET

Bills discounted comprise both Treasury Bills and ordinary Bills of Exchange, the latter including *trade bills* (i.e. those drawn on traders) and *bank bills* (those drawn on banks). The security for Treasury Bills consists of the entire resources of the British Government and is therefore as good as is humanly possible. Bank bills, backed by a well-known bank or acceptance house, are almost as secure; trade bills (of which every kind, good, bad, and indifferent, are to be found in the market) are usually discounted by banks only when they are drawn on firms of high standing and thus represent first-class security. (See Chapter XVI for more about discount rates.)

Cash, money at call and short notice and Bills comprise the liquid assets of a bank. It is generally accepted that, in the interests of safety, these should constitute about 30 per cent of total assets.

Special Deposits with Bank of England. These deposits were introduced in 1960, and constitute a form of credit control by the Bank of England. The joint stock banks must lodge a certain percentage of the assets with the Bank of England when called upon to do so. These deposits cannot be converted into cash; thus the liquidity ratio of the banks is reduced when a special deposit has to be made and so the bank's lending power is restricted (see p. 217).

Investments in British Government securities are the less liquid of a bank's assets, since they are only redeemable at the end of a stated number of years. The value of this kind of asset can and does fluctuate widely with changes in the rate of interest and with people's political and financial expectations. For example, suppose the Government offers $2\frac{1}{2}$ per cent Treasury stock at 100, it can be trusted to pay its $2\frac{1}{2}$ per cent regularly and to repay the stock (if redeemable) at redemption date; but meanwhile, suppose there is a rise in the market rate of interest to 3 per cent, nobody will want to spend £100 on buying the right to draw £2 10s. a year when they can get £3 a year for their £100 elsewhere; the most they will pay for that right is a sum which, by simple rule-of-three calculation, will yield 3 per cent on their outlay—that is, about £83. Thus the holder of the $2\frac{1}{2}$ per cent security who has bought at 100, if he sells when the rate of interest is 3 per cent, takes a capital loss of 27 per cent. If he holds on till the security matures he will avoid that loss, since he will get his full £100; but meanwhile he has a less than perfectly liquid asset in spite of the fact that it can readily be marketed on the Stock Exchange. On the other hand, it is obvious that $2\frac{1}{2}$ per cent or 3 per cent is a more profitable yield than the very low percentage on 'money at call and short notice'.

Advances and loans to customers earned in 1963 about $5\frac{1}{2}$ and $6\frac{1}{2}$ per cent and were thus the most profitable form of credit. They are, however, the least secure and, since they are entirely unmarketable during the period for which they are granted (usually six months) the least liquid.

Cover for acceptances usually consists of the goods concerned in the transaction for which the accepted bill is drawn, and is, of course, equal in value to the acceptances. This form of security is not very liquid as the possibilities of realizing it depend on obtaining a ready sale for the goods.

Profit and Liquidity. A banker's skill is shown in the wise distribution of his assets between different forms of credit. He must keep his position sufficiently liquid for safety—but the more liquid his assets, as we have seen, the less the return on them. He must make a profit—but the most profitable forms of lending, advances to customers and investments, are less reliably convertible into liquid cash in case of need. Moreover, he carries a wider responsibility than that towards depositors and shareholders. His position imposes a certain duty towards the business community, which counts on him to help expand trade and to fend off disaster in bad times, and a further duty towards the country at large, which, through the Treasury, looks to him to provide credit in times of especial national need. Since 1939 the commercial banks have co-operated closely with the Treasury, not only by taking up increasing quantities of the Floating Debt (see page 290), but by granting or withholding credit to borrowers according to Treasury directives.

CHAPTER XV

THE BANK OF ENGLAND

T HE Bank of England is the linchpin of the whole British financial system. It was founded by Royal Charter in 1694, when banking as we know it, with deposit and cheque facilities for the general public, scarcely existed. Its original purpose was to raise capital from the merchant class to help William III and the Government in the war against France.

Development of the Bank of England. In the course of the next century the Bank's Charter was renewed several times, giving it an increasingly exclusive right to carry on large-scale banking business. (Any individual, at that time, could set up as a banker, but the Bank's Charter, from 1708 to 1826, limited to six the number of individuals who could join forces in order to set up a bank, and so ensured that no rival house could grow large enough to challenge the Bank of England; modifications of this Charter in 1826 and in 1833 still left the Bank in a commanding position.) In return, the Bank made repeated loans to the Government, the more easily since foreign trade was rapidly expanding and bringing large capital gains to the City merchants on whose resources it was based.

The Government's Banker. The Bank never engaged seriously in deposit banking, a business which, except for a very few favoured accounts, it left to the private banker. Instead, it concentrated on the management of the Government's account and on the issue of notes. Though it had no nation-wide monopoly of note issue, as it had of joint-stock organization until 1826, there were in fact few private banks still issuing notes in London by the beginning of the nineteenth century.

The Monopoly of Note Issue. By the nineteenth century the Bank was well established and its prestige was high, which was more than could be said for the multitude of small note-issuing banks up and down the country. Note issue, so the experts of the day concluded, was better concentrated in the hands of one chosen body than entrusted to a lot of possibly irresponsible private banks. These were always tempted to over-issue for the sake of extra profit, and over-issue meant not only danger to depositors if too many notes were presented at once, but inflation—excess purchasing power forcing up prices. So in 1844 the Bank Act (see page 188) forbade the country banks to issue additional notes and provided that whenever such a bank closed down, or amalgamated with another, its notes should be called in and replaced, as to two-thirds of their quantity, by Bank of England notes. Thus, by degrees, the Bank of England became the sole note-issuing bank and, with the disappearance of gold coins in our own day, the sole source of new currency.[1]

Leadership of 'the City'. At the same time the Bank gradually assumed another function which, previously, no one had exercised; that of leadership over the whole London Money Market, which by the mid-nineteenth century had become the financial centre of the world. This role of the Bank was not deliberately worked out or consciously assumed; things just happened that way. As the biggest and most powerful financial house, the Bank became the 'lender of last resort' to whom every other financial house turned in emergency; this gave it both power and responsibility. The nature of its power, and the

[1] Except for a very small quantity of notes (now about £120 million) issued by the seven Scottish note-issuing banks. The original charter of the Bank of England, giving it a monopoly of joint-stock organization, did not cover Scotland, which in 1694 was still a separate kingdom. (The Act of Union was not passed until 1707.) The English note-issuing banks, being small and private, had to amalgamate during the nineteenth century in order to achieve adequate scale and stability—and under the Bank Charter Act of 1844 that meant that they lost their note-issuing rights. But the Scottish banks, having had the advantage of joint-stock organization from the start, were big enough to stay independent; so they kept their right of issue.

way it uses that power, will be described shortly; but quite apart from the direct action which the Bank could take in order to influence events in 'the City', it also gradually acquired a quite informal, unwritten but generally recognized title to lead and advise. The importance of this role was all the greater because the tremendous expansion in British industry and foreign trade was at the same time bringing more and more wealth to 'the City' and so making it the chief source of both long- and short-term credit for most of the civilized world.

Thus, before the nineteenth century drew to a close, the three primary functions of the Bank were well established— that is, it was already the Government's Bank, the Banker's Bank, and the controller, directly through the note issue and indirectly through its influence over the money market, of the nation's credit. Its actions, since 1939 have been entirely, and indeed almost passively, keyed to Government policy.

Co-operation with the Government. These three functions grew more and more important during the twentieth century as economic and financial problems grew more complicated, but the actual shaping of policy was, after 1914, more and more taken over by the Treasury, working in close co-operation with the Bank itself. On paper, the Bank was a private business institution; in fact, it acted as a responsible arm of the State. This development was so strengthened by World War II that when, in 1946, the Bank was nationalized, nobody noticed any substantial difference.

Function as Government Banker. Let us take the three functions in order; first, the function of Banker to the Government. The Bank of England does for the Treasury what an ordinary commercial bank does for its depositors: that is, keeps an account for the Treasury into which its revenues are paid and from which its expenses are met. This account appears in the Bank's balance sheet under the heading 'Public Deposits'. It acts as the Government's agent in raising the various long-and short-term loans (National Debt) which are needed from time to time. And it is responsible for offsetting the effects of the

P

seasonal inflows and outflows of Government money, which might otherwise have awkward results on the supply of credit in the Money Market, by buying or selling Government securities on the Stock Exchange. (As we shall see, it formerly used this same method to bring about positive changes, and not a mere smoothing-out, in credit conditions.) In fact, the *management* of the National Debt by the Bank—not just in the sense of simply raising and paying back loans, but to regulate the supply of credit and liquid assets—has become a function of supreme importance.

Finally, as agent of the Treasury, it has nowadays the important job of controlling foreign exchange, that, is, the buying and selling of foreign currencies against pounds. When war broke out in 1939 it was plain that foreign currencies were going to be far too badly needed to pay for essential imports (food, raw materials, munitions) for their holders to be allowed to use them in the normal way to buy or invest abroad for their own private benefit. So a system of *exchange control* was imposed, with regulations making it illegal to exchange pounds sterling for any foreign currency[1] without making application to the Bank of England and getting that application granted. (Before World War II anyone could buy any foreign currency he liked, at any time he liked and for any purpose he liked, either at home or abroad. Before World War I a traveller often did not even bother to buy foreign currency; he simply took a pocketful of gold sovereigns with him.) To-day these regulations, which are administered by the Bank of England, have now been considerably relaxed, but some are still in force primarily to control transactions abroad affecting capital.

Function as Bankers' Bank. The Bank of England similarly holds deposits made by the several commercial banks. The total of these accounts appears in its balance sheet as 'Other

[1] Except the currencies of the Sterling Area; that is, the British Colonies and Dominions (excluding Canada) and certain others, which kept their gold reserves at the Bank of England and were sufficiently united financially, to be treated, from this point of view, as home territory. *See* Chapter XIX.

Deposits—Bankers'. As explained in the last chapter, banks treat these deposits as cash and can draw on them immediately to supplement their actual cash holdings when necessary. They also settle accounts between themselves, according to the daily balances established at the Clearing House, by cheques on their respective Bank of England deposits. As shown below, the Bank of England can act so as to influence the size of these deposits and so—since, as we have seen, the commercial bankers have to keep a proper balance between their liquid reserves and the credit they give—to control the commercial banks' credit policy.

Function as Controller of Credit and Cash. This brings us to the third, and most important, function of the Bank of England; that of controlling the liquid assets of the banks and the amount of credit available to the public. This control is exerted so as to avoid on the one hand an insufficiency which would cause trade stagnation and unemployment (we have seen in Chapter XII how heavily business depends on credit) and on the other an over-supply which would mean inflation.

(*i*) *Control of Liquid Assets.* These consist of cash, call money and Treasury Bills and constitute about 30 per cent of the total assets of joint stock banks. Although only about 15 to 20 per cent of transactions are settled in cash, all major business being done by cheque or bill of exchange, the quantity of cash and the quantity of credit are closely related. The right to *draw* a cheque includes the right to *cash* a cheque. So it would not be safe for bankers to grant so many loans—i.e. rights to draw cheques—as to make it doubtful whether they would have enough notes and coin to honour such cheques as, in practice, people chose to cash. With more notes and coin available they can expand credit, with less notes and coin available they must contract it.

However, in recent years there has been no attempt by the Bank of England to control the amount of actual *cash* holdings by the joint stock banks because they could always convert some of their Treasury Bills into cash if they found their supplies of the latter running short, and so maintain their 8 per cent cash to total assets ratio. The Bank of England therefore has instead concentrated on urging the joint stock banks not to allow their total liquidity ratio to rise above or fall below 30 per cent. For this reason the practice was introduced in 1960 of requiring the joint stock banks to make 'Special Deposits' with the Bank of England, so as to reduce their liquidity. So the total proportion of liquidity is a kind of lever. By comparatively small movements of that lever, the Bank of England can bring about comparatively large changes in the total amount of purchasing power.

(*ii*) *Bank Rate*. The second method of control is one which from 1932 to 1951 was kept almost entirely in reserve, and whose restoration since then to the rank of a main instrument of policy has caused a great deal of argument: that is, the method of changing what is called the *Bank Rate*, the rate at which the Bank of England discounts first-class Bills of Exchange. This serves as a kind of standard for all short-term interest rates; it is the rate with reference to which all borrowers and lenders calculate. With Bank Rate at such and such a level, the rate on deposit accounts in the commercial banks is (subject to a minimum) so and so, that on the slightly riskier Bills of Exchange is so and so; and so on. Thus, by raising or lowering the Bank Rate, the Bank of England can either make all credit dearer (and so diminish the amount demanded and cause the total of purchasing power to shrink) or make all credit cheaper (and so increase the amount demanded and cause total purchasing power to expand).

Partly, such changes act merely as a signal, followed by the rest of the banking and financial world without further pressure. But, particularly when the changes were large and rapid, as they frequently were before 1932, they could also exert a powerful direct influence because of the Bank's position as 'lender of last resort'. If the Money Market's rate were too low, and the demand for credit consequently too high, the Bank would be the only lender which could satisfy it—and no one wants to take a loss by borrowing from the Bank, in order to meet his liabilities, at a higher rate than he is getting from his debtors. That risk can only be avoided by keeping all market rates in step with Bank Rate. Recent experience has shown, however, that Bank Rate in modern conditions constitutes a less supple and effective method of control than once it did. In particular, it is by no means certain that high interest rates and dear credit do have a deterrent effect on business men contemplating long-term investments as was once believed.

(*iii*) *Open Market Policy.* The third method, now used mainly as an adjunct to Bank Rate, is called *Open Market Operations.* It is a magnified form of that offsetting process of buying and selling Government securities, mentioned on page 210. The securities concerned may be Treasury Bills bought on the Discount Market, or long-dated Government securities bought on the Stock Exchange; the principle is the same.

Traditionally, this process was used by the Bank of England to restrict the quantity of cash, and thus in turn to restrict also the lending powers of the joint stock banks. As explained on page 200, it is now generally recognized that because Treasury Bills are in practice freely convertible to cash, the lending policies of the banks cannot significantly be affected by influences that alter only their cash ratios, without affecting their total liquidity. Nevertheless, the Bank of England still makes use of Open Market Operations, partly because it is to some extent possible to use them to affect the total liquid assets held by the joint stock banks, and partly because of the effect of these operations on interest rates.

It is worth first describing the function of Open Market Operations as this was formerly understood, since the mechanism has not altered, and its effects have changed less than the theory which is supposed to explain them. Suppose the Bank wishes to restrict the volume of credit in order to check inflation. It would sell, say, £10 million worth of Government securities. The buyers would pay for them by cheques drawn on their accounts at the commercial banks in favour of the Bank of England. The commercial banks would honour these cheques out of their respective Bank of England deposits, which would thus be reduced by £10 millions. Now, we have seen that the banks' deposits at the Bank of England are regarded by them as equivalent to cash, and that the proportion of their deposits held in cash is traditionally about 8 per cent. Theoretically, therefore, to keep this proportion intact the banks would be driven by the reduction in their deposits at the Bank of England to make proportionate reductions in their day-to-day loans to the discount market or in their advances to customers, the total reduction in credit resulting being of the order not of £10 millions but of £125 millions, as an 8 per cent cash-to-deposits ratio would give a leverage of $12\frac{1}{2}$ to 1. Conversely, by buying Government securities, the Bank would put more money, through the hands of sellers of those securities, into the commercial banks' accounts, and thus would make it safe for them to expand credit in a similar proportion. There are several things wrong with this traditional analysis. The first, already mentioned, is that the banks are not seriously concerned about a change in the *composition* of their liquid assets—they worry only about the *total* of these assets. Thus they are not directly affected by a fall in their cash ratio, if it merely means that the cash is converted into Treasury Bills. They will not call in their advances or sell their investments just because their cash ratio falls below 8 per cent. Nor will they worry if, having started out (as is quite often the case) with a comfortably large ratio of liquid assets to deposits—say, 33 per cent or 34 per cent—they find that this liquidity ratio has been reduced to 31 per cent. It is only when the ratio drops below the accepted level of 30 per cent that they will be forced to reduce credit. And when this happens, the leverage exerted is not $12\frac{1}{2}$ to 1, but at best about $3\frac{1}{3}$ to 1 (the proportion of deposits to *total* liquid assets), so that a reduction of £10 millions in their liquid assets is not likely to bring about a reduction of credit of more than about £33$\frac{1}{3}$ millions. Moreover, the actual leverage may be even lower than this, since it is now thought that when the Bank of England buys or sells Government securities, a part of the increased or decreased cash holdings of the joint stock banks is taken up by the public.

In spite of all this, Open Market Operations are of value.

In the first place, they still have some direct influence on the banks. More important, Open Market Operations by the Bank of England, by providing the Money Market with either an ample or a scarce supply of Treasury Bills, influence the rate of interest for short-term money, thus effectively backing up the standard for interest rates set by the official Bank Rate. And finally, Open Market Operations have a practical effect as a signal to the joint stock banks of the kind of credit policies which the Bank of England wishes them to apply. It hardly matters that the banks can, when their cash balances at the Bank of England fall, avoid reducing their loans and advances by holding Treasury Bills; they know that the signal has been given to reduce their lending, and that if they disregard it, they may find the Bank applying pressure by less gentle means—as, for instance, by increasing the proportion of their assets which are to be placed on Special Deposit (see page 217).

Other Forms of Financial Control. The Bank of England and the Treasury have developed further means of controlling credit. The Act of 1946, by which the Bank of England was nationalized, converted the informal influences which it had previously exercised into a legal right to give directions to the joint stock banks. These usually take the form of a request to banks either to curtail their advances to customers generally or to be more selective in their lending, e.g. to cut down their loans except to the export industries and to farmers.

The Bank Return. Every week the Bank of England issues a 'Return' or statement of its accounts. The one issued on 29th November, 1962 is shown in Table VIII on the next page. It is issued in two parts, relating to the Issue Department and the Banking Department, because under the Bank Act of 1844 these two types of business must legally be kept separate. The Issue Department return shows on the one side the amount of notes, whether in public circulation or held in the Banking Department, on the other the backing for these notes, which is overwhelmingly 'fiduciary'. There is only a historical distinction between 'Government Debt' and the 'Other Government

Securities' which comprise most of the Issue Department's assets; the small 'Other Securities' holding represents loans to the Indian and Dominion governments. 'Coin other than gold coin' explains itself. Before 1932 'Gold Coin and Bullion' would have stood at a very much higher figure, but in 1939 this reserve was transferred to a special account, the Exchange Equalization Account, which had been used since 1932 (for reasons explained on page 272) to prevent inconvenient changes in foreign exchange rates.

TABLE VIII—BANK OF ENGLAND RETURN

ISSUE DEPARTMENT

	£		£
Notes issued:		Govt. debt .	11,015,100
In circulation	2,330,099,990	Other Govt. se-	
In banking		curities	2,362,966,953
department	45,260,070	Other securities	755,641
		Coin other than	
		gold coin ..	262,306
		Fiduciary issue	2,375,000,000
		Gold coin and	
		bullion† ..	360,060
	£2,375,360,060		£2,375,360,060

BANKING DEPARTMENT

	£		£
Capital ..	14,553,000	Govt. securities	303,083,393
Rest	3,407,626	Other securities:	
Public deposits	13,171,088	Discounts and	
Special deposits	80,800,000	advances ..	59,182,353
Other deposits*		Securities ..	20,237,209
Bankers ..	243,424,379	Notes	45,260,070
Other accounts	73,258,691	Coin	850,759
	£428,614,784		£428,614,784

* Including Exchequer, Savings Banks, Commissioners of National Debt, and Dividend Accounts.   † Taken at 250s. 3d. an oz. fine.

The Banking Department's return also shows some historical survivals of no present importance. The 'capital' of £14.5 millions used to belong to private shareholders and now belongs to the Government; the 'Rest' is a form of reserve, not really different from other capital. The 'Public Deposits' are those made by the Government and its Departments; this item swells or shrinks over the year according to the inflow of revenue from taxes and National Savings and the outflow of expenditure on the Government's activities. 'Special Deposits' were first introduced in 1960. The joint stock banks can be ordered to place a certain percentage of their deposits with the Bank of England in order to curtail their lending power. These deposits remain 'frozen' at the Bank until the Treasury decides that a proportion or the whole, depending on economic conditions, may be released. (See page 204.) 'Other Deposits: Bankers' is, of course, the total of the commercial banks' balances with the Bank of England, already discussed; 'Other Accounts' comprises the deposits of the Indian Government, Foreign and Dominion Banks, and a few other privileged customers, such as the Ecclesiastical Commissioners, for whom the Bank performs ordinary banking business.

On the Assets side, 'Government Securities' shows the amount of Bonds and Treasury Bills held by the Bank; it is this total which rises or falls when the Bank undertakes Open Market Operations, with a corresponding fall or rise in the 'Other Deposits: Bankers' mentioned in the last paragraph. Of the 'Other Securities', 'Discounts and Advances' represents both the value of the bills of exchange discounted by the Bank for its ordinary customers (and the credit extended to them by way of loans or overdrafts) and the value of bills *re-discounted* for the Discount Houses (that is to say, in effect, of credit advanced to the Money Market).

The 'Securities' item is made up of the bonds and short-term bills of governments other than that of Great Britain, and also debentures representing loans to a few industrial firms and to semi-public finance institutions such as the Finance Corporation for Industry and the Industrial and Commercial Finance Corporation, set up to supply industry with medium-term credit for periods longer than the commercial banks allowed, but too short (as a rule) to make an issue of shares worth while.

Finally, the item 'Notes' corresponds to that on the liabilities side of the Issue Department Return. This and the silver coin constitutes the country's final reserve of legal tender.

CHAPTER XVI

THE MONEY MARKET

LIKE any other market (cf. Chapter VII), the Money Market is a means of bringing buyers and sellers together and establishing a price which will balance supply and demand. The difference between it and other markets is that what is bought and sold is not goods or services but different kinds of credit, supplied by those who have funds to spare at the moment, and demanded by those who need more funds than, at the moment, they have got. We have seen how wide is the range between types of credit, from that needed to finance a new steelworks to that needed to carry a bill three days from maturity, and from that demanded by a small shopkeeper to that demanded by a government. Corresponding to this wide range, there is really not one single Money Market but a whole complicated system of specialized markets.

We naturally associate the Money Market with the City of London, because that is where most of the banks and finance houses which constitute the market are to be found. It must be remembered, however, that wherever there is a bank, however remote, there exists the means of bringing together lenders and borrowers.

Pre-eminence of London before 1914. Up to the outbreak of World War I the London Money Market was the chief market for credit, whether long or short term, of the whole civilized world. Bills were discounted and accepted not only for commercial transactions concerned with goods exported from or imported to Great Britain, but for trade between other countries all over the globe. Not only the British Government, and British enterprise, but foreign governments and foreign business men, looked to London as the natural source of long-term loans and the natural channel through which to invest. There were, of course, other large financial centres, but none approaching the pre-eminence of London. This pre-eminence was the result partly of the wealth created by nineteenth-century technical and commercial progress, and partly of the financial skill, aptitude, and reputation for straight dealing built up through long years of experience by London bankers and financiers.

Effect of Wars and Depression. After World War I this pre-eminence diminished; a much poorer Britain could no longer supply large quantities of long-term foreign credit, a much richer America was in a better position to do so. The big depression of the 1930s, which cut down international trade even more than it did trade in general, because every country tried to keep up employment by keeping out imports, greatly reduced the demand both for short-term loans and long-term investments; and the abandonment of the Gold Standard in 1931 (see Chapter XIII) made foreigners less enthusiastic about using a less reliable pound. Finally, World War II left us with no spare capital to lend and indeed with an urgent need to borrow capital ourselves; while the widespread trade and currency restrictions which continued after the war prevented the Money Market's activities from returning to their old pattern.

Nevertheless, the Money Market adapted itself to changed conditions and still plays an important part not only in home financial affairs but in those of the outside world. In the Sterling Area it remains as pre-eminent as ever. The following are the various institutions which directly or indirectly form part of the machinery of the Money Market: the Bank of England; the commercial banks (including the Scottish, Irish, the Dominion, Colonial and foreign banks); the Discount Houses; the Merchant Bankers; the Investment Trusts; the Insurance Companies; and the Stock Exchange.

The Bank of England and the commercial banks have already been discussed. The term 'Money Market' does not properly include them, but they are obviously essential to that market's working, and the Bank of England, in addition, wields powers of control over the cash and credit in which it deals.

The Discount Houses and Bill Brokers. These are really highly specialized banks. There are about twelve, the number having been considerably reduced by amalgamation and closing down during the lean 1930s. Up till that period the discount houses were, as their name implies, specialists in the discounting of foreign bills of exchange (see Chapter XIII). When the volume of these bills fell off in the depression years, they had to turn to other outlets for investment and rely on advances to the Government by way of Treasury Bills, which, as we have seen, carry a lower rate of interest and are accordingly less profitable.

During the war years the volume of Treasury and trade bills available to the discount houses shrank. Their facilities and experience were used by the Government in handling the new medium- and short-term securities.

Since the war, their business has edged back towards normal. The Government once again relies on Treasury Bills for its short-term finance; and the expansion of overseas trade has increased the supply of bills of exchange requiring to be discounted—though not to the old scale. In addition, the discount houses have retained from the war years the function they then acquired of being the principal dealers in short-term Government securities (i.e. securities due for repayment within three years).

Methods of Discount Houses. Whatever the type of bill discounted, the discount houses work with a comparatively small supply of capital of their own and supplement this by borrowing short-term funds from both home and foreign banks, which, as we have seen, make them available at a low rate of interest as and when they find it convenient. The discount houses' profit is made out of the difference between this very low rate which the banks charge them and the higher rate which they charge the drawer of the bill. Their skill consists partly in judging how big a volume of business they can handle, given the current 'easiness' or 'tightness', that is, abundance or scarcity, of loanable money, and partly in judging the element of risk attached to each bill, according to the record and current standing of the acceptor, and adjusting their rates of discount accordingly.

The Merchant Bankers. Most of the surviving merchant banks or private banks were originally family businesses, and for the most part trading rather than banking firms in the first instance, though with the lapse of time they have come to concentrate their activities on finance rather than on actual dealing in goods. A minority were finance houses from their beginnings; some of these were originally foreign firms which moved to London from Continental centres. (The Rothschilds are a case in point; there is a network of Rothschild houses, still closely linked, after two hundred years, by family ties, in a number of European centres as well as in London.)

For the most part the merchant bankers handle all kinds of banking business, but their depositors among the general public are comparatively few. To varying degrees, they specialize in two particular kinds of financial operation; the accepting of bills, and the 'floating'—i.e. issuing to the public—of long-term loans and share issues for companies and for Dominion and Foreign Governments. Hence they are often referred to as 'Acceptance Houses' or 'Issuing Houses'. Most of them fulfil both functions, though there are some Issuing Houses which do not carry out acceptance work.

Acceptance. In its simplest form, acceptance is merely guaranteeing a bill; i.e. taking the responsibility of meeting it if the person on whom it is drawn fails to pay up. (Authors of old-fashioned novels, looking for a comparatively blameless way of getting their heroes into serious financial trouble, often made them good-naturedly perform this service for a friend, and find themselves sold up when the 'friend' defaulted.) The advantage of getting a bill guaranteed by someone better known and with bigger resources than oneself is obvious; it can be discounted

at a better rate—it is worth more in ready cash—because of the
reduced risk of default which the discounter has to carry. Thus
it is worth while to pay something for the use of an acceptor's
name and reputation. Professional acceptors do not, of course,
lend their name in the lighthearted manner of a Victorian
novelist's hero; it is their business to know their client's standing and the conditions of the trade or the country with which
the transaction is concerned, and to act accordingly. Also, and
again unlike the Victorian hero, they do not accept more bills
than, on a conservative estimate of risks, they can honour.
Consequently, a bill which has been accepted by a merchant
banker is known to be safe. Such bills are termed *bank* bills, as
distinct from *trade* bills, which are those accepted by traders
only. The difference in discount rates is illustrated by the
following excerpt from *The Times* of 11th May 1963:

Bank Bills	3 months $3\frac{7}{8}$–3 per cent
	6 months $3\frac{7}{8}$–4 per cent
Fine Trade Bills[1]	3 months 5–$5\frac{1}{2}$ per cent

The merchant banker, however, does much more than
merely lend his name. On the basis of his special knowledge of
a particular country or region he is able to act as agent for
traders or banks of that area in their commercial relations with
Great Britain. Often a foreign bank will arrange with a London
merchant banker for a large credit of perhaps several hundred
thousand pounds. The traders of that country, by arrangement with their bank, will then be able to take advantage of the
credit; they can pay for the goods which they buy in Great
Britain by bills drawn directly on the merchant banker.

Credits for Foreign Trade. Again, a firm in the United
Kingdom may wish to sell goods to a merchant in a foreign
country. Instead of the British firm drawing bills on the foreign
merchant, of whose credit standing it may know very little,
it will arrange to draw them on an acceptance house which
is familiar with the country concerned and the credit-worthiness
of its firms. Thus it obtains, instead of a 'trade bill' of dubious

[1] i.e. backed by a well-recognized name.

negotiability, a 'bank bill' which any discount house will be glad to buy. The acceptance house will arrange to receive payment through its branch or agent in the importing country, and will cover itself against the risk of default by holding certain 'documents of title',[1] such as bills of lading, so that if the worst comes to the worst it can claim the goods which are the subject of the transaction and recoup itself by selling them.

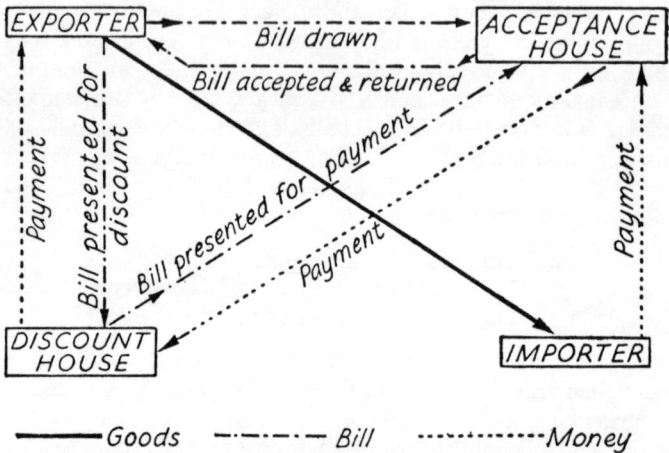

FIG. 25—THE FUNCTION OF ACCEPTANCE HOUSES

Issue Business. A completely different activity of the merchant bankers is their function as Issuing Houses. In the past they have played a very important part in acting as agents for Dominion or foreign governments or firms who wished to obtain capital in this country. In 1939 Great Britain had about £4,000 million of capital invested overseas. Most of this had been raised on the London Money Market during the prosperous century before 1914, when large amounts of liquid capital seeking a profitable outlet could be readily channelled into the vast capital projects—railways, docks, factories, public utilities —needed for the economic development of the 'new' coun-

[1] This legal phrase described documents which enable the holders to establish a legal claim to the goods which they represent.

tries overseas. The merchant bankers responsible for raising these loans in the first place also acted as agents for paying interest or dividends to the British investor on the borrowers' behalf. Since 1939, the merchant bankers' activities in floating foreign loans have almost ceased; a new foreign issue must have Treasury sanction and is a rare event. They do, however, raise considerable sums for investment in the Commonwealth and they also handle debt services for the British foreign investments which still exist.

The merchant bankers also act as issuing houses for industrial and commercial firms in the United Kingdom who wish to raise long-term capital—which, as we have seen, is not provided by the commercial banks. This raising of capital for home purposes has in fact made up most of their work for the last two decades.

'Underwriting' of New Capital Issues. In effect, they act as intermediaries between the public and the business firm in need of capital. They do not invest or lend their own capital on long term; what they generally do is either to buy up the whole of the share issue, and then to offer it themselves to the public by announcements in the Press, turning their capital back into liquid form as the public buys the shares, or to 'underwrite', i.e. guarantee, the sale of the issue, so that the firm offering the shares can be relieved of the risk of having any left unsold on its hands and consequently being short of capital. (There are frequent references to these transactions in the City columns of the Press.) A single issuing house rarely takes on the sole responsibility of underwriting an issue, but shares it out with other houses.

Apart from these special functions, the merchant brokers do ordinary banking business, accepting deposits and safeguarding securities. Their clients, however, are mostly governments, firms, and private individuals in the foreign countries with which each is particularly associated by past experience.

Other Issuing Houses. Besides the merchant bankers there are other firms which act as issuing houses. Some specialize

Q

entirely in providing long-term capital. Of these, some again specialize in one particular branch of industry, e.g. mining. Unlike the ordinary issuing houses, these actually invest their own capital on long term, holding a proportion of the newly issued securities as part of their own resources. A similar function is carried out, though only as a side activity, by the *insurance companies* and *building societies*. (The latter do not do any building, but lend money on the security of house property, borrowing from the public, at a lower rate of interest than they charge their clients, in order to be able to do so.) The sums received in premiums by insurance companies each year amount to some millions of pounds. Some of this money is invested in Government securities—obviously, an insurance company must be in a position to meet claims in cash and some in ordinary shares without delay—but a portion is diverted to financing, mainly on mortgages, building construction and various industrial projects. The same applies to the surplus funds of the building societies. Finally, a certain amount of issuing work is undertaken by stockbroking firms, which follow the same procedure as the issuing houses proper. But the main work of the Stock Exchange is of a different kind entirely and requires separate treatment.

Investment Trusts. These are joint-stock companies whose entire capital is invested in a wide range of securities and shares. By buying the shares of an investment trust, instead of investing directly in the shares of particular enterprises, the ordinary investor without special knowledge to guide him is able to spread his risks.

A further development in this direction, in recent years, has been the appearance of the Unit Trusts whose capital is held mainly in ordinary shares. These institutions receive small deposits from the public who are thus able to put their savings into a wide selection of ordinary shares without the expense and formality of Stock Exchange transactions.

The Stock Exchange. All the Money Market institutions so far discussed are primarily concerned with *new* credit. The

Stock Exchange is primarily the market for what one might call second-hand credit. It provides the means by which holders of existing securities who wish to sell, and would-be holders who want to buy, can be brought together. It is a highly professional closed market; ordinary members of the public cannot themselves operate there, and the privilege of doing so has to be paid for at a high price. The would-be Stock Exchange member must, after having undergone a period of two years' training with a Member Firm, acquire a Nomination, which costs about £1,200 (depending on the demand for membership). He must be proposed and seconded, and then be interviewed by a committee of the Stock Exchange Council. If elected, he pays an entrance fee of £1,050 and an annual subscription of £189.

Brokers and Jobbers: a Typical Transaction. Stock Exchange operators are of two distinct kinds: *brokers* and *jobbers*. The brokers deal with the public as agents; the jobbers buy from, or sell to, the brokers exclusively, and act as principals on their own account. The easiest way to describe the function of the Stock Exchange is to see what happens in the course of a single transaction. Mr. Brown, let us say, has received a legacy of £500. It is sitting in his current account at the bank, earning nothing. He could put it in a Post Office account and get 2½ per cent interest, but he would like something better and is prepared to forgo the certainty which the Post Office offers in order to get a higher yield.

If there happened to be an attractive new issue advertised in the Press he could write direct to the issuing house and apply for £500 worth of the new shares at their advertised price; but none of the current new issues strikes him as attractive enough. He has been keeping track of the movements of share prices as recorded in the daily Press, and has noticed that F. W. Woolworth's Ordinary 5s. shares have been changing hands at steadily increasing prices, the previous day's rise having been from 44s. 3d. to 44s. 6d. On the strength of past dividend payments and his judgment of future prospects, he believes this rise will continue. He therefore instructs his broker (who has an office outside the Stock Exchange and can be approached by tele-phone or letter) to buy 200 Woolworth's Ordinary shares at any price up to an outside limit of 45s. (this leaves him a small margin). What happens next?

The broker has not got the shares himself; so when the Exchange opens he looks for a jobber who will be able to supply them. Jobbers are always specialists, each dealing only with a particular type of share or stock, e.g. Government securities. Jobbers sharing the same speciality are always to be found in the same part of the 'House' (the Stock Exchange trading area). The broker, then, knows where to look. But he does not, when he finds an appropriate jobber, offer to buy the shares from him. He merely asks their price, not saying whether he wants to buy or to sell. The jobber then quotes two prices, a higher one at which he will sell and a lower one at which he will buy; in this instance perhaps '44s. 9d., 44s. 3d.'. Nowadays, jobbers are sometimes unwilling to quote their prices and to enter into a very large deal without first knowing whether the broker intends to buy or sell.

This sixpenny spread (it might be wider or narrower accord-ing to the jobber's estimate of how risky it is to deal in these particular shares) is known as the 'jobber's turn' and is his profit margin and source of livelihood. When the broker is satisfied that he cannot get better terms by bargaining or by looking elsewhere, he will accept the offer and reveal that he is a buyer. Both parties then record the deal in their notebooks; and next day their respective clerks meet and arrange for the actual legal transfer of the shares to their new owner, the draw-ing up of a deed of transfer, the notification of Woolworth's so that their list of shareholders may be amended, and so on. For transactions in British Government stocks, payment is made at once; for others, it is postponed to the end of the 'Account', a fortnightly period. At that date the broker pays the jobber and collects from Mr. Brown the price of the shares—£447 10s.—plus his commission and the amount of the Stamp Duty or Government tax on the transfer document. From Mr. Brown's point of view, the transaction is over.

Importance of the Stock Exchange. Where did the shares come from which the jobber sold to Mr. Brown's broker? He may have been holding them for some time—the jobbers' holding of shares is a kind of buffer stock, building up when there are more people wanting to sell, running down when there are more people wanting to buy, and thus doing something to keep prices stable. But either recently—possibly the same day—or at some earlier time, he has bought them (at the lower of the two prices he was quoting at that date) from a broker whom some other client, say a Mr. Jones, has instructed to sell.

In effect, what has happened is that there has been a transfer of the Woolworth's shares by way of the Stock Exchange machinery from Mr. Jones to Mr. Brown. Mr. Jones has the cash—and Mr. Brown has the shares he wants. Mr. Jones could not have got his money back from Woolworth's—he was not a short-term creditor but a part owner; Mr. Brown could not have asked Woolworth's to sell him shares, because they were not making an issue at the time. The Stock Exchange has given to the shares a liquidity which they would otherwise lack, and ensured (by way of the competition between jobbers) a single market price for them. If there were no such certain means of turning securities back into cash, and of varying one's holding, investment would be a much less attractive proposition. The Stock Exchange also helps to safeguard the investor by imposing strict rules of conduct on its members, who are responsible for fulfilling their contracts even should they be let down by a client, and by admitting to its list of 'official quotations' only the shares of firms which its Council regards as reliable. In all these ways it helps to mobilize free capital and so contribute to economic progress—to which free capital is essential.

'Right' and 'Wrong' Kinds of Speculation. Unfortunately, the same machinery which does this essential job can be used for that harmful kind of speculation which widens, instead of smoothing out, price changes, and so increases instead of decreasing the wasteful element of guesswork in business. It will be remembered, from the discussion of commodity markets in Chapter VII, that the informed speculator does a useful and

indeed essential job. Buying cheap what is plentiful now, selling at a profit when the glut is over, he spreads supplies more evenly over time and so benefits both producers and consumers. In the same way the informed speculator on the Stock Exchange, who buys a promising share in order to sell it at a profit when the promise of a high yield is fulfilled, evens out its price; he makes that price a more reliable index of the firm's fortunes and credit-worthiness. Obviously, a firm whose shares are quoted at a high price will be better placed either to borrow on short term or to issue new shares; the high price shows that its assets are valuable and its prospects good.

But the uninformed speculator who goes by rumour (sometimes set afoot by interested parties) buying blindly and selling in a panic, produces quite the opposite effect. So do the operators who make it their deliberate practice, by judicious setting-off of buying and selling waves, to stimulate these uninformed speculators to optimism or pessimism. The kind of upward and downward movements thus caused can give a totally false impression of credit-worthiness, so that one industry may be over-expanded and another starved of capital, with general misdirection of the national resources. It was of New York's Wall Street, not the London Stock Exchange, that Lord Keynes said that capital development had become 'the by-product of the activities of a casino', but the danger of securities becoming mere gambling counters is always present and has sometimes been only too well realized. Here is an often-used argument for taking capital development outside the market process altogether and making it a matter of official credit allocation. The trouble with central allocation, however, is the difficulty of making it correspond either to the technical possibilities open to industry or to the preferences of consumers for more of this rather than more of that. Judgment of these things (remember Chapter XII) is business judgment, and it is an open question whether the advantages of central allocation—disinterestedness, the long view, the possibility of ignoring the effects of Stock Exchange fluctuations when this seems desirable—outweigh the disadvantage of losing the profit-and-loss yardstick provided by free dealings in credit and securities.

CHAPTER XVII

THE VALUE OF MONEY

IT is time to hark back, after the technicalities of the last two chapters, to a more general view of money and its importance in economic affairs. Its most obvious job, as we saw in Chapter XIII, is to serve as a *medium of exchange*, thus making possible the complex exchanges of goods and services which could be managed only with great inconvenience, or sometimes not at all, by barter. But it has the equally important job of serving as a *measure of value*. The value of commodities is reckoned in money. So are the values of land and of human energy. This fact can be looked at in two ways. If things have a value in terms of money, then money has a value in terms of things. When it takes more money to buy a given assortment of things, we say that their *prices* have risen; it is only another way of describing the same change to say that the *value of money* has fallen. More of it is now needed to buy a given quantity of goods than was needed to buy the same quantity in the past.

Real and Monetary Influences on the Value of Money. Many different causes may bring about a change in the general price level, or, in other words, a change in the value of money. These causes, however, fall into two broad classes; those acting through the *goods* side of the comparison and those acting through the *money* side. These are generally called, respectively, *real* and *monetary* influences.

If the supply of goods in general is cut down (as by a blockade or a natural catastrophe) while people are still getting the same money incomes and are still trying to spend the same amount, then prices will rise—that is, the value of money will fall. Or, if people's attitudes change so that, with the same supply of goods forthcoming, they try to spend more and to save less, the same result will follow, even without a change in their total incomes. In the first case, the same amount of spending money is chasing a diminished supply of goods; in the second, a bigger amount of spending money, derived from the same incomes, is chasing the same amount of goods. Both these causes (and, of course, their opposites, an increase of goods or a decrease in actual spending) are independent of anything which the central monetary authority can do; they are not started off by any action on the part of the Bank of England.

Of course, some goods can become scarcer, and other goods more plentiful, without affecting the value of money at all; and some people may take to spending a bigger part of their incomes, while others take to spending less, without affecting the value of money at all. It is the big, general movements which count. Big, general movements are, on the whole, rare; the real, non-monetary, influences working to change the value of money are in practice unimportant beside the *monetary* influences, those springing from the actions of Governments and Central Banks. Although there have been ups and downs, the actions of Governments and Central Banks have, as a matter of historical fact, generally been such as to *reduce* the value of money; to bring about, that is, some degree of *inflation*.

Inflation. The meaning of this word is, literally, a blowing-up, a swelling-out. When the supply of money coming into people's hands is blown up or expanded without a proportional increase in the supply of goods in general, then (except in the unlikely event of everyone deciding to save the whole surplus instead of spending it), that extra money will enter the market for goods in general and, by the familiar process of competition, drive up prices. If one lot of prices is kept down by controls, then it will drive up other prices still more. If no controls are imposed, then the price of necessaries will rise along with everything else; wage-earners will feel cheated and demand higher pay to meet the higher cost of living; costs of production will consequently rise in the wake of prices; with the bigger wage incomes once again entering the market to drive up prices, and with higher costs in the background, a further price rise will follow; and so again and again in what is called the *inflationary spiral*.

War as a Cause of Inflation. What starts the process? Why are incomes inflated in the first place? The most frequent cause is war and post-war dislocation. The evident and simplest starting-point is the decision of a Government, faced by the enormous expenses of war, not to raise the necessary funds by taxation or by long-term loans, but merely to drop whatever limits may have been set to the issue of currency and print a lot more paper money for its own use. That money is spent on paying the armed forces, on settling with contractors (who in turn pay it out to their suppliers and their workers), on renting land and factories, on the salaries of wartime administrators and their staffs. None of these recipients are producing goods in the ordinary sense, goods which go to make up the standard of living. Indeed, unless they were all previously idle, they are actually withdrawn from the production of such goods, thus decreasing the supply. But they all want to spend the money they get on goods in the ordinary sense; and so, as indicated in the last paragraph, prices rise—the value of money falls. When extra government spending is financed by taxes or long-term loans there is no such direct inflationary effect, because private spending is cut down by much the same amount as public spending increases. There is some inflationary effect if tax rates increase very steeply, because people who find it hard to cut their spending very severely may stop saving, or draw on past savings, in order to maintain their standards; and there is an indirect inflationary effect when taxes remain very high for a long time, because people begin to calculate what any transaction—such as a wage bargain—will bring them *net of tax*, and make demands accordingly. But neither is comparable, in size and violence, with the effect of actually inflating the supply of cash by direct Government issue.

Inflation through the Credit System. As one might realize from a study of the last two chapters, matters need not begin with a big printing of new notes. They may begin with short-term Government borrowing, from the Bank of England and the Money Market, on Treasury Bills. These do not circulate among the general public, so they do not drive up prices in the same direct and obvious way. But they do appear in the books of the banks as safe, liquid, negotiable securities, so that the banks feel able to increase their loans—and that means more purchasing power in the hands of borrowers in general. Since 'every loan creates a deposit' (see page 196), they increase the amount of bank money—the total of bank deposits —by several times their own volume. Sooner or later, cash has to be increased too; for otherwise the banks' cash ratio would fall below the safe minimum, and the Government, which started the whole process as a matter of public policy, is bound to safeguard their position.

Broadly speaking, that is the mechanism of inflation as we have seen it in Great Britain during and since World War II, and as is shown by the following table:

TABLE IX—INCREASE IN NOTE CIRCULATION AND BANK
DEPOSITS, 1938–62

	Average Quantity of Notes in Circulation (£ million)	Average Quantity of Bank Deposits (£ million)
1938	486	2,277
1946	1,358	5,097
1955	1,760	6,454
1962	2,327	7,611

Though these figures are striking, they represent a mild rate of inflation compared with what happened in Germany after World War I, and in Hungary and China after World War II. There, inflation reached a point where the currencies became practically waste paper, prices having risen so high that a barrow-load of money, of a face value of millions, was needed to buy a basketful of groceries. (One odd result was that as the price of postage rose, people having bought stamps a week or so earlier found there was not room on the envelopes for enough stamps to meet the new rates; so that a letter from Germany in 1923 was apt to arrive with a dangling flap of paper attached, entirely covered with stamps.) Between these extremes and the British experience of roughly a 170 per cent price rise one might quote the example of the French, who have seen the franc fall to about one-tenth of its 1938 value.

It is possible, moreover, to have a considerable inflation even on a strict metallic standard which allows no increase, directly or indirectly caused, of unbacked paper money. During the sixteenth century there was a substantial increase in the quantity of silver coinage in Western Europe, because of the influx of silver from Spain's New World empire. This undoubtedly helped to bring about the persistent rise in prices which marked that century. Again, in the nineteenth century, it is possible to trace in the upward movement of prices the effect of the new gold discoveries, first in California and later in South Africa (see Layton and Crowther, *Introduction to the Study of Prices*). *Anything*—whether an increase in the supply of the standard monetary metal or an action by Government or Central Bank on the supply of notes and credit—*which increases the quantity of money available is likely to increase prices*.

Deflation. Conversely, anything which decreases the supply of liquid assets is likely to decrease prices. So the way to lower the price level and restore the value of money is, on the face of it, simple; it is to reduce the supply, by methods described in Chapter XV. This process is called *deflation*. Between 1920, the peak of the inflation induced by World War I, and 1925, the Bank of England successfully carried out a policy of deflation. The Bank Rate was raised to 7 per cent (compared with $2\frac{1}{2}$ per cent until the end of 1951), thus discouraging borrowing and cutting down the volume of bank deposits. Government spending was drastically cut and the amount of floating (i.e. short-term) debt was reduced accordingly; in December 1920 the value of Treasury Bills outstanding was £1,102m., in 1924 it was £626m. The result was that over these five years prices in general were roughly halved; a pound in 1925 was worth, in goods and services, twice what it was worth in 1920.

The cost inflation which has been a feature of our economy of the 1950s and early 1960s could probably be checked by such a vigorous deflationary policy. Unfortunately the necessary action (high interest rates, curtailment of lending and reduction in government expenditure) would, almost certainly, reduce productivity and cause considerable unemployment—a policy which, nowadays, no government would be willing to pursue. (See page 275.)

Effect of Changes in the Value of Money: (i) Distribution. If inflation or deflation took place, as it were, all of one piece, they would have no effect on economic life one way or another. If everyone were to wake up one morning and find that they had twice as much money in their pockets and bank accounts as the night before (and could expect their future incomes to keep the same proportion) but that all prices in the shops, rents, etc., had doubled, each one of them would be precisely as well off as before. And the same would hold good if, instead of being doubled, incomes and prices were halved.

But, of course, that is not what happens. Increases in money incomes reach some people before they reach others; so do decreases. Some people's incomes are rapidly adjusted to a change in prices; others are adjusted slowly or not at all. When prices rise, holders of fixed-interest-bearing securities (such as Government bonds, or debentures) lose buying power in proportion to the increase; when prices fall, they gain. The same thing is true of beneficiaries from pensions and annuities and from social insurance payments. Wage earners suffer from inflation to the extent that their earnings rise less rapidly than do prices (as they are apt to do) and gain from deflation to the extent that their earnings fall less rapidly than prices (as, again, they are apt to do). Business men, on the other hand, generally gain from inflation because, as we have seen, production takes time, so that costs incurred at an early stage, when prices are lower, are covered with an extra big profit margin when goods are sold at a later stage, after prices have risen; and, conversely, they generally lose by deflation because costs are incurred at a higher price level and returns received at a lower. (Both their gains and losses are less than they look on paper, because at the next round the inflationary gain is partly swallowed up in replacing materials, fuel, worn-out equipment and so forth at higher prices, and the deflationary loss is partly recouped by the fall in the prices of these same necessaries of production.) Investors have sought to share in the inflationary gains of business in recent years, and also to provide themselves with a 'hedge' or protection against the continuing decrease in the value of money, by buying shares in preference to fixed-interest-bearing securities, such as government stocks.

In general, debtors score in an inflation because the real value of their debts (i.e. value in terms of actual goods) is reduced; creditors, for the same reason, lose. In a deflation, their positions are reversed. One reason which tempts monetary authorities to inflate, and discourages them from deflating, is that inflation reduces the 'burden of the National Debt'. Taxes come in in a bigger flow to match the higher price level, but holders of Government bonds only have to be paid their interest at the old level and thus get a smaller share of the national income. In deflation, on the other hand, taxes on the generally lower money incomes yield less, interest has to be paid at the old rate, and the holders of Government bonds get a bigger share. The 'burden of the National Debt' is very much a figure of speech, since it is members of the nation who get the income concerned (see Chapter XXI); but for various reasons which will be clearer after we have studied National Finance, this out-of-one-pocket-into-another transaction has, when it gets beyond a certain scale, its inconvenience for the Exchequer.

(*ii*) *Employment.* This effect of inflation and deflation on the way the real national income is distributed is not, however, the whole story. If it were, stopping an inflation and restoring the old balance would be a comparatively simple matter. The trouble is that inflation and deflation have very different effects on the volume of business done, on actual production, on the level of employment. Inflation stimulates the business man. He sees bright prospects of profit as eager buyers, with extra money in their pockets, snap up his goods at higher prices. He speeds up his activities. He takes on more workers; he also buys more equipment, plans extensions to his works, and increases his orders for raw materials, all of which actions stimulate other business men to speed up *their* activities and take on more workers themselves. When all the most suitable workers are engaged the less suitable ones are taken on; the untrained, the elderly, the 'bad bargains'. Except in the most difficult areas where some highly localized trade may be failing to share the general prosperity, unemployment dwindles away to practically nothing. This is, obviously, a very strong argument for inflation—if one could keep inflation up indefinitely without reaching a breaking-point.

Looking at the position since the war ended in 1945 the level of unemployment in this country (and in most of Europe) has generally been very low (1 to 2 per cent) as compared with the inter-war years (9 to 22 per cent). Labour shortages and unfilled vacancies—in most areas and in most occupations—have led employers to bid against one another to secure and retain workers. Trade Unions have, therefore, been in a powerful position to obtain higher wage rates—for the price of labour, like the price of commodities, goes up when supplies are short. Wage increases which correspond with increased productivity will not cause cost inflation; but, though technical progress and more efficient methods of production do lead to a fairly steady rise in industrial productivity, in times of full employment it is difficult to check 'wage drift'—the tendency for wages to rise faster than productivity. So in Britain for much of the time since 1945 we have had an inflationary spiral—rising wages, higher costs of production, increased prices and then further demands for wage increases to match the higher cost of living. Monotonously the break has come, generally because booming home trade has attracted imports exceeding our export earnings and so led to a balance of payments crisis.

Deflation, on the other hand, discourages business. Prices fall, pulling down profits or turning them into losses; sales fall off; with less cheerful prospects, business men put some workers on short time, dismiss others, reduce orders to their suppliers, thus discouraging them; and so a chilly wave of depression spreads and unemployment rises. That happened on a very serious scale during those five years from 1920 to 1925 while a deflationary policy was triumphantly halving prices. It is the memory of this grievous side-effect of the obvious, frontal attack on high wages which prevented the same methods being used after World War II. We shall return to this question of deflation, inflation, and the volume of employment in Chapter XXII, which deals with the nature and causes of 'good times' and 'bad times'—prosperity and depression—in economic life.

Index Numbers. Changes in the general price level are obviously harder to measure accurately, and in a way that really means something, than changes in particular prices. Particular prices can be measured against money; general price changes involve, as we have seen, the value of money itself. The difficulty is got over, more or less adequately, by the use of *index numbers*, which can be applied to either particular or general price movements. Suppose one wishes (choosing a particular example) to compare the changes over a period of years in the average price of wheat. First one must choose a base year and find the average price of wheat for that year (say 120s. a quarter). This price is represented by 100. Then if in subsequent years the price per quarter is 135s. and 150s. respectively, the index for those years will be $\dfrac{135 \times 100}{120}$, and $\dfrac{150 \times 100}{120}$ respectively—that is, 112·5 and 125; and so on for other prices. That is a *simple* index number.

The Cost-of-Living Index. Where a larger number of different commodities are concerned a *composite* index number is compiled. This may cover wholesale or retail prices. The best known example of such an index is the Ministry of Labour's cost-of-living index of 1962. The original cost-of-living index was compiled on the basis of data collected in 1904 to measure changes in the cost of living of a typical working-class family, and was drawn up in the following way. First, a list was prepared of essential, generally used commodities and services, such as bread, meat, clothes of a certain standard, rent, light and fuel. The total value of all items was calculated for the base year, and converted to 100 just as in the wheat example. Supposing the aggregate cost of food, etc., amounted to 25s.; if that represents 100, then if the current value of the same assortment were calculated in subsequent months to be 25s. 3d., 25s. 6d., 25s. 4d. the index for those months would be 101, 102, 101·6. In practice, the Ministry of Labour employs officials who take weekly samples, all over the country, of the commodities and services included in the index. An average of these sample prices is calculated for each item and so a representative set of prices for the whole country is obtained.

Limitations of a Retail Price Index. The cost-of-living index is only a rough-and-ready tool for measuring changes in the price level, because of the difficulty of deciding what goods to include and what to leave out. Getting them all in would be impossible—think of the number of officials needed to keep track of the prices not merely of bread and meat and clothes but of pet dogs, fancy stationery, restaurant meals, comics, motor launches, and bubble gum, to mention only a few random examples. Moreover, a single index covering everything would mean very little to each particular group in the community, because once general necessities are accounted for, different people buy different things. The people who buy race-horses do not usually buy cooked tripe, the people who buy Rolls-Royce cars do not usually buy candles. To put things more generally, there are a great many things bought only by the wealthy and well-to-do, so that their prices, whether increasing or decreasing, do not affect the majority of the public, and there are many more things important to the poor which are either unimportant to, or completely ignored by, the rich. Thus, to get a true picture of changes in the cost of living, there should be a series of indexes for different classes of the community, divided per-

haps both according to income and by other tests, e.g. life in
town or country.

Weighting of Index Items. Since the index measures
changes over time, another difficulty arises; any group, rich or
poor, changes the nature of its consumption as time passes.
New commodities appear, old ones drop out. In 1904 one of
the items in the clothing section of the index was red flannel,
then widely used for underwear; it would be hard to find anyone buying red flannel now except perhaps for fancy dress.
Safety-razor blades and toothpaste, on the other hand, were
excluded, as not being generally used by the working class at
that date. These curiosities were put right in 1947, when the
Interim Index of Retail Prices was begun. Further revised indexes have been constructed in 1956 and again in 1962 to take
into account the change in the pattern of consumer expenditure
resulting from higher living standards. However, any index
relating to a long period is bound to be falsified, to a greater or
lesser degree, by this sort of change in buying habits.

Finally, it must be very much a matter of judgment, when the
index is compiled, what importance to attach to any particular
item. Some necessaries, which must be included because they
are necessaries, are bought rarely and in small quantities—like
toothpaste. Others are bought in large quantities every week,
like potatoes. Obviously it would not do to construct an index
which moved just as much, up or down, with movements in the
price of a tube of toothpaste as with movements in the price of
a pound of potatoes. So the more important commodities are
'weighted', i.e. counted several times over, so as to ensure that
changes in their prices show up in a way proportionate to their
importance. Evidently, a wrong weighting can be only a little
less misleading than no weighting at all; and a weighting which
was correct in 1939 may have become wildly incorrect by 1949.
On the other hand, if the weights are altered to suit new circumstances, or some items are dropped altogether and replaced by
others, the index numbers before and after the change are no
longer strictly comparable.

Nevertheless, the index is better than pure guesswork, which

R

is the only alternative. It is accordingly used wherever it is important to know what changes have taken place in the cost of living; notably in the fixing of wages in certain occupations where it has been agreed that wage rates shall vary, by an agreed amount, with every change of so many points in the index. Apart from actual written agreements, it is also used as evidence for or against wage increases in other occupations.

CHAPTER XVIII

INTERNATIONAL TRADE

INTERNATIONAL trade—that is, transactions between residents of different countries—has certain special characteristics and problems of its own which need separate treatment. In spite of these special characteristics and problems, it is always necessary to remember that it is carried on for exactly the same reasons as trade between persons or firms in a single country. In international trade, as in home trade, buyers look for the best value for money, sellers look for the buyers who will give them the best price. In international trade, as in home trade, there is specialization between firms and regions, according to the distribution of particular factors of production and the historical developments of the past. In international trade, as in home trade, transactions may be concerned either with *goods* or with *services*; though personal services, for obvious reasons, play a less important part, transport is an obvious example of a service sold to, or bought from, foreigners, and so are insurance facilities or the kind of financial work done by the City of London which is described in Chapter XVI.

International Trade a Special Case of Long-Distance Trade. The difference between international and home trade is partly just an exaggeration of the difference between short-distance and long-distance trade, within a single country. Trade over long distances means bigger transport costs for goods produced, so that there can be a bigger spread between the prices charged for the same commodity in widely-separated places than there is in places close together. It also means a greater difficulty in shifting the factors of production, not only because of transport costs but because one factor of production—labour—is supplied by human beings who on the whole generally prefer to remain in the part of the world with which they are familiar. On the average, distances in international trade are greater than in home trade (though this is, of course, not always true of particular transactions; compare a deal between firms in Rotterdam and Antwerp with a deal between firms in Vancouver and Montreal), and to distance is added rather more risk (because those taking part in transactions are likely to know less about markets, supply conditions, etc., in a foreign country than in their own) and a very much greater unwillingness on the part of workers to move to places not merely remote but strange in language, habits and laws.

Special Characteristics of International Trade. Part of the differences between international and national trade arises, however, from quite another cause; from the fact that nations are politically separate, with separate governments pursuing different economic policies, having their own separate currencies and national banking systems, imposing special taxes on transactions between their own citizens and foreigners, and, for the most part, putting obstacles in the way of immigration. Some (like our own since World War II) also prevent the free movement of capital.

In general, the government of a single country is supposed to use its powers for the common benefit of all the regions of that country, perhaps raising taxes paid mostly by residents in the richer regions for the benefit of residents in the poorer regions but never neglecting or actually attacking the interests of any; whereas it generally feels little or no responsibility for the welfare of residents in foreign countries, which it is quite willing to injure if its own nationals can be thereby benefited. So whereas trade between the residents of Staffordshire and the residents of Lancashire is carried on under equal laws which favour neither especially, trade between residents in, say, Belgium and residents in Egypt is subject to interference by Belgian regulations made exclusively in the interest of Belgians and by Egyptian regulations made exclusively in the interest of Egyptians.

Finally, political influences enter in. In a troubled world, with international war always a possibility, international trade, which increases mutual dependence, is regarded by all governments as needing to be regulated with an eye to strategical requirements.

To sum up, the study of international trade is the study of trade under conditions when:

(1) Distance and variety of climate and natural conditions are particularly great.

(2) There are special obstacles to the movement of capital and labour.

(3) Separate currencies are used by the parties to the transactions.

(4) Special taxes or other restrictions are imposed on the movement of goods, whether for economic, political or social reasons.

Gains from International Trade. Like all other trades, international trade is the result of specialization; in other words, of the division of labour. It provides the bigger market which makes more specialization possible (remember Chapter IV), and greater specialization in turn, by increasing productivity, ensures that each national working group shall have a bigger surplus of its own special product with which to buy the products in which others are specializing. Of course, nations never specialize as closely as particular towns or smaller regions do, any more than towns or regions specialize as closely as particular firms do. There is much more variety of skills, tastes, and resources within the national boundaries than within those of a single town or region. But they all specialize to some degree, for just the same reason as do towns and regions —basically, because they have different assortments of natural resources and human skills. The inhabitants of each English county live a great deal better than they could if they had to produce everything for themselves—with Devonshire, say, having to make do with wood for fuel and Lancashire having to feed itself entirely from its own farmland.

In fact, if one thinks in terms of counties, it is obvious that the more closely peopled ones could not live at all and that the less peopled ones would live at a medieval standard. In just the same way, nations need (in order to live at anything near their modern standards) to draw on goods produced outside their own frontiers. Even huge areas such as the United States and the Soviet Union cannot avoid drawing on the outside world for certain essentials of modern life such as tin and rubber. For smaller and less variously endowed areas it is even less possible to be self-sufficient at a tolerable standard of life.

Uneven Distribution of Natural Resources: (i) Climate. The economic resources of the world, the factors of production—natural resources, capital, labour—are irregularly distributed over the globe, and this in itself makes strongly for specialization. To take the most obvious example, different areas have different climates and soils; tropical crops such as rice, cocoa, tea, sugar-cane, spices and bananas will not grow in a northern climate, and wheat and other 'white crops' thrive better outside the tropics. It is technically just possible to grow tropical crops in Britain, or even, if one really felt inclined, north of the Arctic Circle, in an artificial climate under glass; but there are so many other, more productive uses for building materials, fuel, and labour that no one would think it commercially worth while. It is obviously a better proposition to use materials and fuel and labour in a line of production in which they will yield bigger results, and buy one's bananas and so forth with the proceeds.

(ii) Mineral Wealth. Other kinds of natural resources, particularly mineral deposits—metals, coal and oil—are also very irregularly distributed over the globe. As we saw in Chapter IV, the cost of transporting any particular mineral narrowly settles the location of any industry which uses much of it; thus heavy industrial areas coincide with coal deposits. It is true that the development of electrical power has already changed the geographical pattern of industry in Great Britain; and when atomic energy comes into its own it may bring about bigger changes still, making industrial development possible where now lack of

power prevents it, and perhaps greatly altering both the nature of world trade and its existing flows. It is also true that commodities which normally depend on particular natural conditions for their production may be very nearly reproduced synthetically—rubber is an important example. But although particular natural resources may become more or less important as techniques change, their distribution cannot be altered; they cannot themselves be moved from one part of the world to another. Of course their products can—that is what international trade consists in—but that is another matter. So the distribution of natural resources has a profound effect in determining the pattern of international trade, that is, the nature of the goods imported and exported by different countries.

Uneven Distribution of Skills and Capital. Labour and capital are not irrevocably fixed as natural resources are; they can be moved from place to place, though social and political obstacles make this movement far less than the corresponding movement inside the national areas. If they did move as freely as goods themselves, then the basic reason for many particular trade-flows would disappear; but in fact this freedom does not exist, and the distribution of capital and of human resources remains uneven. So does that of the business ability which handles the factors of production, though enterprise (which can exert itself at a distance) is effectively much more mobile than technical skill or mere muscular power.

Because different kinds of skilled labour are unevenly distributed between different countries, the countries where any particular kind of skill is scarce must import from elsewhere those goods for whose production that skill is necessary. Those where skilled workers in general are scarce, the 'backward' countries, have to specialize in producing things for the production of which skill does not matter much, and buy all skilled-labour products from abroad. (The unskilled can become skilled by training, but we have seen what an advantage is given by a long local tradition of skill, and its lack is a corresponding handicap.)

Britain, poor in most natural resources, is particularly rich in skilled labour—industrial, commercial, and professional—and can accordingly specialize in skilled labour products such as engineering, and commercial services. In the same way, the uneven distribution of capital resources between nations makes it necessary for those lacking heavy capital equipment to specialize in producing those things which do not demand heavy capital equipment, and to buy from abroad those that do. (Again, capital equipment can be produced by a newly-developed native capital-goods industry; but as we saw in Chapter IX, the very poverty which goes with absence of capital equipment makes it difficult to spare resources from daily living to build for the future.) Thus on top of the forces which bring about division of labour between localities (and hence inter-local trade) inside any country, there are special forces bringing about division of labour between nations (and hence international trade).

The Motives of International Trade. It should be obvious that a country will normally import those commodities which it cannot produce itself at all (e.g. tin imported by a country having no tin mines), those which it can produce only at great expense (e.g. tropical crops in a northern country), and those which it cannot possibly produce itself in adequate quantities (e.g. food and timber in a densely peopled country like Britain or Belgium). Or rather, to put it more accurately and even more obviously, the merchants of a country, who usually are the people actually doing the trading, will normally buy from abroad things for which there is a market at home, but of which home supplies either do not exist at all or exist only in inadequate quantities or at fancy prices. (One must qualify with the words 'normally' and 'usually', because of those strategic, political and social considerations mentioned on page 245. A government may decide that for reasons of national safety it must encourage the production, and enforce the use, of synthetic substitutes for raw materials which cannot be produced at home; Germany, Russia and the United States have all taken this line about rubber, and Germany fought the last war largely on synthetic petrol produced from coal. It was very expensive, but it did escape the blockade difficulty.) Further, a certain amount of international trade is now carried on by governments themselves, though it is still a small proportion of the whole.

All the same, one must remember that expressions like 'a country will import this', or 'a country will export that', are really only a kind of convenient shorthand. Buying or selling abroad, like buying or selling at home, are done by individuals and firms who expect to make a profit by moving things from places where they are plentiful, and therefore cheap, to where they are scarce, and therefore dear, and thus filling consumer needs. Readers are urged to bear this in mind, and, whenever they are tempted to imagine 'Great Britain' (or 'France' or 'America') making a national decision to buy or sell this or that, to remind themselves that, apart from bulk-buying schemes originating in the needs of war, it is quite exceptional for anything of the kind to happen.

From the point of view of a government having power (even though it may do little or no actual trading itself) to influence and control the flow of trade between its own residents and those of other countries, there are genuine 'national' decisions to be taken. Should the shift of population from country to town, for instance, be checked by a particular tariff on imported food? (Remember what was said about this in Chapter V.) We have already seen, in Chapter III, that the profit motive is not an absolutely safe guide, that bargains willingly entered into by both parties may have such undesirable side effects that they cannot be left uncontrolled; that, in fact, a good deal of State intervention is needed even in home economic affairs. International trade raises questions of its own from this point of view of public, as distinct from private, advantage.

Why Import what can be made at Home? One question of this kind, on which a good deal of confusion exists, may be put like this: obviously it is to a country's advantage to import goods which cannot be produced at home at all or which can only be produced under an enormous handicap, like

that of the wrong climate. But is it to her advantage to import
goods which could easily, from the technical point of view, be
produced at home? For example, why should Great Britain
import motor cars, mouth organs or mouse-traps? Why, in
1962, did she import manufactures to the value of £1,443 millions, some of them from countries less well equipped and less
well provided with skilled workers than herself? Would it not
really have been better to have made them at home?

The answer is that the equipment and the labour which
could, so far as technical possibilities went, have produced those
things in this country were already busy producing something
else. They were working on lines of production in which their
particular advantages over the equipment and labour of other
countries were even bigger than they would be if applied to the
production of those imports. To substitute home production
for imports, one would have to take the necessary labour and
equipment away from their present uses—thus actually diminishing their total yield. It would be just as though a busy lawyer
were to refuse a well-paid brief in order to find time to do his
own typing, just because he could type faster than his clerk; or
as though a woman doctor, just because she could cook better
than her maid, were to turn away patients in order to do her
own cooking. Or one can think of a football team—one player
may be both the best available centre-forward *and* the best
available centre-half-back, but he cannot play in both positions,
and the position where his superiority is most marked is the
position where he ought to play.

In economic affairs, owners of labour-power and capital find
out where their superiority is most marked by finding out
where they can earn most; the self-betterment motive (where is
the highest wage? where is the highest salary? where are the
highest profits?) guides the division of labour. This is just as
true of the specialization which leads to foreign trade as of the
specialization which leads to trade between localities. It is all
part of the same process; the process by which the division of
labour, as we saw in Chapter IV, increases total production
and the general standard of living above what could be attained
by self-sufficiency.

Reasons for Trade Barriers. Then why do governments intervene and put special obstacles in the way of this particular kind of specialization? Why is free trade between nations not taken as much for granted as free trade between London and Portsmouth or New York and Los Angeles? There was a time, during the nineteenth century, when it looked as though international trade barriers would follow internal trade barriers (such as existed in many countries in the Middle Ages and later) into oblivion. Great Britain, in particular, pursued an almost completely Free Trade policy from the 1850s up to 1932; at that date, however, she went back to a system of 'protective' tariffs, which most of the leading nations in the world had never abandoned and which America, in particular, had greatly strengthened in the previous few years.

A good deal of Government intervention, one can safely say, has been due to sheer muddle-headedness and lack of understanding of the principles of international trade. But that is not the whole story. It is possible to argue for particular kinds of intervention (by tariff, prohibition of imports, exchange control or otherwise) on a number of different grounds. Here are the main ones:

(i) *Grounds of National Safety.* Unlike trade between localities, trade between nations is trade between markets which may be cut off from one another by war (see page 245). It may be considered unwise to allow specialization to reach the point when the country concerned would lack the means to manufacture arms for its defence because, for instance, its residents had specialized overwhelmingly in the production of light consumer goods and left it to possibly hostile or inaccessible foreign suppliers to produce steel and machinery. Even if an *economic* loss results from hindering this specialization in order to encourage the growth, or prevent the decline, of a native steel industry, the *strategic* gain may be regarded as well worth while. The lower standard of living resulting from lesser specialization is part of the cost of defence, just as the maintenance of the armed forces is part of the cost of defence, and is incurred for the same reason.

(*ii*) *Grounds of National Development.* We saw in Chapters IV and V that the pattern of the division of labour depends a good deal on historical accident—on the way things chance to have happened in the past. With an intelligent and hard-working population and great natural resources, a country may remain unindustrialized because in the short run it pays everyone better to go on buying foreign goods, produced by long-established, low-cost foreign concerns, than to buy the products of a native industry still in the high-cost, small-scale, experimental stage. In the long run, its government may consider, industrialization might pay handsomely, enabling all sorts of human ability and potential skill to develop and reap a reward. So to cover the time of transition it may be worth while to put obstacles, in the shape of protective duties, in the way of manufactured imports, and by making them more expensive encourage consumers to buy the home product.

If all calculations are correct, the 'infant' industries will lower their costs as they grow to full stature and achieve the economies of scale (see Chapter VI) and will no longer need to be protected; the pattern of international trade will have changed and the world as a whole will be richer for the development of new resources. The initial fall in the standard of living, as consumers are cut off from cheap and good-quality foreign goods, is a price paid for a better standard in the future; it can be looked on as a sort of forced saving, a sort which has to be undertaken by joint action, through Government control, or not at all.

The trouble about this perfectly valid argument (which was first worked out late in the nineteenth century by economists in Germany, whose situation, compared with that of Britain, was a perfect example) is that no 'infant industry' has ever been ready to admit that it was grown up and ready to stand on its own feet. So the pattern of international trade has always gone on being pushed out of the shape which a real weighing-up of comparative advantages would have brought about.

(*iii*) *Grounds of Stability.* This is a very popular but very tricky argument. Competition, as we have seen, leads to the expansion of better-placed and more efficient firms, which can offer the best terms to labour and capital and accordingly get them, and to the contraction of worse-placed and less-efficient firms, which are unable to offer such good terms to labour and capital and accordingly lose them. This is an excellent thing for consumers—the public at large—as it leads to their getting better and cheaper goods more conveniently. But it is naturally uncomfortable for those firms which have to contract; and it may also be exceedingly uncomfortable for those workers who lose their jobs by the contraction.

Now, if the competition is between firms in the same town or region, a displaced worker has only to move from the contracting to the expanding firm; he may take a little time to find his way to a new job, but he suffers no serious loss or hardship. But when the competition is between firms in different countries the picture is far less cheerful. The expanding firms are far out of reach of the displaced worker; some highly skilled, venturesome and confident men may be ready to migrate to where their trade skill is in demand, but they are likely to be a minority and—especially nowadays—to find migration barriers blocking the way.

For most, the only way to get back into employment is to take another sort of job altogether. That other job may, of course, be ready and waiting. The changing pattern of international trade works both ways; in the foreign country where the industry concerned is expanding, other industries will be feeling the draught as their workers and supplies are attracted away, and their higher costs, with consequently higher prices, will be opening up new opportunities for the outside competition of sellers offering better value. But even if other jobs are available, the chances are heavily against their being just the right jobs for the displaced specialists. There is a real loss involved for those on whom the burden of change falls; a loss to set against the general public gain. The gain is spread thin, but continues; the loss affects only a few and only for part of their working lives, but it may be severe. 'Cheap imports throwing British workers out of employment. . . .' 'The cotton industry in danger from Japanese competition. . . .' Everyone has seen such phrases. The new pattern of international specialization, appearing when competition has done its job and everyone has settled down again, may give better standards all round than the old; but how much dislocation and discomfort and particular hardships are worth putting up with for the sake of that gain in standards? Nowadays people are inclined to say: 'Let's have a bird in hand, it's worth two in the bush', and to support any Government decision which takes the edge off competition from abroad. Their cost of living may remain higher than it need do, but they are less likely to have to change their jobs—or so they feel.

In fact, however, it is doubtful whether a country like Great Britain, which depends so heavily for so many essentials on being able to buy abroad with the proceeds of her exports, can safely follow a policy which will make those exports dearer for foreigners to buy. No tariff can protect the job of workers for foreign markets when their customers decide that they can get better value elsewhere.

To follow this argument further would be to get involved in some uncomfortably advanced theory; readers should merely note, first, that stability may be worth paying for by way of interference with international trade; and, second, that it is extremely difficult to be certain that when one has paid for stability one will actually get it.

(iv) *Grounds of Preserving Rural Society*. Some people believe that there is something intrinsically valuable in preserving a rural population. They consider that it is desirable to keep a certain balance between the number of urban industrial workers and the rural farm workers. Although this reason is most commonly used in countries which have a considerable peasant farming population, in practice tariffs, subsidies, and import restrictions are used in most Western European countries to keep the prices obtained by farmers for agricultural products well above the levels at which American or Australasian products could be imported. In this way, more labour and capital is attracted to agriculture, leaving less to be devoted to industry. Economically this is wrong, but it may be right on strategic or social grounds.

(*v*) *Grounds of National Solvency*. A tariff, or other form of interference with international trade, may be used to correct an 'adverse balance of payments'. (This is the technical name for a situation in which the value of a country's imports, both visible and invisible,[1] exceeds that of its exports.) The balance can be put right (as Chapter XIX will show), without putting particular obstacles in the way of particular imports, by using the money-and-credit machinery of the Central Bank to lower prices, discourage imports, and encourage exports at the same time; but we have seen how depressing and uncomfortable this deflationary process can be, and no government willingly takes steps which depress business and cause unemployment. (There will be more to say on this later, in Chapter XXII.) It is much less uncomfortable, in the short run, simply to prevent a certain proportion of imports from entering the country. Great Britain, and a number of other countries, did this during the Great Depression of the 1930s; and, of course, import restriction was our chief but inadequate defence against an adverse balance of payments for a long period after World War II.

The long-run trouble with this kind of defence is that by hitting at other countries' trade it makes them less good customers for the export industries and so is apt to push the balance out of trim again; that it encourages them to impose restrictions themselves; and that it makes it difficult to get back, later on, to a pattern of international trade which really makes the best use of every country's resources, because (see page 253) a renewal of competition would be very painful to particular industries. The restrictions imposed in 1931–2 were never withdrawn, the total volume of international trade never recovered to its previous level, and so the standard of living of the countries restricting their trade remained lower than it would otherwise have been. The existing pattern of specialization is so far from the pattern which would have developed in the absence of restriction that passing from one to the other would be a horribly uncomfortable process, involving great shifts of workers, considerable business losses, sharp changes

[1] See page 261.

in price levels, and a general shake-up which no one would enjoy; nevertheless, the countries of Western Europe are beginning to realize the great advantages which will result by establishing a more liberal system which makes the best use of existing resources.

Liberalization. Attempts to restore a rational pattern have taken three main forms. The General Agreement on Tariffs and Trade (GATT) provides a negotiating framework and set of rules within which, at successive conferences, member countries have exchanged and widened tariff concessions and relaxations of restrictive practices. The Organization for European Economic Co-operation (OEEC), which was set up in 1948 primarily to administer Marshall Aid, provided a closer, more active co-operation between 18 member nations, and contributed powerfully to the expansion of European trade. This body was replaced in September 1961 by the Organization for Economic Co-operation and Development which has wider aims than its predecessor. These aims include not only the promotion of economic growth and stability in Europe and North America but the fostering of economic expansion among the undeveloped countries of the world. More drastically, six nations of Western Europe (Germany, France, Italy, Belgium, Holland and Luxembourg) have taken a succession of bold steps towards economic unity. In 1951, they set up the European Coal and Steel Community, which established a supranational authority and a single market for their coal, iron and steel. This was followed in 1958 by a parallel authority for atomic development, Euratom. At the same time, the Treaty of Rome set up the European Economic Community (the Common Market), a joint body which provides a common economic policy among its members and aims to establish eventually complete freedom of trade and movement of labour and capital between the countries of the Community. These countries are, however, to maintain a common tariff (with certain exceptions) against goods which they import from the rest of the world. Britain belongs to the GATT and the OECD, but not to the Common Market; negotiation for British membership took place in 1961–63, but eventually broke down. Britain is, however, a member of the European Free Trade Area (EFTA) which, although it has less ambitious aims then the Common Market is nevertheless working toward eventual free trade in industrial products among its seven members (Britain, Austria, Denmark, Norway, Portugal, Sweden and Switzerland).

Wider Issues. Readers will have realized that all these questions of international trade policy, even those which seem to have to do only with standards of living, really take one outside the purely economic field. As soon as one starts asking: 'Is it *fair* that people now working in the cotton industry should suffer so that we can all buy cheaper sheets and shirts?' one is getting away from economics into questions of right and wrong. As soon as one starts asking: 'Is it *better* to be richer or to have fewer worries about losing one's job?' one is getting into questions of psychology. As soon as one starts asking: 'Ought we to break down the barriers and try to make the whole world one market for labour?' one is getting into questions of national character, and of how people with different backgrounds and standards mix, and of the value to be set on national tradition. However, anyone who has really digested this chapter ought to be able to avoid thinking of foreign trade as a sort of warfare, or of good value for money as a thing to be avoided if it is offered by a foreigner, or—on the other hand —that international transactions can be left to themselves just as safely as transactions between London and Bradford.

S

CHAPTER XIX

THE BALANCE OF PAYMENTS

As we saw in the last chapter, a nation is, economically speaking, something more than just another regional group; it has a currency of its own, which the regional group has not, and a central bank exercising control over money and credit, and hence over the price level, which the regional group has not; it is bound to rely for its standard of living on its own directly or indirectly used production,[1] while the regional group's standard is (as explained on page 244) at least partly the responsibility of other groups within the same nation; its government can and does make economic decisions in the light of strategical requirements, which local authorities have neither the need nor the power to do. For all these reasons *the balance of payments* of a nation is more important and significant than that of a regional group; moreover, since goods are checked at frontiers, and services rendered internationally involve foreign currency transactions which can also be checked, it is possible to measure the national balance of payments, which would be virtually impossible for a town or county. (Attempts to find out about the flow of trade between Scotland and England have been frustrated by this difficulty.)

What is the Balance of Payments? This balance of payments is the balance of incomings and outgoings of money on account of transactions between a nation's residents and those of other countries. If on balance (taking into account goods bought abroad and sold abroad, services rendered to and received from foreigners, and interest and dividends received

[1] Leaving aside, of course, such exceptional circumstances as its being in receipt of foreign 'aid'.

from and paid out to foreign debtors and creditors) income from abroad exceeds spending abroad, then the nation as a whole is accumulating capital. If the balance is the other way, the nation as a whole is running its capital down or getting into debt, and is suffering from an unfavourable or 'adverse' balance of payments.

These changes in its *international* economic standing may, of course, be accompanied by quite different changes in its *internal* fortunes; perhaps the easiest way to understand this is to compare the nation to a single family. The family as a whole may live more or less comfortably according to how good a cook the mother is, how good a handyman and gardener the father is, how useful are the children's hobbies; its different members may individually be more or less comfortable according to how the food is shared out and who gets the best chairs and beds and so on; but however important these family matters may be, the family must in the long run live within the income which its breadwinners earn from the rest of the community. It can temporarily live beyond its earnings by drawing on its balance or selling out investments; it can run into debt within the limits of its credit-worthiness; in an emergency, it may perhaps get help from a better-off neighbour—but the comparison breaks down when one gets to social services; there is no international Welfare State to safeguard the unfortunate or the shiftless national group.

Of course, the national group depends much less than does the family group on 'outside' transactions, because nations are less narrowly specialized than families. Much more of the national standard of life is, in a manner of speaking, a matter of home cooking. But if a national group wants to maintain the standards which specialization makes possible—standards much higher, for reasons discussed both in the last chapter and in Chapter IV, than could be attained by national self-sufficiency—then it has got to make specialization pay; it has got to earn, by selling its produce and its services to foreigners, enough to pay for the produce and services which it buys abroad. The question whether any country is achieving this or failing to do so, and the margin of success or failure, can be determined by studying the officially published statistical statement called the Balance of Payments.[1]

The Balance Examined. Here, in summary form, is one such statement:

TABLE X—UNITED KINGDOM BALANCE OF PAYMENTS: CURRENT ACCOUNT, 1962.

DEBITS	£ million	CREDITS	£ million
Imports (f.o.b.)	4,059	Exports and re-exports	
Government	407	(f.o.b.)	3,988
Shipping	720	Government	36
Interest, Profits and Dividends	457	Shipping	681
Travel	240	Interest, Profits and Dividends	765
Migrants' funds, etc.	98	Travel	220
Other services	344	Migrants' funds, etc.	119
(including civil aviation, royalties, education, commissions)		Other services	
Credit balance	67	(including expenditure of foreign government agencies in this country, earnings from insurance and merchanting)	583
	£6,392		£6,392

The first items—*imports and exports*—explain themselves; they include the total value of all goods imported and exported during the period concerned. Import and export values may be quoted either 'f.o.b.', as here, or 'c.i.f'. These mysterious initials stand for 'free on board' and 'cost, insurance, freight'; this latter method of quotation means that the exporter includes in his selling price not only the cost of the goods themselves but the cost of insuring them during transit and of shipping them to the port of destination. If, on the other hand, prices are quoted 'f.o.b.', they include only the cost of trans-

[1] The Balance of Trade of a country is a narrower conception and is concerned only with imports and exports of actual goods.

porting the goods to the port of embarkation and loading them on board; it is the buyer who pays freight and insurance charges. One has to watch this distinction because 'c.i.f.' prices are naturally higher than 'f.o.b.' prices, and only 'f.o.b.' prices give a true picture of the value of a country's exports. The insurance and freight elements in the 'c.i.f.' price may appear on either side of the balance-of-payments picture, according to whether a British shipper is paying freight and insurance charges to foreign firms, or a foreign shipper is paying freight and insurance charges to British firms.

Government. The main items are on the debit side, and consist of military expenditure abroad, colonial grants, aid to developing countries and contributions to international organizations. The credits are mainly the result of expenditure on behalf of U.S. forces stationed in this country.

Shipping. This item on the debit side means that British firms and individuals incurred debts to foreign shipowners to the extent of £720 millions for transporting goods and passengers. On the credit side it similarly means that United Kingdom shipowners earned £681 millions by carrying goods, and providing passages, for foreigners. Thus, shipping constituted a net 'invisible' import worth £39 millions.

Interest, Profits and Dividends. These were other 'invisible' items. The debit side records payments to foreigners on account of the capital which those foreigners had invested in this country (shares or debentures held abroad), and the credit side similarly records payments to British firms or individuals on account of capital which they had invested abroad. (The original process of investment, normally just the same for home and foreign firms, is described on pp. 11–13.

This 'invisible' credit item has shrunk considerably since 1939, as during the first two years of World War II (before Lease-Lend) the national need for extra imports was so great that the Government had to requisition (i.e. buy compulsorily) a large part of the overseas holdings of British investors and sell them to foreign buyers, in order to raise the necessary sums in foreign currency; and this process has continued since the War, e.g. with the sale to the Argentine Government of the British-owned Argentine railways. In 1939, individuals and firms in Great Britain owned about £4,000 m. of capital invested abroad in all kinds of forms; they held the stocks of foreign and Dominion governments and of foreign local authorities and public utility companies (gas, electricity, waterworks, tramways) and the debentures or shares of industrial, commercial, mining, plantation and other enterprises. Sometimes they controlled these enterprises as well as owning them. Of this £4,000 m. there remains about £2,500 m.; the return from this capital provides us with an income which does not have to be earned by current production. Like the investment income of a family, it is the result of the accumulated savings of the past.

Travel Expenditure. When people from this country travel abroad they incur expenses abroad; they pay fares to foreign railways and board-and-lodging bills to foreign hotels, and they buy goods in foreign shops. To do this, they need to get foreign currency, giving pounds in exchange. In effect, they are 'importing' these goods and services, even though they do not actually bring them home to consume them. So travel expenditure abroad is a debit item in the balance of payments; and sums spent by foreign travellers in Great Britain, sums obtained by giving up foreign currency in exchange for pounds, similarly appear on the credit side.

Migrants' Funds. This consists of money sent back by immigrants to their families abroad, and gifts from individuals to relatives or friends in foreign countries and vice versa.

Other Services. These include payments and receipts in respect of civil aviation, education, royalties, commissions and banking. Included in credits are the expenditure of foreign government agencies in Britain and net earnings in respect of insurance and merchanting transactions.

Capital Movements. All these items we have examined above make up the *current* balance of payments, with credits currently accruing and debits currently incurred. But the current balance does not give the whole picture. Beside the current account there is the capital account. Firms and individuals may be investing in foreign securities—which have to be paid for just as foreign goods and services are paid for, but which later yield an income; or they may be issuing shares, or raising loans, to be taken up by foreigners—who similarly have to pay for these securities in the first place, but will have to be recompensed with an income later. Naturally, the more favourable its current balance, the easier it is for a country to 'export capital', that is, to invest abroad. (With an adverse balance, a country can usually only export capital by shipping gold, the one form of money which every national bank will accept.)

We come round, from another angle, to the explanation of Great Britain's tremendous activity as an international lender during the century preceding 1914, a matter already touched on in Chapter XVI; during all that period, she had a strongly favourable balance of payments. After 1914 the export of capital from Great Britain dwindled and almost vanished. This was partly because foreign exchange rates (that is, the rates at which pounds and foreign currencies could be exchanged for one another) had become so unstable as to make foreign investment disproportionately risky, partly because the areas where most investment had been done in the past were now economically more mature and less anxious for loans, and partly because the credit margin in the current balance of payments had practically vanished. Indeed, it was only the flow of income from past investments which kept a debit margin from developing.

World War II and the Balance of Payments. The Second World War had an even more drastic effect, not of course only on British trade but on world trade in general. Trade between continental Europe and the rest of the world was reduced to a trickle by the Allied blockade. The United Kingdom, entirely cut off from Europe and partially cut off from more distant supplies by the Axis blockade, had to rely more and more on the New World, particularly the U.S.A. and Canada, for food, raw materials and munitions. After 1941 these were taken care of by 'Lease-Lend' (or in its Canadian form, 'Mutual Aid'), under which goods and services needed for war purposes were supplied without payment; but by the time Lease-Lend began, it had become necessary to requisition and sell more than a third of Britain's total foreign capital holdings. With the income from those holdings no longer coming in, correspondingly less has been available, ever since, to pay for current imports.

Nor is this all. On the whole, Britain exports manufactured goods and imports raw materials; so the cheaper raw materials are in comparison with manufactured goods, the further her exports will go in paying for her imports, and conversely. Now, after the war raw materials were much more expensive, in comparison with manufactures, than previously. It took the price of two ships, for instance, to buy as much wheat as the price of one ship used to buy. This change against us of the *terms of trade*, as economists call it, obviously made a healthy balance of payments much harder to attain. And matters were all the worse, when the war ended, because so many of both our customers and our suppliers had been more devastated by war than we ourselves; which meant that both we and they had to get supplies, if we were to get them at all, from the undevastated New World.

U.S. Aid to Europe. As America and Canada did not want to see their allies collapse, Lease-Lend was replaced only a few months after it ended by a couple of large loans to Britain, the 'Washington credits' of 1946, and by international, mainly American, gifts under the United Nations Relief and Rehabilitation Administration (UNRRA) to Europe. Later on, when it became obvious that both Britain and Europe were in danger of economic collapse, for lack of essential imports after these emergency aids had run out, America shouldered a still bigger responsibility under the European Recovery Plan—ERP or 'Marshall Aid', so called after General Marshall, the American administrator who devised it.

Under Marshall Aid the United States Government made available to all the countries of Western Europe, free of charge and according to their needs as jointly determined, the goods they required to re-equip themselves or to keep themselves during the re-equipping process. The goods were imported in the ordinary way, but the American exporters were paid not by the countries receiving them but by the United States Treasury. In effect, the trading deficits of the Marshall Aid countries were filled by the American taxpayer.

When after four years the Marshall Aid scheme came to an end the balance of payments situation of the countries receiving it was still far from satisfactory, but the scheme did accomplish its essential job of getting them back on their feet. Substantial American aid is still provided in a different form, by the supply to different countries (directly or by means of finance) of military equipment and other goods needed for defence. American funds have also been made available in order to finance technical advice and help to under-developed countries particularly in Asia, Latin America and Africa.

The Washington credits, UNRRA, and Marshall, Aid were all emergency measures. As a long-term agency for making credits available, there has been set up an International Bank, under the auspices of the United Nations, with capital subscribed by the members but mostly from the United States. It is through this and similar official international agencies, rather than through private financial houses drawing directly on the private investor, that most international lending seems likely to be accomplished in the future.

Multilateral Trade. Getting back to the current balance of payments, we have to notice another important thing about it. It shows how we stand towards the world as a whole: it does not show how we stand towards each of the separate countries with which we trade. Now, of course, we do not deal with the rest of the world in a lump; we deal with different countries, some of which are on balance our customers and others of which are on balance our suppliers.

We have always, for the last century and more, bought more
from America than America has bought from us; we have
always (except for a few years during the war) bought less from
India than India has bought from us. And the same has been
true of other countries. They balanced particular debit accounts
with particular suppliers out of the credits they earned elsewhere; just as a private individual pays his creditors, say, the
butcher or the gas company, with the earnings of his services to
his employer or customers or clients. This is called *multilateral*
(many-sided) trade, and can be illustrated, in its simplest form,
by the following diagram:

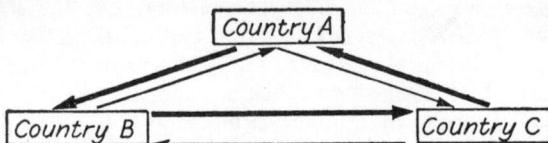

FIG. 26—MULTILATERAL TRADE

Country A has an export surplus with country B, and so
acquires more of B's currency (or, more probably and exactly,
bills of exchange payable in B's currency) than are needed to
pay B's traders for imports supplied. At the same time, A has
an import surplus with C, and thus acquires less of C's currency than is needed to pay for imports from C. Meanwhile, B
has an export surplus with C (and a consequent surplus of C's
currency) but an import surplus with A (and a consequent
deficit of A's currency). Looking at the matter from A's point
of view—though one could repeat the argument at any corner
of the triangle—A can square matters with C by transferring to
C her surplus holdings of B's currency, which C will use in turn
to settle accounts with B.

Bilateral Trade. The alert reader will have realized that
this kind of many-sided transaction, just like many-sided
transactions between individuals, depends on the existence
of some trustworthy and acceptable money. It is not strictly
necessary for all these countries to use the same currency

or even the same metallic standard; so long as all their currencies can be freely exchanged for one another, any debt can be settled in any currency which the debtor happens to have earned.

But if there are obstacles and prohibitions in the way of free exchange, international trade is crippled, just as individual trade is crippled by the necessity for barter; with totally inconvertible currencies, it becomes a matter of straight-line swaps, no country bring able to buy from any other a greater value of goods and services than it can directly supply in exchange. (This is known as Bilateral Trade.) Customers and suppliers must coincide exactly; and if the most promising customer has nothing to supply which is really wanted, and the best supplier does not happen to want one's exports (and it would be extremely odd to find a double coincidence of wants everywhere), then international trade falls to a fraction of its potential value and (another way of saying the same thing) the benefits of the international division of labour are lost. The loss is all the worse when inconvertibility follows on a long period of free exchange, because firms and industries have everywhere adapted themselves to specialization, and adapting back again is a slow and wasteful process.

Ever since 1931, more and more restrictions on convertibility have brought about more and more restrictions on normal, multilateral, international trade. The restrictions began with the Great Depression and became much more widespread, and much tighter, during and after World War II.[1] Fortunately, the economic recovery and expansion during the late 1950s and subsequently made it possible for most countries to remove, or at least considerably to relax, their exchange controls. To understand why exchange controls were devised, kept in being for many years, and then gradually dismantled, we must look further into the question of how national currencies are in fact exchanged against one another and what settles the rate at which these exchanges take place. For the last time, we must investigate a particular market—the market bringing together the buyers and sellers of foreign currencies.

[1] See page 257.

CHAPTER XX

THE FOREIGN EXCHANGES

IN the market for foreign currencies, where does the supply come from and for what purpose is it demanded? The last two chapters, to say nothing of earlier ones, should supply the answer. On any particular foreign exchange market—say in London—the demand for foreign currencies comes ultimately from people who need them to settle with foreign creditors for the goods, services or securities which they have bought abroad; the supply is provided by those people who have acquired foreign currencies as payment for goods, services or securities which they have sold abroad. French francs, for instance, are *demanded* by importers of French wines or potash, by passengers on French liners, by tourists on the Riviera, by purchasers of shares in French firms. They are *supplied* by exporters to France of machinery or tinplate, by shippers of French goods on British (or other) freighters, by Frenchmen attending foreign conferences, by French purchasers of shares in firms outside France. These traders or shippers or travellers or investors did not, even when such transactions were free, generally do the actual exchanging themselves; they went to their banks, and the banks might either handle the transaction themselves or, in turn, get specialist foreign exchange brokers to act for them.

The foreign exchange market was always, in fact, a highly professional market in which skilled dealers worked in very close competition, buying and selling not only for immediate needs but speculatively (like the dealers in commodities described in Chapter VII). But the supplies and the demands which that market brought together were, in the last resort, those of firms and individuals concerned with buying or selling, on foreign markets, goods, services and securities. It is on the movements of trade in these things that the state of the foreign currency market depends. The fact that to-day the market in foreign currencies is an official market, with legally fixed rates and a single authority controlling purchases and sales, does not alter this rock-bottom situation, any more than the imposing of a fixed price and the setting up of a government monopoly alters the rock-bottom supply-and-demand situation in a commodity market (see the tomato example in Chapter VIII).

Demand and Supply of Foreign Currencies. If, for instance, British and other buyers consider French goods, services and securities particularly good value, and buy them accordingly, the result is a big demand for French francs with which to do the buying. If they think them poor value, and so buy elsewhere, then the demand for francs falls off. That demand, whether large or small, will be met out of the supply of francs currently being offered on the market by their holders (Frenchmen and people having claims on Frenchmen) in order to buy pounds and other currencies needed to pay for goods which these holders are importing into France. And so for every other currency, including the pound itself. To link up with the last chapter, *the demand for, and supply of, any country's currency depends on that country's balance of payments— on capital account as well as on current account.*

The Offsetting of Claims. The procedure of exchange varies; it can be extremely complicated, and its details are best left to specialist textbooks. Essentially, what happens is that banks, finance houses and specialist dealers 'clear'—that is, offset against one another—claims in different currencies held by their clients; e.g. a claim by a British shareholder on a Brazilian railway for so many cruzeiros can be offset against a claim by a Brazilian coffee exporter on a British importing firm for so many pounds (see Fig. 27). The 'claims' may be bills of exchange, cheques, telegraphic transfers (i.e. cheques sent by cable) or any other kind of instrument; the offsetting may be done within a single financial house handling the affairs of both home and foreign clients, or between financial houses in the same country, or between corresponding houses in different centres. The principle is the same in each case.

For offsetting to be possible, supply and demand must match. There must be a two-way traffic. It need not, as we have seen, be equal between any two countries; it can be, and in normal circumstances generally is, extremely roundabout. But unless, taking particular surpluses and deficits together, the flow of transactions results in an even balance of supply and demand for each currency, these offsets will leave a margin to be transferred in some other way. What happens then?

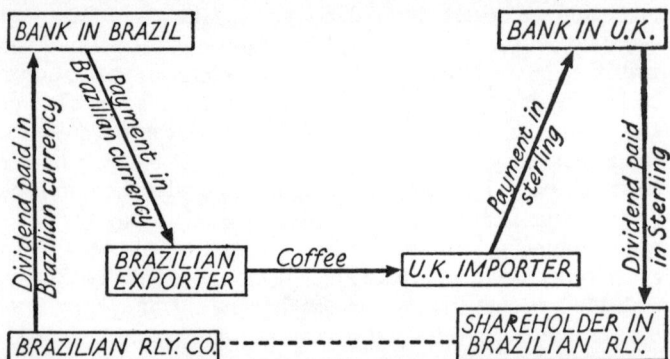

FIG. 27—PAYMENT OF FOREIGN DIVIDENDS

It all depends what are the rules concerning the particular currencies in question. Currencies may be on the gold standard (see Chapter XIII); they may be on no standard at all and exchangeable at any rate which holders and buyers care to agree on; or they may be exchangeable only at a rate legally fixed by the monetary authority of their country. During most of the nineteenth century the gold standard was the rule; between World War I and World War II free exchange was (with exceptions) more usual; since World War II Great Britain, like practically every other country except the United States (which is on a form of gold standard), has had controlled exchange rates.

*Influences affecting the International Value of Curren-
cies.* Where the rate is free it is easy to see what happens;
exactly the same thing happens as in any other market—with
supply exceeding demand at current rates, the price is driven
down by the competition of sellers; with demand exceeding
supply at current rates, the price is driven up by the competition
of buyers. As we have already seen, demand and supply are
derived from trade in goods, services and securities; so it is
easy to see what influences may cause a country's currency to
become dearer or cheaper in terms of other currencies. It will
become dearer if, on balance, that country's goods, services and
securities become more attractive to the rest of the world than
are goods, services and securities available elsewhere; if there
is a specially large demand for its exports or its shipping; if the
profit prospects of capital invested in its enterprises seem particularly good; if its government and local authorities offer
better interest on loans than do others; or if people think these
conditions are likely to arise in the future and so want to put
themselves in a position to benefit by them by getting hold of
the right currency.

A currency will become cheaper, on the other hand, if on
balance the goods, services and securities concerned become
less attractive to the rest of the world than are goods, services
and securities obtainable elsewhere; if the demand for the
country's exports and shipping and so forth falls off; if the
profit prospects of capital invested in its enterprises are darken-
ing; if its government and local authorities offer less good
terms for loans than do others; or if people think these conditions are likely to arise in the future and so do not want to be
left holding a less useful currency.

The biggest single influence on the value of a country's currency in terms of other currencies is exerted by changes in that
country's price level. If that level is rising, compared with price
levels elsewhere, then its goods and services will be less attractive to foreign buyers, whereas foreign goods and services will
be more attractive to its nationals; exports will fall off (and
with them the demand for its currency) and imports will rise
(and with them the supply of its currency). Smaller demand and

bigger supply mean a fall in value. A falling price level has, of course, just the opposite effect. Thus inflation and exchange depreciation go together, and so do deflation and exchange appreciation.

Official Stabilizing Agencies. Swings of value either way —particularly those caused not by real changes in the flows of trade but by shifts of opinion about future prospects—can be damped down, even where there is no legal fixing of exchange rates, by the establishment of an official buying-and-selling agency which can buy surpluses of any over-plentiful currency and keep the market supplied, from its holdings, with any temporarily scarce one. During the period of free exchange in the 1930s the British Treasury set up the Exchange Equalization Fund for this purpose; it was particularly necessary just then because, for political reasons, a great deal of what was called 'refugee capital' or 'hot money' was being moved from one capital to another in search of safe investment, and these erratic movements made the demand for different currencies bob up and down in a way which had very little to do with underlying economic conditions and which was very inconvenient for traders. Since World War II there has also been set up a much bigger international agency, the International Monetary Fund, which serves a somewhat similar purpose, holding scarce currencies available for buyers and absorbing plentiful currencies from sellers. (Its clients are governments, not private dealers.) But neither a one-country Exchange Equalization Fund nor an International Monetary Fund can go on indefinitely staving off the effects of a basic trading situation which is bringing about a roaring demand for one currency (e.g. dollars) and a general lack of interest in another. For a lasting balance the basic trading situation itself must be adjusted.

How the Gold Standard Worked. The great advantage of the gold standard (see Chapter XIII) was that it did keep the basic trading situation in adjustment. People could exchange gold-standard pounds against gold-standard francs at any rate they chose, but in fact they did not choose to exchange them at any rate very different from the ratio between the amounts of gold for which each was legally convertible. Suppose the conditions of trade were such that there was a surplus of francs; that francs were, in conditions of free exchange, getting cheaper, so that French importers needing sterling had to give up more francs to get that sterling. They had an alternative open; their francs might be cheap in foreign exchange, but they had the right to buy gold with them from the Bank of France at a fixed rate, and once they had that gold they could ship it to England to be used to buy sterling, also at a fixed rate. Shipping gold costs something, in freight and insurance, so exchange rates under the gold standard can move a little way each side of the 'mint par rate'—that is, the ratio between the gold contents of the different money units. But as soon as they reach the 'gold-point' on either side, the point at which shipping gold becomes cheaper than paying a premium for the scarce currency, the movement stops.

The Gold Standard as Price Stabilizer. And that is not the end of the story. We saw, in chapters XIV, XV and XVII, two things; first, that in a gold-standard country the amount of cash and credit available, the volume of purchasing power, depends closely on the amount of gold at the Central Bank; second, that the level of prices in general depends closely on the volume of purchasing power. And we have just seen that the balance of payments in turn depends very largely on the level of prices, low prices bringing in custom and discouraging sellers, high prices discouraging customers and encouraging sellers. So under the gold standard, *so long as Central Banks confronted with gold inflows or outflows adjusted their currency and credit policy accordingly* (see page 189), *and so long as prices responded smoothly to the consequent changes in the volume of purchasing power,* the balance of payments of each country was automatically kept very narrowly in adjustment.

It might be adjusted by borrowing; in that case the value of its currency would be kept up, and a possible gold drain averted, because foreign buyers were purchasing its securities.

T

Conversely, it might be adjusted by lending, a country having a surplus on current transactions spending its surplus holdings of foreign currency on buying foreign securities (nineteenth-century Britain again). But it could not get into the kind of situation which was typical just after World War II, in which the flow of imports and securities can only be kept down by direct Government control and legal prohibition, and the flow of exports can only be kept up by legally preventing makers from selling at home. Nor could there develop the situation in which, out of all the currencies of the world, some are 'soft'—i.e. easily obtainable—and others 'hard'—i.e. very difficult to get hold of—at current rates.

Why the Gold Standard has not been Restored. Why was the gold standard dropped? That it should be dropped in war is understandable enough. Gold and foreign currency must be kept for special war imports, and it would be too inconvenient to finance the enormous Government spending programme which war makes necessary entirely out of loans and taxes—new money is wanted for this purpose, and new money cannot be convertible on the old terms. But why do we not find the gold standard, with all its usefulness to foreign trade, and hence to international specialization and the standard of living, restored in peace time?

There were special reasons why the first return to the gold standard, after World War I, was a failure. For one thing, although, as we have seen, there was a big deflation between the end of the war and 1925, when partial convertibility was restored, it had not gone far enough by 1925 to make the pound equal in buying power to a legal pound's worth of gold at the restored pre-war rate, and so to a legal pound's worth of other gold-standard currencies. This disparity had the effect of making our goods more expensive to foreigners than before the return to gold, since foreigners had to give up more of their own currency in exchange for the pounds required to buy them. So British exports (which, as we saw in Chapter V, were already depressed) were further discouraged, and Britain suffered chronic balance-of-payments difficulties.

The old-fashioned remedy would have been to deflate still further, but while a small dose of deflation—the kind needed to adjust a small initial movement away from balance—may be not too uncomfortable for anyone, a big dose means business failures and general depression and unemployment on a big scale; and Britain had had a big dose, with all these unpleasant results, already. Moreover, the country which at this time was enjoying a big gold inflow by reason of its favourable balance of payments—the United States—was not expanding its currency to match, so that there was no rise in United States prices to right the balance from that side. In any case, higher and higher United States tariffs were preventing other countries from earning gold and dollars by selling to America even such goods as would otherwise have been cheap enough to appeal to American buyers.

Given this unbalanced state of affairs between two of the world's biggest trading nations, the whole position of world trade was shaky. When the big depression of the 1930s came along, America stopped using even a part of her favourable balance to lend abroad. Everyone wanted to sell securities for cash and notes for gold; Britain had a political crisis, the calls on the Bank of England for gold bullion grew bigger than could be met, and convertibility was suspended again in September 1931—which amounted, of course, to the abandonment of the gold standard.

Free Exchange Rates: Exchange Controls. From then until the outbreak of World War II, exchange rates, with some exceptions, were free to move according to people's estimates of the buying power and future prospects of each currency. The exceptions were a small group of countries (France being the most important) which grimly deflated their currencies and clung to the gold standard, and another, larger group, of which Nazi Germany was chief, which imposed exchange controls of the kind later imposed in this country. (The main difference between the Nazi controls of the 1930s and the British controls of the 1950s was in the penalties for infringement: for the latter, fines or imprisonment, for the former, beheading.)

The effect of these controls, which prevented Germans from obtaining or using foreign currency for any but government-approved purposes, was to cut down and distort international trade and put difficulties in the way of other trading countries. British exporters to Central Europe, for instance, would find that no one would buy their goods, however competitive their price and quality, because the countries concerned had exported goods to Germany and could only get payment by taking German goods in exchange, no payments in marks being allowed. The German goods might be not at all what they wanted—Rumania, for instance, once sold a lot of wheat to Germany and had to take payment almost entirely in aspirins and mouth-organs—but the alternative was not to get paid at all. They reduced a significant proportion of international trade to wasteful and clumsy straight-line swaps. But they did do what, from the German point of view, was their main job: they enabled Hitler to use all available foreign exchange to buy what Germany needed to prepare for World War II.

Moreover—this is the important point—they showed how the technique of control could be used to ensure that what the Government thought essential should be bought in preference to other things, and from the sources the Government thought advisable rather than from other sources. The aim did not have to be, as in Germany's case, military strength; it could be any aim the Government chose—better nutrition for the mass of the people, stock-piling of raw materials against a scarcity more distant than ordinary speculators would take into account, or, more generally and more frequently, *the maintenance of an internal price level whose reduction would involve depression.*

Exchange Control for Stable Prices and Full Employment. It is this last point, more than any other, which accounted for the maintenance of exchange restrictions, in practically every country of the world but the United States, after World War II. Britain imposed them in 1939 for war purposes. Exchange rates were legally fixed; the sale of sterling for currencies outside the Sterling Area (i.e. to countries other than those keeping their gold reserve in London) was forbidden, the Bank of England providing whatever foreign currency was needed for approved purposes; all imports were subject to licence; the great bulk of necessary foreign buying was done by the Government itself, the previous importers serving it as agents.

After the war there was some gradual and piecemeal relaxation; some imports were freed from specific licensing, others were allowed on a larger scale, approval was given more easily for the use of foreign currency (as, for instance, the purchase of francs and lire for holidays in France and Italy). But the pound, like most other currencies, remained inconvertible into gold and only convertible into other currencies through the official channel and at the official rate; the export of capital —i.e. the buying of other countries' securities—outside the sterling area was forbidden altogether except for a very few approved projects; and much of the import trade, especially in food-stuffs, remained for many years in official hands and was carried on by procedures sometimes not far removed from straight-line swaps. Thus the extra pounds generated by war expenditure and post-war 'cheap money' policy (see Chapter XV) were prevented from getting out into foreign trade and constituting a demand for foreign currency beyond what could be offset by exports; and this made it possible, as we shall see in Chapter XXII, to maintain high profits, high wages, and high employment without running immediately and automatically into balance-of-payment difficulties.

Return to Convertibility. One cause of post-war currency difficulties was the world-wide dollar shortage or 'dollar gap' arising from the fact that America was buying much less from the rest of the world than the rest of the world was buying from her. Dollars, therefore, became a hard currency, a currency whose value, left to itself, would rise much higher than the official rate of exchange. To help fill the dollar gap America made generous loans and gifts (see page 264) and encouraged the use of part of the Marshall Aid to ease another problem, the breakdown of multilateral trade.

Within the Sterling Area (i.e. the Commonwealth countries,

except Canada, and a few non-Commonwealth countries) the
pound was freely transferable and trade restrictions few. But
inside Europe, and between Europe and the sterling area
countries, trade and currency restrictions in large degree prevented goods moving between countries except as part of a
bilateral balance agreed between Governments. Marshall Aid
funds, to assist in getting multilateral trade going again, provided a central pool of working capital for the European
Payments Union (E.P.U.) when it was set up for the offsetting
of debits and credits between the nations of Western Europe.
Each month under these arrangements any nation which had a
net surplus in its balance of payments with fellow E.P.U.
members, after all offsetting over the period had been carried
out, got part of the surplus in gold and part in credit on the
E.P.U.'s books. Any nation, on the other hand, which had a
deficit paid part of that deficit in gold and was debited in the
E.P.U.'s books for the rest. From time to time E.P.U.'s resources were strained as individual countries repeatedly had
large credits or large debts, but in general the system worked
well and enabled the main countries of Western Europe gradually to remove restrictions on trade and exchange movements
among themselves—and, through Britain's participation, with
the sterling area countries too. More slowly, restrictions on
imports from America were also removed as the dollar gap
was closed, thanks partly to expansion in exports to the United
States, but even more because of heavy American overseas
spending on military and economic aid, largely to non-Euro-
pean countries. In December 1958, all the important member
countries of E.P.U. finally felt strong enough to wind-up
E.P.U. and declare their currencies *convertible*; for Britain
this meant that all new foreign-owned holdings of pounds
sterling could be freely converted into gold, dollars or any
other currency at the official rate of exchange.

Throughout these changes sterling maintained a somewhat
precarious balance. In 1949 the values of the pound and the
dollar were so badly out of step that Britain changed the official
exchange rate, devaluing or cheapening the pound so that it
cost only $2·80 instead of $4·03 as previously (and around

$4·80 before the outbreak of war in 1939). At the same time in 1949, or shortly after, most other European currencies were devalued against the dollar, though the extent of the devaluation varied. Sterling's devaluation helped British exports, but subsequently world demand for pounds continued almost every alternate year to fall below the supply at the current rate. Progressive relaxation of trade and exchange controls— nowadays the only substantial restrictions are those on capital movements—meant that the Chancellor of the Exchequer had increasingly to depend upon the joint effects of his annual Budget and of the controls on credit and interest rates exercised through the Bank of England if he needed to adjust the balance of the British economy in order to aim at the highest level of economic activity attainable at home without an adverse balance of payments. Some of the problems which this involves are examined in the next two chapters.

The whole matter of foreign exchange is indeed, at the time of writing, in a state of almost day-to-day transition. Readers of the latter part of this chapter are strongly advised to remember this and, if they suspect out-of-dateness, to check its account of these matters from current sources.

CHAPTER XXI

PUBLIC FINANCE

THE last two chapters of this book are concerned with the incomes and the expenditures of government as such. In every field of economic activity which we have studied so far, the Government has entered in in one way or another. But the way governments finance their own activities, and the effect of these activities on the economic life of the countries concerned and particularly on the level of employment, need separate treatment. The public finance studied here is the public finance of the United Kingdom. Other countries have different systems, but the principles involved are much the same everywhere.

Why Governments Need Money. Governments have a number of jobs to do, all of which cost money. Some of these jobs have to be done by governments because they are not of a kind which can possibly be done by private individuals and groups. (We touched on this question in Chapter III.) The armed forces, the diplomatic service, representation on the United Nations and other international bodies, the law courts, the police force, the fire services, the roads, the harbours, the sewers, the inspectorate enforcing health regulations—these and many others have to be provided, and paid for, jointly by the citizens whom they serve, through their elected governments and local authorities.

Above this minimum of publicly-provided 'musts' there is the great range of services which could at a pinch, and in theory, be provided individually but which, if left to individuals, might not get provided in the right quantities or reach all those needing them: e.g. education, or medical, dental and optical services. Then, besides providing services directly, the State must (according to all decent modern opinion) look after the helpless and unfortunate among its citizens, paying pensions or benefits to the sick, the unemployed, widows, orphans and the aged; in Britain, it also helps parents to bring up their children by providing family allowances.

Progressive and Regressive Taxation. Some of these Government services are partly self-financing. Every economically independent member of the public makes a weekly payment, the price of his or her National Insurance Stamp, towards the cost of sickness and unemployment benefit, maternity benefit, retirement pension and funeral benefit—what is sometimes called 'cradle-to-grave' security. But this payment does not cover the whole cost of these benefits, which, like the other social services, the housing subsidies, and everything else provided 'free' by the Government, has to be financed out of taxation. Since the rich pay heavier taxes than the poor (we shall see later how they are graded), while the poor make more use of the social services than the rich, the net effect is to redistribute a large proportion of the national income and bring about a greater degree of economic equality than would otherwise exist. This has not always been so. The taxes imposed by medieval princes were apt to be raised from the poor and spent on the rich, and so to increase inequality. Indeed, the pattern of Government spending and money-raising in Britain had this effect, on balance, up to within the last couple of hundred years. A tax system which makes incomes more equal is called *progressive*, one which increases inequality is called *regressive*. Within a tax system any particular tax may work either way, as we shall see; but the net effect is what matters most.

The ordinary revenue of the British Central Government is collected for it by the Board of Inland Revenue, which is responsible for the various kinds of direct taxation (see below); by the Customs and Excise authorities who look after most indirect taxation; and by a number of miscellaneous agencies dealing with other sources of income (e.g. the Post Office).

Direct Taxation. The Inland Revenue collects direct taxes, that is, taxes levied on wealth as such, which are paid directly to the Department by the individual or firm concerned. The main forms of taxation in this class are: Income Tax, Surtax, Death Duties, Profits Tax and (really out of place among the others) Stamp Tax. Income Tax is the highest yielding of these providing nearly a half of the total revenue—in 1963 £2,818 m. out of £6,794 m.

Under the 1963 Budget the 'standard' rate of income tax was 7s. 9d. in the £, but very few people's tax came to exactly 7s. 9d. in the £ of their income, because of exemptions and reduced rates. People with incomes under £180 were totally exempt. Unmarried men and women paid no tax on the first £200 of their incomes, and married men paid no tax on the first £320. Every dependent child in the family entitled them to another £115 to £165 of exempted income. Then there was a further allowance on earned income (as distinct from rents, interest and dividend payments): two-ninths of the first £4,005 and one-ninth of the next £5,940 of net pay after deducting ex-expenses, superannuation contributions, etc. There were other reliefs and allowances (e.g. for aged dependent relations, and for certain kinds of insurance policy) considerably explained in detail in the notes accompanying forms for the return of income. Finally, even when the taxable level was reached after all deductions, tax was not at once chargeable at the full rate; on the first £100 of taxable income the rate was 4s. in the £, on the next £200 it was 6s. and on the remainder it was 7s. 9d. —the so-called 'standard rate'. In fact, no one who was not also a surtax payer (see below) paid as much as 7s. 9d. in the £ on his income as a whole.

Income Tax: An Example. All this may be made clearer by a concrete example. Under the Budget of 1963 a married man earning £900 per annum, with one child, and no claim for other reliefs, was assessed as shown on the next page.

Of course, allowances, deductions and the standard rate of tax itself can vary from year to year according to the views of the current Chancellor of the Exchequer (who is responsible for drawing up the Budget) and the situation with which he is confronted. The example below is given purely as an illustration, not as a true description of what the £900-a-year man, with a wife and one child, will be paying at the date when this page is read.

TABLE XI—AN INCOME-TAX ASSESSMENT

Gross Income		£900
Personal Allowance as married man	£320	
Child (age 11) Allowance	£115	
Earned Income deduction (i.e. 2/9ths of £900)	£200	
Total allowance to be deducted	£635	
Taxable Income		£265

Tax payable at 4s. on £100 = £20 0 0
  ,,   ,,   ,, 6s. ,, £165 = £49 10 0

Total tax payable on £265 = £69 10 0

Surtax. Surtax is levied (as well as Income Tax) on taxable incomes above £2,000 per annum (since 1961, above £4,000 if all the income is earned). Starting at £2,000 this tax is at 2s. in the £ for incomes in the lower ranges, and then increases progressively until for taxable incomes of £15,000 and upwards it is at 10s., which, with Income Tax, amounts to 17s. 9d. on every additional pound. A man with an income of, say, £25,000 a year, who takes on an additional piece of work yielding £400, retains only 400 × 2s. 3d.—i.e. £45.

Estate Duty. When a person dies leaving more than a small minimum amount of property, a proportion of the amount has to be paid to the Exchequer. This tax is the Estate Duty, generally called the 'Death Duty'. The rate rises as the 'estate' increases, ranging from 1 per cent on an estate of £4,000 to £5,000, to the maximum rate of 80 per cent on estates of £1 million or over.

Profits Tax. This tax, first introduced during World War II, is levied on the profits of joint-stock companies and corporate bodies, whether distributed or not (though at a lower rate for undistributed profits), in addition to the Income Tax and Surtax levied on the interest and dividends received by individual shareholders, and at a flat rate regardless of the size of the shareholders' incomes. Under the 1963 Budget the rate stood at 15 per cent for distributed profits.

Stamp Duty. This is really an indirect tax for the collection of which the Inland Revenue is responsible. Most financial transactions call for the use of documents of one kind or another—cheques, receipts, Bills of Exchange, deeds of transfer relating to property, and so on. All these must carry a stamp— of a value of 2d. on cheques for any amount and on receipts for any sum above £2, and of values depending on the scale of the transaction on other documents.

Indirect Taxes: Customs, Excise and Purchase Tax. The Board of Customs & Excise collects customs duties and excise duties. These are known as *indirect* taxes, because they are included in the retail price of a commodity or service, so that the person responsible for paying them in the first place— the manufacturer or importer or promoter—is not the person on whom the burden finally falls. Customs duties or tariffs are taxes levied on goods entering the country from abroad and are generally charged proportionately to the value of the commodity concerned, though they may be 'specific', that is at so much per lb. or other physical unit of measurement. Excise duties are taxes levied on goods manufactured and sold within the country, like purchase tax, and the beer and spirit taxes; they are also levied on some forms of public entertainment where an admittance charge is made.

Apart from what it gets through ordinary taxation, the Government also raises revenue from other sources. Some Government trading yields a profit. Licences on cars, guns and dogs are also revenue earners—the motor licences being by far the most important.

Standards of a Good Tax. These taxes have not been imposed, and fixed at their particular rates, at random. In deciding what taxes to levy, and at what rates, in order to bring in a given revenue, any Chancellor must be guided by certain general principles. He must know whether a tax will cost much or little money to collect—from the revenue point of view it is obviously not worth while to impose a tax which will cost more in tax-collectors' salaries than it brings in. (When the customs tariff was overhauled in 1825 it was discovered that many items were, on balance, actually costing the Exchequer money.) He must consider whether it can be easily evaded, for example, by false and uncheckable returns; it is no use counting on revenue from a tax which can only be collected in full from a scrupulously honest minority. (Countries most of whose taxpayers are peasant farmers, living largely on their own produce and keeping no accounts, find it impossible for this reason to rely much on income tax.)

He must consider the taxpayer's convenience in the time and manner of levying the tax; a tax charged long after the actions (receipts of income, purchases of commodities) which incur it, or a tax which is impossible to calculate beforehand, may put taxpayers to very severe inconvenience indeed. (That is one reason why PAYE, 'Pay-as-you-earn', income tax on wages and salaries, is preferred to the old annually-paid income tax which taxpayers had often not put by enough to meet.) He must consider the fairness or otherwise of the tax; does it take more money from the rich man, who is best able to bear it, than from the poor? or does it fall on all taxpayers equally? or on the poor harder than on the rich? Income tax and surtax are obviously 'fair' taxes in that they increase progressively with income; purchase tax, graded so as to hit luxury articles harder than necessities, is probably (though it is hard to say) roughly neutral; the beer and tobacco taxes are regressive, since the poor (apart from teetotallers and non-smokers) spend a bigger proportion of their income on these things than the rich do.

He also has to consider the incentive effect of the tax, the extent to which it encourages or discourages work, saving and enterprise. Obviously, the £25,000-a-year man mentioned on page 283 has little incentive to do an extra £400-worth of work for £45 net earnings, and investment in risky enterprise is discouraged by the prospect of standing any losses that may arise and paying over 15 per cent of any distributed profits (plus income tax) to the Exchequer. On the other hand, the need to earn more, gross, in order to keep the same income, net, may make some people work harder; how do these two possibilities balance out?

Finally, there are side-effects to be considered; will a very heavy tax on this luxury article squeeze its producer right out of production, and if this happened, would it be a good thing? In the national interest (as the Chancellor and his colleagues see it) is it desirable to reduce or to encourage the consumption of *this* thing or *that* thing? Some examples of changes in taxation, particularly important for their side-effects, as distinct from their revenue effects, are the increases in excise duties on spirits after the war, narrowing the home market and so making more available for export; the increases, over the same period, in petrol tax, designed partly to drive traffic back to the railways by making road transport more expensive, and partly to gain dollars by reducing British consumption of a dollar-earning commodity; the increase in purchase tax on electrical apparatus in 1951, aimed at slowing the increase in the consumption of electric current and so avoiding power cuts.

Looking further back, the beer and spirits duties have always been regarded partly as a defence against drunkenness; the 'death duties' were designed not only to raise revenue but to break up great estates and redistribute property; and of course the main purpose of most import duties is not to raise revenue, but to make imported goods more expensive and so, by preventing consumers from seeking better value for money than home producers can provide, to 'protect' the particular home industries producing those goods.

Conflict of Standards. Naturally, it is rare to find that a tax scores full marks under all these heads. Considerations of fairness and considerations of incentive are apt to collide head-on. Only progressive taxation can be 'fair' according to modern ideas of social justice; but the effect of progressive taxation is to put a special penalty on any extra effort, extra thrift, or extra enterprise which earns extra income, since that extra income bears a progressively higher tax than the lesser amount earned by lesser effort, thrift and enterprise. In the lower income ranges, considerations of fairness also collide with considerations of convenience, and cheapness of collection. Persons whose incomes are just below income-tax level pay a lot of tax indirectly, while persons whose incomes may be only half as much may pay hardly any less. But trying to collect, by the fairer method of graded income tax, the same amount of revenue from those people as they now pay in tobacco tax, would mean an enormous increase in form-filling, PAYE staffs, and so forth; and, moreover, since people do not say to themselves every time they buy a packet of cigarettes: 'I am now paying 3s. 4d. tax on 1s. 2d. worth of tobacco', they 'feel' the tobacco tax less painfully than they would a 3s. 4d. deduction from their pay-packets.

The Budget. Each year's Budget represents a careful balancing of all these pros and cons and—as we shall see in the next chapter—of much wider considerations. The Budget is the Government's balance-sheet of estimated revenue and expenditure for the coming financial year, which the Chancellor presents for the approval of the House of Commons at the beginning of April. During the previous weeks the House has already discussed and approved, in principle and in general outline, the amounts to be spent on the State's various activities during the financial year which the Budget is to cover. (This is known as 'voting Supply'. The details are debated and voted on later, after the Budget.) Thus the Chancellor knows roughly what expenses the Government is committed to, and in his Budget speech he lists and explains the taxes by which he intends to raise the necessary revenue. If the House approves, it passes the 'Budget resolutions' which give the Government temporary power to proceed. Then, in the ensuing months, the details of the proposed taxes are debated and voted on; these are contained in the *Finance Act* which embodies, in legal form, all the revenue provisions of the Budget.

Here is a summary of a Budget Estimate:

TABLE XII—A BUDGET ESTIMATE (1963–64)

Estimated Revenue (in £ millions)		*Estimated Expenditure* (in £ millions)	
Income Tax	2,789	National Debt, etc.	790
Surtax	190	Defence	1,904
Death Duties	279	External Relations	220
Stamp Duties	73	Agricultural Subsidies, etc.	399
Profits Tax	398	Industry and Transport	444
Customs and Excise	2,732	Grants to Local Authorities	794
Motor Duties	160	Education	184
Broadcast Licences	43	Health and Welfare	829
Miscellaneous	175	Other Local Services	108
Deficit	90	Law and Order	124
		Benefits and Assistance	690
		Civil Service	323
		Science, Art and Miscellaneous	120
	6,929		6,929

If there is a surplus it is used partly on meeting what is called 'below-the-line' expenditure—expenditure on capital outlays which do not enter into the ordinary Budget estimates, such as loans to the Nationalized Industries, to the G.P.O. and to local authorities. There may remain a 'true' deficit; there may even be a deficit 'above the line' that is in the Budget estimate itself as in the 1963–64 Budget. If there is a deficit of any kind, then the extra money has to be raised in other ways, notably by borrowing.

The National Debt. The liabilities which the State incurs by borrowing from its citizens constitute the *National Debt*. Most of these liabilities have been incurred in time of war. The enormous expenses which modern war involves cannot be met out of taxation alone; even a very steep increase in practically all kinds of taxation only succeeded in covering half the cost of World War II. This is partly because taxes are imposed on income and various forms of spending, not on capital, and it is capital which a belligerent government needs; partly because taxes high enough to do the trick and bring in enough for capital needs, would have a devastating effect on incentive—and the last thing one wants in wartime is for people to decide that work is not worth while. So the gap between tax revenue and total expenditure is filled by loans; and as we have seen these loans themselves cause a general expansion of money and credit, of which, in taxes and more loans, the Government can get most of the benefit.

It is sometimes argued—but quite wrongly—that in so far as the cost of war is met out of taxation it is paid for at the time while in so far as it is met by borrowing the burden of payment is always shifted to later generations. If the borrowing in question is borrowing from abroad this shift is a real one. The resources needed for the war are imported (for the moment) without payment; later on, they have to be paid for by means of exports for which, in turn, no payment is received. But internal borrowing is another matter. It does not, like external borrowing, in any way reduce the load on the nation as a whole; wars have to be fought by to-day's fighting men (who therefore cannot to-day be producing useful goods and services) armed with today's weapons and munitions (whose production means the transfer, to-day, of more workers and other resources from the production of useful goods and services). 'Posterity' bears a real burden in that it has to go on supporting widows, orphans and the disabled; to restore damage; and to make do with impaired or run-down capital equipment. But the immediate cost, the cost which the loans cover, falls squarely on the nation at the time when it is incurred, just as much as that part which is covered by taxes.

'*The Burden of the National Debt*' is in fact very much a figure of speech. For while the amount concerned appears to the Chancellor, and through him to the taxpayers, as a debt on which interest must be painfully paid, it appears with equal truth to the holders of Government securities as a credit from which an income is painlessly derived; and the holders of Government securities are the taxpayers themselves!

U

Of course, taxpayers and security-holders do not exactly match. Practically everyone pays taxes; not everyone holds Government securities. To an active business man whose capital is all tied up in his business, with nothing left for investment in Government bonds, the National Debt is a debt indeed; he must help meet it and he gets no return from it. To a retired person with a substantial holding of War Loan it is a major source of income, only a fraction of which has to be returned as his share of the 'debt burden'.

How far popular opinion is really wrong in regarding a large National Debt as burdensome and disadvantageous is, however, a matter on which economists do not altogether agree. Some—a minority—hold that its only disadvantage is the comparatively tiny administrative expense of collecting the necessary interest out of one national pocket and paying it into the other. Most agree that it does impose two more important disadvantages; it transfers more wealth than would otherwise be necessary from the active, earning, enterprising part of the nation to the passive, the retired, the sitters-still; and since it must do so by way of taxation it means a worse worry for Chancellors trying to avoid damaging effects on incentive. But how important these disadvantages are is very hard to estimate.

How the National Debt is Made Up. Apart from foreign loans, the National Debt is made up of three kinds: *funded*, *unfunded*, and *floating* debt. The difference lies mainly in the time of repayment. *Funded* debt is either irredeemable (the Government, in effect, offers a perpetual income in return for perpetual ownership of the capital sum concerned) or redeemable at no fixed date (the lender cannot get his money back from the Government unless and until the Government chooses to repay him). In either case, of course, the individual holder of the security can get cash if he wants it by selling the security, through the Stock Exchange, to someone else. *Unfunded* debt must, by the terms of issue, be paid back on or before a fixed date; while *floating* debt, which consists of Treasury Bills and Ways and Means advances (from the Bank of England), must be paid back at the end of three months, six months, or within the year, as the case may be. These three kinds of debt amounted in 1962 to about £28,674 millions.

Interest Rates on Government Securities. The loans comprising the funded and unfunded debt are issued by the Treasury. The rate of interest which they carry depends partly on current interest levels in general (see Chapter XII) and partly on the length of time due to pass before the debt is redeemed. Since the risk of default on British Government securities is too tiny to worry about, the rate is lower than on loans to less stable governments or to institutions and firms. But the longer the period before redemption, the higher the rate tends to be, since the longer is the period during which the investor must, if he wants his money back, take his chance of selling his holding at a satisfactory price on the Stock Exchange.

On the Stock Exchange, the price of Government securities is free to move, like that of any other security, according to supply and demand. These depend on many factors. One, and a very important one, was noted on page 204: with a rising rate of interest, low-interest-bearing securities become less attractive, the demand falls off and holders can only dispose of them at a loss, while with a falling rate of interest high-interest-bearing securities become more attractive, and holders can take a profit. The cheap money policy of 1945–7, with interest rates at $2\frac{1}{2}$ per cent, meant large profits for holders of old securities yielding 4 per cent interest; the later rise to 3 per cent and beyond imposed losses on those who had bought $2\frac{1}{2}$ per cent bonds during the cheap money period. If one looks at the prices of different Government issues as they are listed on the City page of any daily paper, one can see how they all fit the current rate of interest—allowing for the difference in redemption dates, £100 invested in any of them will bring approximately the same return.

Another factor, really one step further back since it affects the rate of interest itself, is the amount of borrowing being done by the Government's competitors. If a Commonwealth government or a big municipality, for instance, launches a loan, a lot of demand is soaked up which might otherwise have been directed to Government securities, and is a factor weakening their price. And the same applies to a certain extent to issues of debentures and shares by private firms. How powerful their competition is depends partly on the credit-worthiness of the firms concerned and partly on whether investors are in the mood to venture, to risk their money for profit, or to play safe and stick to fixed-interest-bearing assets. A great deal of the skill exercised by Treasury officials, the Bank of England, and the Issue Houses consists of timing new issues, purchases, conversions and redemptions so as to fit the current state of the market[1]. This again is a matter frequently discussed in 'City Page' editorials.

The Funded Debt consists of 2½ per cent *Consols* and of other types of undated stock. The Treasury is under no obligation to redeem these securities by any fixed date; but it could in principle do so. In fact, 'sinking funds' have from time to time been set up in order to accumulate the means of redemption. During the nineteenth century the Treasury bought back considerable quantities of securities from their holders and then gradually reduced the Debt. For many reasons, this policy has been abandoned in our own time.

The word 'funded' came into use in the eighteenth century, when a special fund was assigned to meet the interest payments on each particular loan. (Hence the term 'funds' as applied to British Government securities in general.) Later, these special funds were 'consolidated' into one. The Consolidated Fund is that part of the national revenue which is set aside by Statute to meet not only interest charges on the National Debt but also the cost of the Queen's Civil List, the salaries of judges and of the Leader of the Opposition, and other miscellaneous payments. This Fund does not have to be voted annually, as do

[1] A loan is said to be issued at 'par' if, for example, stock to a face value of £100 is sold for £100. It may, however, be issued at a price either above or below par; by this means, the effective rate of interest which the buyer gets on each £100 invested can be finely adjusted to suit market conditions at the time of issue.

other Government revenues; thus it remains above any political battles which may arise over controversial items.

Local Government Expenditure. Not all collective spending is done by the Central Government. Local authorities—County Councils, County Borough Councils, Borough Councils, Urban and Rural District Councils and Parish Councils—perform according to their various legal powers and obligations a number of local services; these are financed partly by the rates, which are a special kind of local tax, partly by Central Government grants and partly by income from their own trading activities. These services include the upkeep of secondary roads, the provision of schools, the carrying out of certain public-health measures, the maintenance of the police forces and fire brigades, street cleaning and lighting, refuse collection, and in some places the supply of water, besides many other minor and optional activities. For purposes of capital expenditure, the more important local authorities have legal powers to borrow money.

The Assessment of Rates. Local rates began with the raising of money by each parish in order to adminster the Elizabethan Poor Law, which made the parishes responsible for maintaining the poor who could not fend for themselves. In those days it was generally difficult or impossible to assess the amount of a man's income, and tax him accordingly, but the size of the property which he owned or occupied was a fairly reliable pointer to his wealth. All property was therefore assessed at a rateable value corresponding fairly closely to its annual rental value, and this practice has been continued to the present day. The 1961 Rating and Valuation Act, which came into force in 1963, does in fact base rateable value upon the current market value of property, subject to modifications in a few cases. Until 1948 the local authorities themselves did the assessing; the Local Government Act of that year transferred the work of assessment to the Board of Inland Revenue, but the collection of the rates is still done by local councils.

The actual amount of rates paid by an individual is settled as follows: Suppose the total assessed rateable value of all property in a local government area is £4 million, and that the total proposed expenditure of the authority amounts, after allowing for Central Government grants, to £1 million in one year, then a rate of 5s. in the £ will be levied, so that an occupier of property rated at £200 will pay £50 in rates. Beginning at the foot of this page and continuing on the pages following, is printed a statement showing how the rates were spent in a recent year in the County of Kent, and the Borough of Dover —it can be found printed on the back of every rate demand note presented in the latter area. The first item in column one, 'Borough and Liberties', relates to the administration of justice in the Borough and certain areas which are outside its boundaries but within its jurisdiction.

Weakness of the Rating System. This system of providing for the needs of local government by levying rates on property has in the past been open to several objections, most of which have now been met. In the first place, while the assessed value of the property may remain the same from year to year, the income derived from it by its owner—and hence his ability to pay—may vary considerably. A very thriving business, and one actually making a loss, may both pay just the same amount, which is neither fair nor convenient. As regards agriculture, this disadvantage was overcome by the 1929 Derating Act, which relieved all agricultural land and buildings entirely from rate payment; industrial, commercial and transport undertakings, which were then relieved, now pay their full share.

BOROUGH OF DOVER
RATE SERVICES FOR THE YEAR 1963–64
STATEMENT OF EXPENSES

The following statement shows how the rate in the £ is made up. It sets out in relation to the Borough Council, the Kent County Council and the Kent Probation Committee in terms of rates in the £ the expenses, after deducting fees, rents, recoupments, etc., of the services and the amounts of Government grants and other moneys receivable.

The estimated products of a penny rate for the period of the rate are: Kent County Council £285,896; Dover Borough Council £4,875.

Purpose	Kent County Council		Dover Borough Council		TOTAL	
	s.	d.	s.	d.	s.	d.
Boroughs and Liberties				0·60		0·60
Burials				2·30		2·30
Care of deprived children		3·08				3·08
Education	10	0·63			10	0·63
Entertainments and publicity				1·51		1·51
Fire services		4·93				4·93
Highways and Bridges	1	0·36	1	2·88	2	3·24
Housing			1	1·54	1	1·54
Land drainage and coast protection		1·72				1·72
Parks and open spaces				8·92		8·92
Police	1	6·49			1	6·49
Public Health Services		9·95		5·07	1	3·02
Public Library and Museum				3·37		3·37
Refuse removal and disposal				4·36		4·36
Registration of electors		0·30				0·30
Services for aged, infirm, etc.		3·56				3·56
Sewerage and sewage disposal				1·16		1·16
Street lighting				3·60		3·60
Planning and Development		0·94		0·12		1·06
Other services and expenses		3·51		3·56		7·07
Contributions to district councils under S.56 Local Govt. Act, 1958		0·13				0·13
	14	11·60	5	2·99	20	2·59

Deduct: Credits, Housing Subsidies, Govt. grants, etc.   10   5.48

     9   9·11

Add: Kent Probation Committee   0.37

     Transitional payment   0.52

Rate in the £ payable by ratepayer   9   10.00

As a consequence of changes made by the Local Government Act, 1958, most rating authorities need to levy a lower rate in the £ than they would otherwise have done. Some, however, need to levy a higher rate. Under S.15 of that Act the gaining authorities are for a period to contribute part of their gains to the losing authorities to make good a diminishing part of their losses. The item 'transitional payment' represents the payment of the Borough Council as a gaining authority under this arrangement.

FIG. 28—RATE DEMAND NOTE (*slightly simplified*)

A second weakness of the rating system lay in the fact that the local authorities whose needs were greatest often had the least rateable value in their area from which to raise money. A local authority in a 'depressed area' consisting mostly of poor streets and run-down factories would have few resources to draw on, but more, rather than less, needs to meet—more claims on public assistance, deficits on municipal trading, and so forth; while a wealthy and prosperous town would have fewer needs and much greater resources. This meant that poor localities, forced to levy high rates on their limited rateable values, discouraged the new enterprises which they particularly needed. This disparity has been partly evened out by a complicated system of Exchequer grants designed both to meet the needs of local authorities for money to pay for their social services, and to compensate them for the loss involve in derating. Certain of these Exchequer grants are for specified purposes: housing, highways, police, while a general or block grant is made towards the cost of education, fire services and National Health Service and other minor services. As the Central Government's contribution to local finances grows more important, so it gains more control over the way in which the money is spent; so that local authorities are less independent than they used to be.

Municipal Trade. The third source of local government revenue is income from corporate property, and profits of municipal trade. The former item explains itself. Municipal trading is the provision by the local authority of water, gas or electricity supplies, local bus services, and sometimes restaurant or laundry facilities. With the exception of the last two (and possibly of buses; here not all economists agree), these services are by their nature bound to be monopolies (see Chapter III) and, even in the days when private enterprise was looked upon as the only natural and normal sort, the possibility that monopoly powers might be abused led to fairly general willingness to see them in disinterested public hands.[1] Any profits

[1] Municipal gas and electricity undertakings, like privately owned gas and electricity companies, were taken over by the Gas Council and

from municipal undertakings are normally used to 'relieve the rates'—that is, to pay for other activities which would otherwise have to be paid for by the ratepayer. Whether it is really sound to run municipal enterprise at a profit, instead of just breaking even, is a question on which there is some disagreement. On the one hand, such profits make it possible to run better local authority services (spend more on schools, for instance); on the other, it is argued that these better services should be paid for by the community in general, in rough proportion to their wealth, and not by the people who happen to ride on the municipal buses or swim in the municipal baths, who may quite well be poorer than those who use neither. This question of the price policy of public undertakings is a great deal wider than a matter of trams and swimming baths; it arises acutely whenever an industry is nationalized. But to discuss this question would be to get involved in advanced theory for which this is not the place.

Local Authority Loans. Like the Central Government, a local authority may wish to embark on a heavy capital expenditure programme. Local authorities do not, mercifully, finance wars between themselves, but they do build houses, civic centres, concert halls, public baths, libraries and so on. To raise the whole amount in one lump through increased rates would put a very heavy burden on the ratepayer; so the local authorities generally borrow for such purposes, thus spreading the charge over a long period of perhaps sixty years. The security for such a loan is usually the rates, which are increased by the comparatively small amount needed, over the period, to meet the interest and repayment charges.

In the years immediately following World War II the local authorities' demand for credit was particularly heavy because of the need for new houses and new schools. Joined with all the similar demands of private industry trying to reconstruct and expand, and of the Public Corporations trying to develop their capital equipment, this demand would, if left to itself,

British Electricity Authority respectively when those industries were nationalized.

have driven up the rate of interest to a very high level and more-over those whose need was most urgent might have been unable to pay the high interest rates. As we have seen, the Government wanted interest rates kept low, so, as in every case where a lower controlled price is substituted for a market price, rationing had to be introduced. All loans for local authorities had to be made through a government department, the Public Works Loan Board, which sifted the applications. All this is now changed, however; local authorities can either borrow from the Treasury or on the open market, but in both circumstances they borrow at rates comparable to those charged to other borrowers.

The Decline of Local Autonomy. Thus, taking together the control which the Central Government exercises by way of Exchequer grants and the transfer by nationalization of a large part of municipal enterprises to the centrally-controlled Corporations, the local authorities have lost a great deal of their power to manage their own affairs. Whether this is a good or bad thing is partly an economic question—does the public at large get better or worse value for money when these collective services are controlled, and paid for, nationally or locally? —but partly also a political question—are local citizenship and local responsibility valuable enough things for one to have to worry about a decline in their importance? The problem, which is not for economists alone, is to strike a proper balance between these possibly conflicting considerations.

CHAPTER XXII

PROSPERITY OR DEPRESSION?

So far, we have considered public finance simply from the point of view of the balancing of collective spending against collective income; and if this book had been written thirty years ago it would have stopped at that point. It is now generally realized, thanks largely to Lord Keynes[1], that there is a great deal more to the problem of public finance than the mere striking of a balance and the proper distribution of total spending and of the total tax burden. *It is public finance which settles, to a very large extent, whether there shall be prosperity or depression, high employment or unemployment.*

Boom and Slump. Now, in a way this is obvious enough. We saw in Chapter XVII that a government which overspends its income and makes up the difference by creating a lot of fresh purchasing power can start off a raging, tearing, inflationary boom; and we saw too (the years following World War I are a striking example) that a government which drastically deflates the supply of money and credit produces just the opposite effect—a general trade slump. But up to quite a short time ago most economists held that these things only happened because the monetary system had been interfered with; that if governments would only keep their hands off, and particularly avoid the kind of inflationary spree which always means deflation later, everything should in theory go smoothly. In practice there had indeed always been swings between good and bad trade between high and low business activity, and very painful and wasteful these sometimes were; but on the whole economists

[1] Particularly to *The General Theory of Employment, Interest and Money* (1936).

explained them by particular causes not especially connected with public finance. Good times and bad, they said, were due to the contagious effect of business men's optimism and pessimism, or to the stickiness of particular prices, or to the fact that big new discoveries start waves of business activity which naturally die down in time, or (getting nearer, now, to public finance) to the limits imposed by the gold standard on the volume of currency and credit available to finance the growing needs of trade.

To be perfectly frank, no one believes that the whole truth about booms and depressions is known even yet; and readers should take warning that the account of modern theory which follows is a very drastically simplified one—more simplified, by comparison with the sort of thing which experts discuss among themselves, than the rest of this book. Still, there is no doubt about the almost universal agreement among economists on one point; that business activity cannot keep itself steady without deliberate action at the centre. The economic system is not, as the older economists thought it was, self-balancing.

Achieving the Economic Maximum. To see why this is so we must go back and pick up a number of threads from previous chapters. First of all, we noted in Chapter I the great obvious economic fact that there is not enough of everything to give everybody as much as they could possibly want. With only so much land, so much resources of raw material and energy, and so much human effort available, and with only so much technical knowledge of how to use these things, there is a maximum possible output of the goods and services which make up the standard of living. The aim, and the limit, of economic activity is to achieve that maximum; to choose between possible different ways of using the resources available so as to get from them, taking present and future together, the best possible result. The fact that it would be pleasant to get a still better result, that the best that can be achieved is still short of people's notion of how well they ought to live, is beside the point. It is just as well to bear this obvious fact in mind, because when for any reason the economic system is obviously failing to get maximum results, people are tempted to feel that the possibilities of improvement, just because they are obvious, are also unlimited.

Specialization and Unemployment. In Chapters II, III and IV we saw that production is organized in an extremely complicated way so as to link together an enormous number of specialist activities, activities of individuals carrying out specialized detailed processes, activities of firms producing specialized products, activities of local groups or nations concentrating on the use of special local resources and local skills. Particularly—this is especially important—we saw that there is a division of labour between enterprises producing for present consumption and those producing for the future—i.e. the capital goods industries. And we noted that as soon as specialization came in, with production for distant markets, there arose the danger of unemployment for specialists whose market for any reason failed them and who, because they were specialists, could not immediately and without serious loss turn to something else.

Difficulties of Adaptation to Change. In Chapter V we saw, from the example of British industry, how deeply rooted is specialization and how hard it is for the structure of established industry to adapt itself to changing circumstances; in Chapters VI and VIII we saw how changing circumstances—changes in supply, changes in demand—make different prices necessary to exactly clear the market of particular goods coming forward, and how accordingly, prices which do not fit the market situation leave either unbought goods piling up or unsatisfied customers in the queue. In Chapters X and XII we saw how, by buying or hiring the factors of production, enterprises incur costs and, particularly if they are heavy-industry enterprises, commit themselves for the future to programmes which may be very difficult indeed to alter.

Spending Equals Income. Now let us look at all these facts, together with what we know about the national income as a whole and the way it is divided between spending and saving.

The national money income, readers will remember, can be looked at from two sides. It is everyone's receipts—earnings, dividends, interest, rent, and so forth—and since all these receipts must have come from somewhere, it is everyone's spending too. The housewife's spending is the shopkeeper's income, the shopkeeper's spending is the income of his suppliers and his landlord and his assistants and his creditors, and their spending in turn is the income of other people.

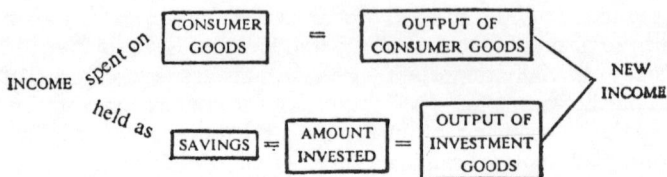

FIG. 29—RELATION OF CONSUMPTION AND INVESTMENT TO TOTAL NATIONAL INCOME. (*If amount invested is less than the amount intended to be saved, output of investment goods decreases and so resultant income is less.*)

Income and spending, taking everyone together, must be equal. If spending falls, income falls; if spending rises, income rises. The word 'spending' generally suggests spending on consumption, buying for the needs of to-day and for direct enjoyment; but if one thinks about it, it becomes obvious that spending on construction, buying for the needs of to-morrow and for the purposes of higher production, is from this point of view—the point of view of providing income for the recipients—just the same thing.

Spending on immediate consumption means income for people supplying finished consumer goods; spending for future purposes, on increasing stocks or equipment, means income for people supplying capital goods of one sort or another.

Saving and Investment. Now, we saw in Chapter IX that provision for the future, net investment over and above the mere keeping up of existing stocks and equipment, can only be brought about by reducing current consumption—remember the primitive village and its new pipe-line needing labour withdrawn from the fields. That is what saving consists in; in reducing current consumption. If—*if*—everything worked smoothly in this complicated and sticky economic world, one could leave the story there; thrifty A, B and C reduce their consumption—i.e. save; enterprising D, E and F borrow the money which A, B and C are not spending and *spend it themselves*, on pipe-lines or machinery or bringing goods from more distant markets or whatever other form real investment may take.

The total of spending is the same; the factors of production are pulled away from serving consumption and set to serve the building up of real investment; presently, when production is increased in consequence, D, E and F make profits, A, B and C draw interest, and there are more goods for everyone to buy.

Only, with all the complications and stickiness intervening, things need not and often do not work out like that. Thrifty A, B and C reduce their consumption; so far, so good. But that does not in itself bring about investment, or set up a pull into new uses of the factors of production which A, B and C are no longer paying for. That pull can only be set up by a direct initiative on the part of D, E and F. And suppose D, E and F are not feeling particularly enterprising; suppose that, after weighing up probable costs and probable sales, they see no attractive prospect of profits to be made out of new factories or improved equipment or more distant trading ventures. Suppose they prefer merely to keep bigger cash balances and play safe. Then there is no counter-balancing pull on the factors of production. A, B and C's reduced spending merely means a lower income for the people they used to buy from, and a lower income for *their* suppliers and employees, and so on, all the way round; the national income is simply pulled down by the exact amount which A, B and C have thriftily foregone. As all the A's, B's and C's will have had their incomes reduced too, with depression cutting their dividends or earnings or throwing them out of work, and as we know that the proportion people put aside for savings depends very much on their income, the end result will be that savings themselves will fall off. *A community cannot, however hard it tries, effectively save more money than is actually taken up for investment.* For various reasons—there are clues scattered all through this book—business men's ideas about the profitability of investment, and hence the amount of investment that gets done, vary very much more, between one time and another, than do people's ideas about the right amount to save.

What Settles the Amount of Investment? Let us see what factors influence the amount of investment. There is the obviousness or otherwise of opportunity, of the extra profit to be made by extra investment. An important new invention like the steam-engine or the automobile or wireless, or the discovery of a new oilfield or easily-worked coalfield, or the overcoming of some technical difficulty which had been holding up practical progress in developing any of these things, will set plenty of alert and enterprising business men scurrying to the City for capital, to the labour market for workers, to producers of machinery and office furniture and so forth for equipment. When all the more obvious opportunities have been taken, and competition has pulled down profits, the scurry slows down; that particular wave of investment is over.

Effects of a Growing Population. One thing which keeps opportunities obvious is a growing population. So many new mouths each year means so much obvious new demand for food; so many new households means so much obvious new demand for houses and furniture; towns growing at such and such a rate means so much obvious new demand for schools and roads and buses and waterworks and power plant. Once that growth stops, new needs become much less obvious; it is much less easy to see which things people are going to choose to spend their incomes on and therefore which lines of production can profitably be expanded by new investment. The nature of technical progress and discovery, then, and the rate of growth, or absence of growth, of the population, are two in-

fluences working on the business man's will to invest. What
about others?

   The Rate of Interest. In two ways the rate of interest is
important: because interest payments themselves are a cost of
production, so that high rates discourage investment and low
rates encourage it; and because, as we saw only one chapter
back, low rates raise the value of existing securities and high
rates lower them, and so their holders have correspondingly
less or more security to offer banks when they want to borrow.
Now ideally, if the desire of savers to save were stronger, at any
time, than the desire of business men to borrow, the rate of
interest ought to sink smoothly down to whatever level represented the right 'price' of lump sums—perhaps, if the desire to
save were strong enough and the desire to borrow weak enough,
to a negative level, a pay-you-to-take-it-away level, at which
savers would actually pay borrowers to look after their savings
for them.
   In practice, it does not work out like that. For one thing,
people may be saving because they are in a desperately cautious
frame of mind and want to have plenty of liquid cash on hand,
and in those circumstances the banks will have to be very
cautious, and stay very liquid, too—which means that terms to
borrowers will not be particularly easy. There are other points
to consider, too. There is the fear of being caught short, with
one's liquid funds tied up at no return to speak of, if rates
rise again. There is the traditional, conventional view that
rates *ought* not to be lower than such and such—say 2 per
cent. There is the risk of default (which is present, however
slight, in almost all borrowing-and-lending transactions, and
which gets *proportionately* more important as the 'pure' interest
rate falls); and there is the sheer administrative expense of
bringing borrowers and lenders together through the banking
and money market system—which itself costs money to run.
All these factors put a 'floor' under the rate of interest which
borrowers actually have to pay in order to get money.
   And if, as actually can happen, their demand for lump sums
is so feeble and hesitant that even a rate of interest right down

to floor-level is too high for most of them, then the will to invest and the will to save get out of balance.

The Quantity of Money. Finally, there is the quantity of money—and now, at long last after all these wanderings, we begin to see where Public Finance may come in. For 'more money about' means a bigger demand for goods, and a bigger demand means bigger profit opportunities, and bigger profit opportunities mean a bigger motive for investment in new production.

The Cause of Depression. Now suppose, as has often happened, that investment has become inadequate. Perhaps a wave of technical progress has spent itself—the big obvious main railway lines are all built, the obvious electrification schemes have all been carried out; anyway, the opportunities most outstanding in the current state of technique and taste have all been taken, and only the smaller, riskier, less attractive ones remain. At once, unpleasant things begin to happen in the capital-goods industries. Instead of building and equipping new plant, they only have to provide for the upkeep and gradual replacement of the old. Their order books get emptier and emptier. They may—remember Chapter X—cut prices, even far below cost, in order to keep going; but no one is going to replace perfectly good machines, barely run in perhaps, just because they can now be bought cheaper.

Their dividends fall off—less income for shareholders, less spending by shareholders. Workers are laid off or work short time—less income for workers, less spending by workers. So depression spreads from capital-goods industry in general to consumer-goods industry in general; and consumer-goods industry, feeling the pinch, places fewer orders even of the replacement-and-upkeep kind with capital-goods industry; everyone starts thinking less about profit than about how to meet liabilities and avoid losses; there are more and more bankruptcies, more and more unemployed, a general stagnation and freeze-up of economic activity. People *need* food and clothes and house-room as much as they ever did, their skill is no less, their actual resources have not shrunk—and yet, by a kind of general paralysis, they are prevented from serving one another's needs. Partially, to the tune of perhaps 25 or 30 per cent of its capacity, the economic system has broken down.

The Need for Public Action. Now this failure is not like a crop failure or a steel shortage or a shipping shortage, the kind of thing which, by way of scarcity and high prices, offers a wide-open, plainly signposted opportunity to alert business men, workers and investors to reap an advantage by filling the gap to everyone's benefit. We saw in Chapter III that the private enterprise, self-betterment motive cannot be entirely relied on to get everything done that needs doing, nor to take all long-run results or side-effects into account. Here is perhaps the most important instance in which public action is the only kind possible. It is to no one's individual advantage, it is not even in anyone's individual power, to do anything which will remedy this general breakdown. The worker who works hard works himself or his mate out of a job; the business man who takes on jobless workers and expands his output fails to sell it and makes losses; the private individual who tries to keep up spending to the old level overspends his diminished income and find himself in trouble with the tradesmen or his bank manager. It is to everyone's private advantage to do just precisely those things which will make the general situation worse; to be still more cautious, put off spending, cut down production. The remedy must be taken at the centre, through the machinery of money and credit; demand in general must be jacked up. *The key to recovery from general depression, and to the avoiding of general depression, is public finance.*

How can Depression be Averted? Again, the clues are to be found in earlier chapters—those dealing with money, price levels, the banking system and its relation to the government (Chapters XIII to XVII). Depression develops and deepens because inadequate investment has brought about, directly and indirectly, inadequate demand; and inadequate demand, by cutting down profit opportunities, has made investment shrink still further. The defence against depression, then, is to sustain investment and demand if they look like falling off, and develop them if they have in fact become insufficient. Essentially, the job is to increase purchasing power and set it flowing where it will do most good. Purchasing power need not, as we have seen, be actual legal-tender money; it can be Government securities which, coming into the hands of the banks, serve as a basis for an easier lending policy. (See page 214.) It can be set flowing by direct Government spending not covered by taxation—*by a deliberate Budget deficit*.

The Budget can be used, that is, so that extra purchasing power flows out into the national economic system along all the channels of Government activity. The flow can be channelled into special, publicly-directed investment in public enterprises —roads, public buildings, the nationalized industries; or it can be spread out by a move towards greater economic equality, an increase of that part of the national income reaching the poor, who spend more, rather than the rich who save more. And every pound which is directly added to purchasing power goes on circulating, and pulling more factors of production back into work as it is spent by successive recipients. This several-times-over action is called by economists the *multiplier effect*. It is limited, because at each transfer some of the extra purchasing power will leak out of circulation into saving, and some will leak out of the national economy by way of payment for imports, and so go to stimulate some other country.

Inflationary Pressure. Since World War II—and it is only during and since that war that this policy has been accepted as the Government's job—there has been little occasion in this country to jack up investment and purchasing power. For most of the time there has been too much purchasing power, rather than too little, too much private investment for current private saving (or the 'ploughed in' profits of industry) to cover; while the amount of public investment called for by the newly-expanded social services, housing, development of the nationalized industries, new roads, and defence, has been more than enough to take up the resources of all kinds of public authority.

The estimates of national income and of its division between consumption and investment, spending and saving, periodically drawn up by Government statisticians, showed for years after World War II not a deficiency of investment and demand needing to be made good by Budget deficits but, on the contrary, a surplus of investment and demand needing to be deflated by Budget surpluses—a grappling-back and writing-off of purchasing power.

The Budget was in fact used for this purpose, though not with sufficient vigour to grapple back the whole surplus and prevent extra purchasing power from driving up prices. That is why so many controls were needed in the early post-war years, when Budgets were at their most inadequate; and it is the main reason for the rise in the cost of living, though the change in the international terms of trade (remember Chapter XIX) has also played its part.

The Budget as Stabilizer. When circumstances change, when a falling off of investment threatens an insufficiency of demand, then the Budget can be used the other way. It should be in fact a kind of governor to the economic machine, increasing or reducing the pressure of steam according to the engineer's reading of the appropriate gauges.

Difficulties of Stabilization Policy. Unfortunately one still has to say 'should'. For one thing, the gauges which must be read before the engineer knows what to do are still rather imperfect. The statisticians can reckon the gap between probable investment and probable saving only rather roughly; and they have practically no means, as yet, of reckoning the appropriate 'multiplier'. Nor, unfortunately, is there any certainty that governments will always have the courage to do the unpopular thing when necessary and use the Budget, and the mechanism of credit, to prevent or cut short inflation. The power to maintain full employment by maintaining the right amount of spending is also the power to push spending too high; and with so many desirable projects, public and private, to spend on, the temptation must always be strong.

International Complications. Moreover, there is the hard fact that while all the machinery for regulating demand and investment is *national* machinery, the situation which it has to deal with is a *world* situation. If one big trading country lets a slump develop, then its nationals become too poor to buy abroad as much as they used to, and its business men see no profit in importing raw materials, and everyone else's trade suffers accordingly; as happened when America developed a great slump in 1930. If another country tries to keep investment and demand at too full a pressure and develops inflation, its prices will be too high or its deliveries too slow for its customers and it will find itself with an adverse balance of payments—as happened to Great Britain after World War II (see page 263). For the money-and-credit stabilizer to work properly, it must be worked by all the main trading nations in co-operation; and they may have very different ideas as to how much Government control the individual citizen ought to put up with, and as to how much unemployment, or how much increase in the cost of living, is tolerable; or on the purely technical indications of whether or not the time has come to turn the tap on or off.

The Use of Economics. One thing which will make it easier, both nationally and internationally, for governments to take the right action and avoid the wrong one, is a sound, sensible understanding by their citizens of what they are trying to do. This is true not only of anti-depression and anti-inflation policy but of all sorts of other things; of taxes and subsidies and controls, of monopoly laws and trade regulations and Factory Acts and the division of activity between public and private enterprise. That is why economics is taught in schools; and that is why, in the last resort, this book has been written.

GLOSSARY

ACCEPTANCE. The act of accepting (i.e. expressing willingness to pay the value of) a bill of exchange.

ACCOUNT. (i) a financial statement.

(ii) the fortnightly period on the Stock Exchange at the end of which payment is made for securities not purchased for cash.

AD VALOREM (*according to value*). A term usually applied to customs duties which are based on the value of a commodity, as opposed to specific duties which are based on units of a commodity irrespective of their value.

ALLOTMENT. The process of allocation of shares among subscribers of new capital.

BEAR. One who sells Stock Exchange securities in the expectation that prices will fall, with the intention of buying them back again later at a lower price.

BILL. This is frequently used as an abbreviation for Bill of Exchange, apart from its everyday meaning of a statement of goods or services that have to be paid for. It is also used in connection with various types of commercial documents, especially Bill of Lading, which is a receipt and document of title given by a master of a ship for goods taken on board.

BOND. In general, a legal promise of any kind, frequently applied to loans raised by a government.

BUILDING SOCIETY. A permanent building society is a form of business organization the capital of which is subscribed by shareholders and is used to provide loans to enable people to build or buy houses for themselves, the interest and capital being repaid in instalments over a period of years.

BULL. A person who buys Stock Exchange securities with the intention of selling them again at a higher price.

CALL MONEY. Money which is lent by bankers, frequently to bill brokers, stockbrokers or jobbers, for very short periods (up to a fortnight) and which is repayable on demand without notice.

CAPITAL. All forms of wealth used especially for the production of goods and services.

CHAIN STORE (an expression derived from America). One of a large number of retail shops all owned by one firm, e.g. Woolworths, Boots.

311

CHEAP MONEY POLICY. A state of affairs when the financial authorities are deliberately keeping interest rates down.

COMMON STOCK. An American expression denoting ordinary shares.

CONSOLS (Consolidated Funds). This is usually taken to mean 2½ per cent Consolidated Stock—a part of the National Debt which the Government is under no obligation to repay by any fixed date.

CONTANGO. Really a form of interest which is charged to buyers of Stock Exchange securities who wish to postpone payment until the next Settlement period.

CONVERSION. This usually applies to any issue of securities in exchange for a maturing issue.

CORNER. To obtain control over the whole or a large part of the available supply of a commodity in order to sell it at an enhanced price.

CREDIT. Spending power granted by lenders to borrowers. In accounting, credit means all assets and money belonging to a firm.

CUSTOMS DUTY. A tax levied by the Government on goods entering or leaving a country, cf. Excise Duty.

DEAR MONEY. Loans borrowed at a high rate of interest.

DEBENTURES. Loans raised by firms, bearing a fixed rate of interest and repayable by an agreed date. Debenture stock is usually issued in units of £100. Cf. Mortgage Debentures.

DEFLATION. A deficiency of total money demand compared with the total supply of goods and services at current prices. It usually results in a general fall of prices.

DIVIDEND. The payment made out of profits to the holders of shares in a firm; it should be distinguished from interest which is payable on a loan.

EQUITY. An ordinary share.

EXCISE DUTY. A tax levied by the Government on goods produced within a country. Cf. Customs Duties.

FIDUCIARY ISSUE. The part of the currency note issue not covered by gold or silver bullion. Nowadays the greater part of the note issue of almost all countries is fiduciary.

FIXED CAPITAL. Capital which is in the form of goods of a permanent and durable nature, e.g. a ship or machinery, as distinct from floating capital, (q.v.)

FLOATING CAPITAL. Capital which has not yet taken on a permanent and durable form, e.g. stocks of raw materials.

FLOATING DEBT. That part of the National Debt, consisting mainly of Treasury Bills, due to be repaid within three or six months of their issue.

FREE TRADE. The system by which imports are allowed to enter a country without paying customs duties or being subjected to other special restrictions, although Free Traders do not object to duties if they are purely for raising revenue and are balanced by an excise duty (q.v.) on equivalent home produced goods.

FUNDED DEBT. That part of the National Debt which is regarded as permanent and which is either repayable at a distant date or by no fixed date, e.g. Consols (*q.v*).

FUTURES. Titles to primary commodities for delivery some months ahead. They are usually bought and sold to obtain protection against price fluctuations.

GILT EDGED SECURITIES. The safest kind of investments obtainable, e.g. British Government Stocks.

GOODWILL. The likelihood that the regular customers or clients of a firm will continue to patronize it, and hence a marketable asset on change of ownership.

INCORPORATION. The legal process by which two or more persons are brought together as a legal entity.

INFLATION. An excess of total money demand over the total supply of goods and services at current prices. It usually results in a general price increase.

LAISSER-FAIRE. The doctrine that government intervention in economic affairs should be kept to a minimum. It was widely accepted in Great Britain in the nineteenth century as a desirable objective.

LIQUID CAPITAL. Cash or bank deposits which may be used for acquiring capital goods.

LLOYDS. An association of underwriters and insurance brokers situated in the City of London who undertake all types of insurance, but specialize particularly in marine insurance.

MONOPOLY. Perfect monopoly exists when one person, firm or organization has exclusive control over the production and/or sale of a commodity or service.

MORTGAGE. The temporary transfer of titles to land or property from a borrower to a lender as security for a loan.

MORTGAGE DEBENTURES. Loans raised by a company with part of the assets of the company as security.

OVER-CAPITALIZATION. The increase of a firm's capital to such a level that the total value of the firm's revenue is insufficient to pay an adequate dividend.

PAID-UP CAPITAL. That amount of capital which has been actually subscribed by shareholders.

PAR VALUE. Standard or full value. Par value of stock is the value at which it will be redeemed.

PRIMARY COMMODITIES. Unprocessed foodstuffs and raw materials.

PROTECTION. The imposition of customs duties on imported goods with the object of raising their price to the consumer and so protecting the producer of those goods within the country.

RENTES. A French word meaning government securities.

RENTIER (derived from the above). A person who derives part or whole of his income from government securities.

RIG. To 'rig the market' means to force the price of a security or a commodity above or below its true market value, by spreading false information or by initiating a buying or selling campaign.

RING. A number of people who combine to restrict supplies of a commodity in order to force up the price. Cf. Corner.

SETTLEMENT. The period at the end of each fortnight on the Stock Exchange when transactions not made for cash must be completed. Cf. Account.

STAG. A person who buys new shares or securities in the anticipation that the issue will be oversubscribed and that he will be able to sell the securities at an enhanced price.

TARIFF. A list of articles on which customs duties are payable; the term is also used as synonymous with 'duty'.

TOKEN COINS. Coins whose metallic value is less than their face value, e.g. the whole of the present British coinage.

TRUCK. The payment of wages in kind, that is, in the form of goods.

TURNOVER. The total takings or revenue of a firm over a given period.

UNDERWRITING: (i) The provision of a guarantee that the whole of a new issue of shares or debentures will be bought.

(ii) The guaranteeing of marine or other insurance policies by a member of Lloyds (*q.v.*).

BOOKS FOR FURTHER READING

Some of the following books are beyond the needs and capabilities of Ordinary level candidates, but they are mentioned because they are suitable for Advanced level candidates and are worth inclusion in the Economics section of a grammar school library. Those which are of a more advanced nature are marked with an asterisk.

FOR GENERAL READING: F. Benham, *Economics**; A. Cairncross, *Introduction to Economics**; Honor Croome, *Approach to Economics*; J. Harvey, *Elementary Economics*; F. C. Happold, *This Modern Age*; *Oxford Junior Encyclopaedia, Vol. VII, Industry and Commerce*; M. Roberts, *The Estate of Man*; P. Samuelson, *Economics**; G. Williams, *Economics of Everyday Life*; A. L. Youngson, *The British Economy 1920 to 1957**.

FOR CURRENT REFERENCE: *Economic Trends* (H.M.S.O.); *Monthly Digest of Statistics* (H.M.S.O.); *The Economist*; *The London & Cambridge Economic Bulletin*, with *The Times Review of Industry*; the periodic reviews of the main banks: Westminster, Barclays, Lloyds, Three Banks, Midland, District, *Bank of England Quarterly* (these can usually be obtained free on application); *Central Office of Information Fact Sheets*.

CHAPTER

II. F. Geary, *Background to Business*.

III. E. Goodman, *Forms of Public Control and Ownership**; Kelf-Cohen, *Nationalization in Britain*; L. C. Robbins, *The Economic Problem in War and Peace**; Robson, *Nationalized Industry and Public Ownership**; Annual Reports on Nationally Owned Industries (H.M.S.O.).

IV. E. Cannan, *Wealth* (Chapter III on Division of Labour).

V. G. C. Allen, *British Industries*; R. C. Estall and R. Buchanan, *Industrial Activity and Economic Geography*; W. Smith, *Economic Geography of Britain*; *Preliminary Report of the 1961 Census* (H.M.S.O.); *Ministry of Labour Gazette*, May 1960, for numbers employed in different industries by areas.

VI. G. C. Allen, *Structure of Industry in Britain*; E. A. G. Robinson, *The Structure of Competitive Industry**, and *Monopoly**.

VII. C. Fulop (Hobart Paper), *Revolution in Retailing*; M. Hall, *Distributive Trading*; National Savings Committee Booklet, *Markets*.

VIII-X. & XII. H. D. Henderson, *Supply and Demand**; National Savings Committee Booklet, *The Price System*; J. E. Meade, *Planning and the Price Mechanism*; I. Bowen, *Population*; C. Clark, *Growthmanship* (Hobart Paper); J. R. Hicks, *The Social Framework*; W. A. Lewis, *Theory of Economic Growth**; P.E.P., *Population Policy in Great Britain*; Report on Royal Commission on Population 1949 (Cmnd 7695, H.M.S.O.).

XI. E. H. P. Brown, *The Economics of Labour*; M. Dobb, *Wages*; A. Flanders, *Trade Unions*; J. R. Hicks, *The Social Framework*; Annual White Paper on National Income and Expenditure (H.M.S.O.).

XIII-XVII. H. Croome, *Introduction to Money*; G. Crowther, *Outline of Money**; O. R. Hobson, *How the City Works*; W. T. C. King, *The Stock Exchange*; R. L. Sayers, *Modern Banking*; W. Manning Dacey, *British Banking Mechanism**; G. Winder, *A Short History of Money*; National Savings Committee Booklets, *The History of British Coinage*, *What the Banks Do*; *Report of Royal Commission on the Working of the Monetary System*—Radcliffe Report*. (Cmnd 827 H.M.S.O.)

XVIII-XX. R. F. Harrod, *International Economics*; Institute of Bankers, *The City of London as a Centre of International Trade and Finance*; White Paper published by H.M.S.O.—*Balance of Payments*.

XXI. U. K. Hicks, *Public Finance**; H.M.S.O. Reference Pamphlets, No. 10, *The British System of Taxation*.

XXII. Beveridge, Lord, *Full Employment in a Free Society**; D. Dillard, *The Economics of J. M. Keynes**; R. C. O. Matthews, *The Trade Cycle*.

INDEX

317

QUESTIONS AND EXERCISES

The following abbreviations are used to denote the sources of questions which are taken from examination papers.

A.C.C.A.	Association of Certified and Corporate Accountants
C.	Cambridge Local Examinations Syndicate (G.C.E.—'O' level)
C.C.S.	Corporation of Certified Secretaries
C.I.S.	Chartered Institute of Secretaries
D.	Durham School Examinations Board (G.C.E.—'O' level)
I.B.	Institute of Bankers
I.M.T.A.	Institute of Municipal Treasurers and Accountants
I.T.	Institute of Transport
L.	London University (G.C.E.—'O' level)
L.G.E.B.	Local Government Examinations Board
N.	Northern Universities Joint Matriculation Board (G.C.E.—'O' level)
O.	Oxford Local Examinations Delegacy (G.C.E.—'O' level)
S.	Scottish Leaving Certificate (new syllabus: specimen papers published by H.M.S.O.)
S.I.A.A.	Society of Incorporated Accountants and Auditors
W.	Welsh Joint Education Committee (G.C.E.—'O' level)

CHAPTERS II and III

1. Make a list of some of the chief firms and organizations supplying goods and services in the town or district where you live. Tabulate these according to whether they are one-man firms, partnerships, private joint-stock companies, public joint-stock companies, co-operative societies or public corporations.

2. 'John Smith and Co. Ltd.' In this firm's title explain the significance of (a) John Smith; (b) Co.; (c) Ltd. (*L.*)

3. Contrast the characteristics of the following forms of business organization: (a) sole trader; (b) partnership; (c) limited joint-stock company. (*W.*)

4. Discuss the importance of the joint-stock principle in the organization of industry and trade. (*D.*)

5. Compare and contrast a joint-stock limited company and a Public Utility corporation in respect of: (a) ownership; (b) control; (c) disposal of profits. (*C.*)

6. How does a consumers' co-operative society differ from an ordinary company owning a chain of stores? (*L.*)

7. To what extent is it true to say that the joint-stock limited liability company is the most satisfactory form of business organization? (*S.*)

8. What is a joint-stock company? (*A.C.C.A. Inter.*)

9. Name some of the chief industries and services under national or municipal control. Can you suggest any reason why they are so controlled? (*C.*)

10. Distinguish between *public enterprise* and *private enterprise*. Outline the development of public enterprise in Britain in the twentieth century. (*L.*)

11. What is a Public Corporation? Discuss the merits of this type of administration in nationalized industries. (*I.B.*)

12. Make a list of the functions which the Government carries out to-day and which it did not a hundred years ago.

CHAPTERS IV and V

1. What are the main occupations and industries in the area in which you live? What changes have taken place in this respect in recent years, and why? From the last Census report find out what changes have taken place in population; suggest reasons for these changes. What industrial or town-planning schemes have been carried out locally?

2. Show how the division of labour can increase the standard of living of a people. (*D.*)

3. Mr. Henry Ford has, for a long time, preached and practised 'the minute sub-division of an industry'. Explain why such methods are more suitable for the manufacture of cars than of ladies' hats. (*L.*)

4. Show how the extensive division of labour depends on: (a) money, and (b) the existence of an efficient system of transport. (*L.*)

5. 'Division of labour is limited by the extent of the market.' Explain and illustrate this statement. (*C.C.S.*)

6. What considerations would you bear in mind if you had to decide in what part of England you would build a new factory? (*L.*)

7. What do you understand by geographical specialization? (*S.*)

8. What do you mean by the term *standardization of products*? In what ways does the standardization of products lead to lower prices? (*L.*)

9. What are the advantages and disadvantages which may derive from the concentration of an industry? (Illustrate your answer by reference to a particular industry.) (*S.*)

10. Steel manufacture is highly localized, furniture manufacture is widely dispersed. Why? (*L.*)

11. 'Specialization is fundamental in economic activity.' Explain and discuss. (*S.*)

12. Indicate some of the (a) advantages and (b) disadvantages of the division of labour.   (*A.C.C.A. Inter.*)

13. Why were many factories built in the Midlands in the early nineteenth century? Why have many been built around London in recent years? Give examples of the industries concerned in each case.   (*L.*)

14. What are the principal factors which have determined the localization of industry in Great Britain?   (*D.*)

15. The following figures relate to the density of population per square mile:

Westmorland	84
Sussex	699
Lancashire	2,716

Comment on these figures, and give reasons which help to explain the differences in the densities of population.   (*L.*)

16. What industries expanded in Great Britain during the inter-war years? What were the causes of their expansion?   (*N.*)

17. Discuss the reasons why foreign trade is important to Great Britain. Show the ways in which we have increased our exports since 1945.   (*W.*)

18. What forces tend to determine the location of industry *to-day*, and how do they differ from those operating 100 years ago?   (*I.B.*)

19. What economic difficulties would confront a planner who, for social or strategic reasons, wished to distribute industry widely through rural areas?   (*L.*)

CHAPTER VI

1. What are the main advantages of large-scale production? Why in spite of these advantages, do so many small firms continue to exist?   (*W.*)

2. Distinguish between 'horizontal' and 'vertical' combines in industry, giving typical examples of each.   (*L.*)

3. British industry is carried on by firms of many different sizes. Why does the size of firms vary in different lines of production?   (*N.*)

4. What factors may make it profitable to increase the size of a business undertaking? What factors may operate in the opposite direction?   (*O.*)

5. What is meant by an industrial combine? Briefly describe the main types of combines.   (*C.*)

6. To what extent are the economies of large-scale production applicable to agriculture?   (*C.C.S.*)

7. What is a monopoly? What effect has monopoly on price?
(*A.C.C.A. Inter.*)

8. How would you distinguish between competitive and monopolistic conditions? What is the main consequence, so far as price determination is concerned, of the existence of monopolistic conditions?   (*D.*)

CHAPTER VII

1. What significance is attached to the term 'market' in economics What is meant by a 'perfect market'?   (*W.*)

2. What do economists mean by (a) a market; (b) a world market; and (c) a sellers' market? *(L.)*

3. 'Speculation is merely gambling under another name.' Discuss this statement. *(I.T.)*

4. Distinguish between wholesale and retail markets. What are the conditions for a perfect market? *(W.)*

5. What do economists mean by the term *market*? Explain, and illustrate, the statement: 'In any one market, there can be only one price for a given commodity.' *(L.)*

6. Do you consider that the middleman or wholesale dealer performs any useful purpose in our economic system? *(C.)*

7. Some manufacturers sell to retailers through wholesalers; some manufacturers sell directly to retailers; and some manufacturers have their own retail shops. Discuss the merits of each of these retailing methods. *(C.)*

CHAPTER VIII

1. What do you understand by the term 'elasticity of demand'? Which items in a family budget would you expect to have elastic and which inelastic demands? *(N.)*

2. Define the term *demand*. What factors determine the demand for consumers' goods? *(O.)*

3. What do economists mean by 'changes in supply and demand'? How do such changes affect the price of an article? *(L.)*

4. Compare the advantages and disadvantages of (a) rationing, and (b) an uncontrolled price system, as a means of regulating the distribution of goods. *(I.B.)*

5. Explain clearly how price is determined. *(A.C.C.A. Inter.)*

6. Explain how, in a free market, the consumer determines what goods shall be produced. *(C.I.S. Inter.)*

7. Define (a) total utility; (b) marginal utility; and show the importance of the law of diminishing marginal utility. *(D.)*

8. Explain the factors which are likely to affect the elasticity of supply of any commodity. *(I.M.T.A)*

9. What differences are there in the influences determining the price of (a) tomatoes, (b) antique furniture? *(L.)*

10. Suppose you have a considerable increase in the demand for a commodity and that supply is very inelastic while demand is very elastic; what do you think would be the relation between the increase in quantity demanded and the increase in price? *(D.)*

11. 'When goods are scarce they have a price.' Comment on this statement, relating your answer to car parking problems in large cities. *(L.)*

12. Explain the underlying economic causes for the differences which occur in the prices charged for coal: (a) at different times of the year, and (b) at different places in Britain. *(L.)*

13. What is meant by *supply*? What are the main factors which affect the supply of potatoes? *(L.)*

14. British Railways have in recent years been operating at a loss. Some people suggest that the situation should be met by higher fares and freight charges while others claim that fares and freight charges should be lowered. Which course of action would you recommend and why? (*N.*)

CHAPTER IX

1. What meaning is attached to the word 'land' in economics? What are the significant differences between land as a factor of production and other factors of production? (*W.*)

2. In what sense, if any, is it true to say that a country is over-populated? (*O.*)

3. Examine the basis of the distinction generally made by economists between Land and Capital as factors of production. (*N.*)

4. What are the factors of production? (*O.*)

5. Explain the law of diminishing returns. (*D.*)

6. What is meant by the mobility of labour? Why and how do governments try to make labour more mobile? (*L.*)

7. What changes have taken place in recent decades in the size and structure of the population of the United Kingdom? What will be the economic effects? (*O.*)

8. Indicate carefully the part played by capital as a factor in the production of wealth. (*I.T.*)

9. Discuss the main influences affecting the growth of capital in a country. (*A.C.C.A. Inter.*)

10. Explain the importance, so far as productivity is concerned, of the concept of mobility as applied to labour, land and capital. (*I.B.*)

CHAPTER X

1. Does the price of a commodity necessarily equal its cost of production? (*O.*)

2. Discuss the connection between the value of a commodity and its cost of production. (*N.*)

3. What are the different items which make up the *cost of production* of an article? Is it true to say that the price at which an article will be offered for sale depends upon its cost of production? (*L.*)

4. Discuss how the price and output of a commodity may be affected by an increase in the demand for it. (*W.*)

5. Do you agree that cost of production alone determines the price of a commodity?

6. What factors determine the level at which the manufacturer of a commodity fixes its price? (*S.*)

7. Distinguish between fixed and variable cost. Give three examples of each. (*N.*)

8. What do you understand by cost of production? What is its influence on price? (*C.I.S. Inter.*)

9. Explain, and illustrate, the statement: 'An increase in the demand for any commodity will tend to increase its price.' What circumstances, other than an increase in demand, might cause an increase in the price of a commodity? *(L.)*

10. Suppose there occurs a preference for plastic kitchen utensils over enamelled ones. Explain its effects on the prices and outputs of both types of commodity. *(L.)*

CHAPTERS XI and XII

1. What kind of job do you propose to choose when you leave school or college? How much do you expect to earn at first, and in ten years' time? How does this compare with the prospective earnings of other members of the class? What reasons can you suggest for any differences in earnings?

2. What in your opinion is the function of the rate of interest? *(D.)*

3. What are the chief causes of unequal distribution of income between individuals in Great Britain to-day? *(W.)*

4. Describe briefly the main objects of measuring the National Income, and the methods used in doing so. *(O.)*

5. Define the National Income and suggest briefly how this income might be increased. *(I.T.)*

6. In what ways can a country increase its wealth? Show how the national dividend is divided among its producers. *(W.)*

7. Why do wages vary in different occupations? Is it economically desirable to aim at greater equality of wages? *(W.)*

8. A woman teacher is paid as much as a male teacher with similar qualifications, but a woman factory worker is generally paid less than a male factory worker. Why? *(N.)*

9. Describe and give examples of the difference betwen: (a) wages and earnings, and (b) money wages and real wages. *(C.)*

10. What factors affect the amount of rent paid for land in (a) rural areas, (b) the great shopping centres of large cities? *(N.)*

11. There are figures which can be quoted to support either answer to the question: 'Can wages and profits increase only at each other's expense?' Explain how this can be the case. *(N.)*

12. What categories of income are properly described as *profits*? *(O.)*

13. Distinguish between interest and profit. In what ways are a country's savings important for industrial production? *(W.)*

14. To what extent is it true to say that 'rent is a surplus'? *(S.)*

15. Consider the circumstances in which a rise in the rate of wages might injure and not benefit the real interests of the wage-earners.
(L.G.E.B.)

16. Give an account of the determination of wages and point out the function of Trade Unions in relation to this matter. *(C.C.S.)*

17. 'Profits are the earnings of enterprise.' Discuss this statement. *(I.T.)*

18. Why do rates of interest vary at different times, and between different trades and undertakings at the same time? (*C.I.S. Inter.*)

CHAPTERS XIII to XVI

1. What do you understand by the phrase 'a money economy'? Explain the part played by money in our economic system. (*N.*)

2. What different forms of money are used in England to-day? (*L.*)

3. Set out the various ways in which a Debtor may settle his indebtedness to his Creditor. (*S.I.A.A. Inter.*)

4. What part do banks play in modern economic life? Why are they an essential feature of modern economic organization? (*N.*)

5. Compare and contrast the function of British commercial banks and the Bank of England. (*W.*)

6. What is the Bank Rate? Why have movements in this rate often been regarded as of great importance to business people in general? (*L.*)

7. What are the main functions of the Bank of England? (*L.*)

8. Explain the difference between 'legal tender money' (cash) and 'bank money' (cheques). How may a government influence the amount in circulation of each sort of money? (*L.*)

9. Discuss the view that the main function of a banker is to create credit. (*I.T.*)

10. Discuss the assertion that the banks are merely middlemen and can lend only what is lent to them. (*L.G.E.B*)

11. What institutions, apart from the Bank of England and the joint-stock banks, make up the London Money Market? Briefly indicate their functions. (*L.*)

12. Outline the work done by (a) accepting houses, (b) underwriters, (c) stockbrokers. (*L.*)

13. Give an account of the organization and functions of the Stock Exchange and discuss the role it plays in the financing of industry. (*S.*)

14. What are the respective functions of the Broker and the Jobber on the London Stock Exchange? (*S.I.A.A. Inter.*)

15. Explain the connection between the currency system and the banking system of a country. How does each affect the supply of money available for trade? (*I.B.*)

16. British banks have been described as 'dealers in debts' and also as 'dealers in credits'. How far are such descriptions useful in indicating the nature of banking activity and, giving reasons for your answer, do you think it makes any difference which phrase is used? (*D.*)

17. Explain what is meant when it is said that it is important for a commercial bank 'to be liquid'. What forms does the liquidity of a commercial bank take? (*D.*)

CHAPTER XVII

1. What is meant by the value of money and how do we attempt to measure it? (*W.*)

2. Why does the general level of prices change from time to time? How are such changes measured? (*W.*)

3. What is meant by *Inflation*? Why is an inflationary situation regarded as dangerous? (*L.*)

4. What are 'price indices'? (*S.*)

5. Examine the causes of inflation and give an account of the actions which can be taken to counteract inflation. (*S.*)

6. 'Since the last war there has been a rise in the cost of living.' 'Since the last war there has been a rise in the standard of living.' Explain clearly the meaning of these statements, and show how both statements can be true at the same time. (*L.*)

7. What does a Cost of Living index number measure? (*O.*)

8. When is a currency system 'inflated'? Discuss the statement that increased production is the only effective safeguard against inflation. (*I.B.*)

9. How is the general price level determined? (*I.M.T.A.*)

10. What kinds of investment should an investor put his money in if he expects an inflation? (*L.*)

CHAPTERS XVIII to XX

1. With the aid of the *Stateman's Year Book* and the monthly *Digest of Statistics*, find how the pattern of British foreign trade (i.e. the volume, direction and composition of her imports and exports) has changed since the 1930s.

2. What advantages does a country derive from its foreign trade? Are there any disadvantages? (*C.*)

3. What is meant by an adverse balance of (a) trade, (b) payments? How can an adverse balance of trade be remedied? (*N.*)

4. In what respects has international trade in recent years differed from international trade before 1939? (*S.*)

5. What do you understand by 'The Interdependent World'? Illustrate your answer by specific reference to the foreign trade of the United Kingdom. (*S.*)

6. What do you understand by the gold standard? What are the essential features of such an arrangement? (*N.*)

7. The main argument in favour of free trade between nations is a simple corollary from the principle of the division of labour. Explain this statement. Are there any economic arguments in favour of protection? (*W.*)

8. What is meant by the *terms of trade* between two nations? Illustrate your answer by reference to the experience of Great Britain during the past twenty years. (*O.*)

9. 'In 1949 the pound sterling was devalued to 2·80 dollars.' What does this statement mean? How did devaluation affect British importers and exporters respectively? (*L.*)

10. What are the main differences between domestic and international trade? (*I.M.T.A.*)

11. Is it true to say that a country's Balance of Payments always balances? *(O.)*

12. Distinguish between the terms in each of the three following sections:

      (a) Visible imports and invisible imports;

      (b) Visible exports and invisible exports;

      (c) Balance of Trade and Balance of Payments. *(L.)*

13. 'The purpose of a scientific tariff is to equalize costs of production between home and foreign producers.' Comment. *(L.)*

14. There have been: (a) a decline in overseas earnings by British insurance companies, and (b) an increase in the investment of foreign capital in Britain. Explain the effects of each of these on Britain's balance of payments. *(L.)*

15. Why, if Britain is 'off the Gold Standard' at the present time, do we still appear to find it necessary to build up, and take measures to safeguard, a gold reserve? *(D.)*

CHAPTERS XXI and XXII

1. Make a list of the various ways in which you or your parents pay direct and indirect taxes. What benefits are obtained in return?

Find out the various ways in which your local government authorities spend the rates and make a comparison with the expenditure of the Kent County and Dover Borough authorities shown at the end of the chapter.

2. Show the differences (a) between rates and taxes, (b) between progressive and regressive taxes, (c) between customs and excise duties. *(L.)*

3. Examine the case for direct as against indirect taxes. Illustrate your answer by reference to recent Budgets. *(S.)*

4. For what purposes are taxes imposed? *(O.)*

5. The Hon. Ivor Castle, a gentleman of leisure, has two residences, a large holding of government stock, and one child, a son, at public school. Mr. Will Needham, a postman, rents a council house, and has six children under the age of sixteen. Compare the effects on their standards of living of government taxation and expenditure. *(L.)*

6. Give the principal reasons for the increased expenditure of local authorities in recent times. *(C.C.S.)*

7. 'The size of the National Debt is a matter of no importance.' Discuss this statement. *(O.)*

8. State the sources from which a Local Authority derives its revenue and the main headings under which that revenue is expended.

      (S.I.A.A. Inter.)

9. What principles should a government follow in framing a system of taxation? *(C.C.S.)*

10. Assuming that a government must raise a large revenue, state the advantages and disadvantages of imposing heavy taxes on personal incomes. *(L.)*

11. In what ways does the State modify the distribution of wealth and income? (*C.C.S.*)

12. The trade cycle may be defined as a period of prosperity followed by a period of depression. Describe the forces which may bring a period of expansion to an end and usher in a period of depression. (*S.*)

13. In what ways can the fiscal system be used to help ensure 'full employment'? (*I.M.T.A*)

14. What causes general unemployment? (*O.*)

15. Define the terms 'savings' and 'investment'. In what sense can the levels of savings differ from the level of investment, and with what results? (*O.*)

MISCELLANEOUS

1. Why is it that as the demand for fuel increases, Britain uses more oil and less coal? What are the economic effects of this tendency? (*L.*)

2. What factors determine the demand (a) for consumers' goods, and (b) for producers' goods? (*O.*)

3. Every child is taught handwriting. What would be the likely economic effects if every child were also taught typewriting? (*L.*)

4. Do you think that the maintenance of large armed forces reduces the standard of living of the people of a country? (*D.*)

5. In what circumstances may (a) a nation and (b) a private citizen be said to be living on capital? (*O.*)

6. 'An increase in money wages, by increasing demand, results in an all-round increase in production.' Discuss this statement. (*I.B.*)

7. Suppose that everyone were to give up smoking; what economic effects would be likely to follow? (*L.*)

8. What would be the major economic effects of the development of cheap and safe atomic energy? (*L.*)

9. What is economic freedom? Is such freedom compatible with a planned economy? (*I.B.*)

10. Distinguish between the National Wealth, the National Income and the Government Revenue of a country. (*N.*)

11. How would you distinguish between 'productive' and 'unproductive' labour? Give two examples, real or imaginary, of a situation in which, in your opinion, the labour was unproductive. (*D.*)